What People Are Saying About *Writing and Developing Your College Textbook*

"An indispensable resource. Equips readers with the information and the confidence to succeed as textbook authors. I can't imagine proposing or writing a textbook without it."

—Andrew Pomerantz, Southern Illinois University

"An absolutely essential guide for first-time textbook authors and extremely valuable for all academic writers."

—Nancy Johnson Black, Metropolitan State University

"Has been a great help in giving our authors advice and direction. Thanks for providing such a great resource."

—M. Douglas Sanders, Sagamore Publishing

"Offers insights for new and seasoned writers alike. It includes tips not only on writing clearly and effectively, but can also help guide authors in their dealings with publishers."

—Julie C. Benyo, Education Initiatives, WGBH Boston

"Extremely savvy. I can't imagine a textbook writer moving ahead without consulting it first."

—Fran Mascia-Lees, *American Anthropologist*, Rutgers University

"What I especially appreciated is the 'I can do this' feeling that you were able to engender in me as I was reading. I'm sure your book will be very helpful to me as I actually write my textbook."

—David W. Denton, Austin Peay State University

"I picked up a copy of your book and I wanted to drop you a note saying how much I liked it. I'm in the middle of writing a textbook for a major publisher and I wish I had read your book before I began."

—Name withheld on request

"Empowers academic authors and textbook writers to undertake textbook development on their own."

—Jane Erskine, *Reference & Research Book News*

"This is easily the single best book I have seen for the co
ing market and a recommended read for anyone wishin
college textbook." —Harold McFarland, *Readers Pre*

"I am very impressed by your coverage of the many aspe
ment. I am writing a first edition intro math text for a m
I'll use many of your pointers in the development of my

—Reva Narsimhan, K

"Experience helps Lepionka to put herself in the place of
see the questions and issues from both sides. Lepionka's

D1069295

the voice of the helpful but direct editor that writers all crave."
—Michael R. Mosher, *Leonardo Digital Reviews*

"Assuming that her readers are experts in their fields but novices in the field of publishing, Lepionka takes them step by step through the process of writing and publishing a textbook, including how to get a manuscript accepted by a publisher. Well laid out and easy to follow."
—M. Lorenzen, *CHOICE*

"A straightforward guide to creating an easy-to-understand, comprehensive, well-thought-out, accessibly organized textbook for college-level courses. Very highly recommended to aspiring textbook writers regardless of the subject matter." —James Cox, *Midwest Book Review*

"I think your offerings go way beyond simple 'how-to' guides and should be of interest for anyone who wants to understand the world of educational publishing."
—Kay Mohlman, Nanyang Technical University, Singapore

"Lepionka has created the definitive reference on creating supplements to college textbooks. It's a must for anyone searching how to get started." —John Bond, SLACK Incorporated

"Written in plain terms with an eye toward practical usage, [this book] is a 'must-have' for academic writers charged with expanding upon standard textbooks to facilitate student learning."
—*Midwest Book Review*

"I just completed your new book—it is fantastic! What a wealth of information for supplement authors—and to my knowledge your book is the only source of this info. Like your first book, this one is thorough yet concise, clearly written, and a pleasure to read."
—Andrew Pomerantz, Southern Illinois University, Edwardsville

"I wish I had read this book four years ago before I wrote my textbook... [Now, your] *Writing and Developing College Textbook Supplements* is essential, especially because it is so up-to-date and contains so many useful links." —T. L. Brink, Crafton Hill College, California

"I wanted to let you know that *Writing and Developing Your College Textbook* has been an invaluable guide for us this summer as my coauthor and I drafted the writing outline and TOC for a textbook manuscript... Thank you." —Denise Guinn, Regis University

"I just got *Writing and Developing Your College Textbook* this past week and am devouring it. I have been drifting and weaving and bobbing my way to writing a textbook and now I feel like I really have a hand to hold! Thank you. I am absorbing how to do the organizing that I should have done before I started to write...You came, I read, now I'm stopping to do the outline I need to make this effort coherent."
—Heidi Lee Hoerman, University of South Carolina

Writing and Developing Your College Textbook
2nd Edition

A Comprehensive Guide to Textbook Authorship and Higher Education Publishing

Mary Ellen Lepionka

ATLANTIC PATH
PUBLISHING

Writing and Developing Your College Textbook, 2nd Edition
A Comprehensive Guide to Textbook Authorship
and Higher Education Publishing
By Mary Ellen Lepionka

Copyright © 2008 by Atlantic Path Publishing

All rights reserved. No part of this book may be used, transmitted, or reproduced in any form or by any means without the prior written permission of the author, except for brief quotations in reviews of the work.

For further information contact:
Atlantic Path Publishing
P.O. Box 1556, Gloucester, MA 01931-1556
atlanticpathpublishing.com
Phone: 978-283-1531 Fax: 866-640-1412
Email: contactus@atlanticpathpublishing.com

The information and advice in this book are accurate and effective to the best of our knowledge but are offered without guarantee. The author and Atlantic Path Publishing disclaim all liability in connection with the use of this book.

ISBN: 978-0-9728164-7-2
Library of Congress Control Number: 2007906225

Cover and Design by Julie Phinney
Cover art by Stevens Brosnihan
Printed in USA

Publisher's Cataloging-In-Publication Data
(Prepared by The Donohue Group, Inc.)

Lepionka, Mary Ellen.
Writing and developing your college textbook : a comprehensive guide to textbook authorship and higher education publishing / Mary Ellen Lepionka. -- 2nd ed.

p. : ill. ; cm.

Includes bibliographical references and index.
ISBN: 978-0-9728164-7-2

1. College textbooks--Authorship 2. College teaching--Aids and devices. 3. College teaching--Aids and devices--Publishing. 4. Publishers and publishing--Handbooks, manuals, etc. 5. College textbooks--Publishing. I. Title.

LB3045.5 .L47 2008
371.3/2 2007906225

Contents

Preface and Acknowledgements

THIS BOOK IS AN OUTGROWTH of my long and diverse experience as a college classroom instructor, curriculum developer, and professional development editor in educational publishing. For more than 25 years I have helped editors, authors, and publishers achieve commercially successful first editions as well as successful revisions of their secondary, post-secondary, and professional books. As of this second-edition printing I have developed or contributed to the development of 80 textbooks in history, political science, English composition, literature, business, finance, education, sociology, anthropology, psychology, child development, archaeology, criminal justice, and mass communication. Most of the first editions I worked on were successful enough to warrant revision, and I believe most of the revisions increased their market share. I have learned something about making good textbooks that succeed.

In commercial textbook publishing, as in other businesses, success is measured in revenues from sales over the costs of producing the goods and being in business. Sales figures are based on the number of instructors who adopt your textbook and the number of students who buy it for use in the course of study for which you wrote it. Factors that contribute to these figures include the publisher's level of investment; channels for marketing, distribution, and sales; and corporate systems for productivity and efficiency. In my experience, however, the greatest source of success is a truly good textbook.

What makes a truly good textbook? Minimally, a good textbook teaches, using good content and organization expressed in a good voice and style. This book aims to explain in each case what I think "good" means. What makes a textbook truly both good and successful? Development and authorship—and that's what this guide is about. I have seen good textbooks fail because they missed their market or were somehow mismanaged, and I have seen mediocre books succeed initially because of publisher hype and aggressive sales campaigns. I have also seen many textbooks fail simply because the author or publisher abandoned them. Textbooks that are both good and successful, however, become classics in their field, indispensable. They last into their 10th editions and beyond, even outlive their original authors. And they consistently make good money for everyone involved.

My principal goal in writing this book is to empower authors to undertake textbook development on their own to enhance their chances of success. Writing and crafting a textbook and attending to authoring tasks is a time-consuming, complex—some would say monumental—project, even harrowing at times. Publishers may contribute little to this process beyond assigning advances. Even large houses seldom employ more than a half-dozen staff development editors, who tend to be reserved for signings with the highest projections of sales. At the same time, outsourced development projects may lack commitment or quality control. As the textbook author, therefore, you are your best bet.

You are an expert in your field, but you are not an expert in textbook publishing, which is equally sophisticated, multifaceted, layered, and nuanced. This book aims to share with you the knowledge and skills of a higher education development editor that you can use to your advantage as an academic author and textbook writer.

This second edition is revised, updated, expanded, and reviewed. There are two new chapters on recent developments in the textbook publishing industry and on uses of learning objectives in textbook development. New or augmented topics include, among others, recent developments in the business of publishing, market segmentation in higher education publishing, online textbooks and the open access and wikitext movements, textbook pricing problems and solutions, customizing and self-publishing textbooks, working with editors, and managing author–editor relations. I have added many new examples from a greater variety of academic disciplines. While I continue to address authors directly, I have tried in this edition to broaden the audience to their editors as well.

In this edition I had the able and dedicated assistance of Julie Phinney (Richmond, VT), who designed the book interior and the cover, and of my copyeditor, Sarah Cypher, The Threepenny Editor (Portland, OR). Thanks to Stevens Brosnihan (Gloucester, MA) for the use of his acrylic and oil painting, "Pepsis," in the cover design. I also would like to thank my readers, friends from the publishing world, Jane Manley and Deborah Brown, along with my ever-supportive daughter Lara Lepionka. This revision was guided by the generous responses and suggestions of users of the first edition, some of whom are quoted in the first pages of this book. To them all I extend my thanks.

—Mary Ellen Lepionka
January 2008

1

The College Textbook Industry Today

The Textbook Business

WHAT EXACTLY ARE YOU GETTING into when you seek to publish a college textbook? What kind of a business is this? And how can publishing's business models and market forces affect you, your work, and your bottom line? This first chapter addresses these questions up front, before we even talk about textbook writing, because ultimately you must decide where you fit into this picture and what publishing model is right for you. First, how big is this business, and who is in it?

Company Revenues

In 2007 the top nine college publishers were Pearson Education, Thomson Learning, Houghton Mifflin, Bedford Freeman & Worth (Holtzbrinck), Jones & Bartlett, McGraw-Hill, Oxford University Press, John Wiley & Sons, and W. W. Norton. According to statistics for the textbook publishing industry, in 2006 these and other college publishers had total estimated sales of $3.5 billion (Association of American Publishers, 2007). Details vary by source. According to Simba Information Inc. statistics for 2007, the top eight U.S. college publishers were Pearson Education (Pearson is a UK firm) with $1,193 million in revenue; Thomson with $1,014 million; McGraw-Hill with $641 million; Houghton Mifflin with $243 million; Bedford, Freeman & Worth (Holtzbrinck is a German firm) with $162 million; John Wiley & Sons with $161 million; Jones & Bartlett with $84 million; and W. W. Norton with $52 million. Simba (**simbainformation.com**) counts the annual industry total at $3,745 million. Those products served students in 4,216 institutions of higher learning; 86% of those students were undergraduates in private (60%) and public (40%) schools. (For more data on higher education in the US, see **nces.ed.gov/fastfacts**.)

According to the college stores industry (National Association of College Stores, or NACS), in 2006 the market for required course materials in the U.S. and Canada provided $6.195 billion in sales, amounting to 59% of store revenue (NACS *2007 College Store Industry Financial Report*). This revenue breaks down as follows:

New textbooks	0.8%
Used textbooks	7.1%
Course packs	1.1%
Course technology	0.0%

Trade book sales accounted for only 4% of college store business.

Course Technology

The insignificant sales of course technology (mainly software and site licenses) in the NACS financial report, while surprising in light of projections, does not take into account the online components and delivery systems that many textbook publishers offer. Companies have text-dedicated websites on company servers and digitized content with course management software on proprietary Blackboard cartridges or via WebCT. Also, many institutions offering online courses are not mediated through college stores and therefore do not show up in NACS statistics (and at present most college stores would like to keep it that way).

By all other indications, acquiring course content through downloads and subscription will continue to increase dramatically. The largest college enrollment in 2006-2007, for example, was the University of Phoenix Online, which registered 115,794 students (*Almanac 2006-2007, Chronicle of Higher Education*, August 25, 2006). Online sales also will increase for both new and used textbook content now that publishers are selling directly to students over the Internet.

In 2006, sales of textbooks through online retailers such as Amazon were estimated at $350 million, or 3.3% of total textbook sales. As reported in *Bostonia*, according to Eduventures (**eduventures.com**), "The number of online higher education students jumped from 315,219 in 2001 to 1,518,750 in 2006, a year in which online students accounted for 8.5% of all students enrolled in postsecondary courses" (Berdik, 2007). Finally, more institutions, watchdog groups, students, professors, and legislators increasingly demand digitized content delivery as a solution to issues relating to textbook pricing, the cost of higher education, and the dissemination of scholarship.

Textbook Pricing

In 2006 the average price of a new textbook was $53, of a used textbook, $44 (NACS, 2007). The overall annual student expense for books rose, however, from $745-843 in 2004-2005 to $801-904 in 2005-2006 (The College Board, 2007). At the same time, publishers estimate that their after-tax income amounted to only 7¢ on every dollar spent on a new textbook and that 11.6¢ of that dollar went to the author (NACS, 2007).

For Every Dollar Spent on a New Textbook

Publisher costs	57.3¢
Author royalties	11.6¢
Publisher profits	7.0¢
College store costs	19.7¢
College store profits	4.4¢

Criticism and debate have led to (often misguided) local policies and state laws attempting to regulate textbook pricing. In 2004, the California Student Public Interest Research Group (CALPIRG) published "Rip-Off 101," claiming that publishers artificially inflate the cost of textbooks by frequently putting out new editions and bundling them with supplements of questionable pedagogical value (**calpirg.org/reports/textbookripoff.pdf**). CALPIRG estimated the average new textbook cost at $102.44 and used textbooks at $64.80.

What the report failed to appreciate is that publishers routinely have offered textbooks with and without a smorgasbord of supplemental materials. Several alternative textbook packages, combining a student text with selected supplements, are offered under different ISBNs, and instructors have the ability to design their own course packs. Publishers were the innovators in giving instructors the power of customization. If students find expensive "bundles" in their college stores, it is because that is what their instructors ordered for them. Complaints that publishers use deceptive marketing practices to keep adopters ignorant of their options have not been substantiated.

It is true that revision cycles have grown shorter, but publishers defend new editions as the only way they have to protect the profitability of key acquisitions against the used textbook industry. Student complaints have been effective, though. Since 2004, the average price of textbooks has gone down, and publishers have embraced and promoted "debundling" as a sales strategy, despite the fact that it has existed all along. The textbook publishing industry attempts to defend itself against charges of price gouging (successfully or not) through consumer education, for example, at **textbookfacts.org**.

ACSFA's 2007 Report

In 2006, members of the Association of American Publishers participated in a study of the impact of textbook costs on students, conducted by the Congressional Advisory Committee on Student Financial

Assistance. The ACSFA's 2007 report, *Turn the Page: Making College Textbooks More Affordable*, rejected legislated price controls in favor of publisher-initiated efforts to make course materials available more cheaply. This is to be done via online digital clearinghouses where publishers' products and prices can be directly compared, bought, sold, and cobbled together to make unique courses. Such clearinghouses also are to manage permissions for printable, customized course packs that mix and match content from a number of different publishers. Other recommendations include:

- strengthening the used book market;
- building textbook rental programs and buying consortiums;
- bypassing conventional publishers with low- or no-cost, no-frills content;
- creating more textbook lending libraries;
- resisting forced rollovers and retaining older editions; and
- subsidizing students' textbook purchases as needed.

These measures may decrease prices and marketing costs but potentially also decrease profitability for both publishers and authors. (See **ed.gov/ about/ bdscomm/list/acsfa/turnthepage.pdf** to read the full ACSFA report.)

Meanwhile, questions remain unanswered about the roles in textbook pricing of the used book brokers, the college store industry, the retail chains (which may have markups of 50% or more), and the ever-increasing publishers' costs. Publishers point out that competition—for example, among authors for advance money against royalties—could easily offset savings from digitized delivery.

Publishing Industry Trends

The textbook publishing business, like most other businesses, is the slave of consumer demand and customer satisfaction, and is also the driver (and victim) of market forces. In the past decade, to summarize, customers have expressed the following trends.

- Rebellion against forced rollovers and ever-higher prices for slightly revised textbooks published too soon as new editions.
- Greater use of customization. More instructors are skipping expensive textbooks altogether in favor of articles hand-picked from content sites such as **knowledgeplex.org** and **planetizen.org**.
- Demand for lower prices, greater value, and debundled supplements, along with demand for open access textbooks. At freeloadpress.com, for example, students can download textbooks in a variety of subjects for free (along with the advertising that pays for them).

- Increase in new and used textbook sharing, pirating, buying back, renting, and online merchandizing. Amazon, eBay, Half.com and other online retailers have bustling textbook businesses. At **SwapSimple.com** students can trade textbooks among themselves for as little as $2 plus shipping.

Publishers seem to be responding to these marketplace trends in many ways, such as the following.

- Reduced prices and cheaper alternative means of delivery, such as no-frills bargain textbooks (e.g., coverless three-hole punched) and reusable digitized content.
- Quest for new product models such as custom online courses and "shadow texts" (products resembling comprehensive study guides for students who want to get through a course without actually having to buy or read a textbook).
- Direct sales of content to students. For example, at **iChapter.com** (Thompson Learning), students can purchase individual textbook chapters for as little as $2 each.
- Fewer supplements of higher quality, kept optional, sold separately or offered online.

In addition, on a broader front, publishers continue to cope with ongoing, long-standing market challenges that relate to corporate finance and globalization. The following responses to these challenges cut across all the media, information, and entertainment industries.

- Increase in company mergers and acquisitions with aggressive rebranding and a smaller number of projects (potentially at the expense of product diversity and excellence).
- Dedication to economies of scale and principles of standardization, downsizing with outsourcing, and the export of manufactory (potentially at the expense of quality and talent).
- Major investment in content and software development for new technologies, including interactive websites, online courses, and products for handheld computers. For Pearson, for example, Audible has created VangoNotes—audio study guides for textbooks in which students can listen to chapter reviews on their iPods for around $3 apiece.
- Market expansion, customization, and the development of niche markets in response to globalization and new opportunities in rapidly growing transnational markets.

Where will these trends and patterns take us as authors, editors, and publishers in the field of higher education?

Higher Education Publishing Options

Whatever the future holds, and however you cut it—whether you go by the publishing industry's 2006 tally of $3.5 billion in sales, Simba's tally of $3.7 billion, or the college store industry's figure of $6.2 billion—the term "big business" definitely applies to college textbooks. This business is spread, however, among highly diverse companies.

The four main kinds of higher education publishing houses are university presses, scholarly or academic presses, professional association publishing groups, and college textbook divisions of larger commercial publishers. Companies within each category vary widely in the number and size of lists they serve, the number of titles they publish annually—between one and thousands—and the amount of revenue they generate in total annual sales.

Each type of college house has advantages and disadvantages for you as an author. The 200 or so universities and professional associations that publish textbooks, for example, may offer special consideration to members, greater prestige in the academic or professional community, and greater authorial control over the product. These publishing houses, along with many smaller academic presses, sometimes offer a high-quality product; however, they typically invest less in marketing, sales, and distribution. For example, they often lack sales forces in the field, and their products tend to be professional books, supplemental texts, and adult nonfiction trade books for postgraduate readers.

Authors seldom make much money with smaller association-dependent or university-affiliated presses. Worse, authors may be asked to subsidize their publications out-of-pocket, without particular hope of recovering expenses. This kind of academic publishing parallels the operation of vanity presses in the trade book industry. However, as one observer points out:

> A book published by a university press that the author was required to partially subsidize is not regarded the same way in academia as one published by a vanity press. This type of subsidy is sometimes referred to as an author subvention (Parsons 1989). Its purpose is to enable the press to afford to publish a book that is likely to have low sales because the topic is of interest to only a relatively small number of students or other persons. (Silverman, 2004)

In contrast, larger commercial houses offer greater investment in your book and potentially more sales with larger advances and royalty checks. Because of their expense, textbooks, especially those for introductory survey courses, mainly are the preserve of big publishers who are in business to make money. Thus, these publishers focus on serving faculties who teach specific undergraduate courses listed in the course catalogues of colleges and universities worldwide.

The Right Publisher for Your Book

The first step to finding the right type of publisher for your book is determining what kind of a book you wish to publish, why, and for whom. Prospective authors often misidentify their work, thinking they have produced a textbook, for example, when actually they have created a dissertation conversion, a professional book for practitioners, a scholarly book for colleagues, a contributed volume or anthology, a reference work, a course supplement, or a crossover trade book aimed perhaps at the *New York Times* lists of best-selling nonfiction. Here are some rules of thumb for identifying the right type of publisher for what you have in mind.

Association Publications

Professional associations publish books by members and others for practitioners in the specific field or profession for which the association or society exists. Most are nonprofit organizations. Acquisitions are based on membership and author reputation and the relevance or currency of the work for the advancement of the field of study. Most publishing opportunities are in journals, but some larger associations also publish books. Examples are the American Educational Research Association (AERA), the American Mathematical Society (AMS), and the American Psychological Association (APA).

Although associations and societies may publish works for students entering their fields, especially career guides, they usually do not publish textbooks. The American Medical Association (AMA) and American Bar Association (ABA), for example, publish professional books and reference books for practicing members of their professions. The markets for association publications may be comparatively small or narrow, therefore, and not widely distributed. They typically are sold from association or society websites. For complete listings of academic and professional associations, start your search at the Internet Public Library at **ipl.org/div/aon**.

University Presses

University, scholarly, and academic presses publish theoretical discourses, research papers, intellectual syntheses, dissertation conversions, original contributions to a field of study, papers on esoteric subjects, reprints of classics, critical reviews of the literature of a field, translations, and sometimes symposium papers and Festschrifts. Acquisitions are based on institutional affiliation, subject and discipline, and author reputation.

University press publishing operations typically are endowed or subsidized and vary greatly in size and permanence. Examples include Oxford University Press (in revenues one of the top ten publishers of college textbooks today), the University of Chicago Press, Georgetown University Press, Vanderbilt University Press, Texas Tech University Press, and University Press of New England.

In 2007 the American Association of University Presses had 112 not-for-profit member organizations (AAUP, 2007), including other non-profits, such as the Brookings Institution Press, Carnegie Mellon, Teachers College Press, Modern Language Association, and the National Gallery of Art. For a complete list of AAUP members, see **aaupnet.org/membership/directory.html.**

University presses account for only a small segment of the higher education market. In 2006, university presses had hardcover sales of $6.6 million and paperback sales of $5.1 million, a slight decline from 2005 (AAP, 2007). Many not-for-profit publishing arms have found it increasingly difficult to attract sufficient sponsorship or funding to maintain publishing operations and personnel. One solution has been for institutions to join forces. The University Press of New England, for example, is a consortium supported jointly by Brandeis University, Dartmouth College, the University of New Hampshire, Northeastern University, Tufts University, and the University of Vermont. Another strategy has been to publish more trade books—adult trade non-fiction—thereby increasing revenues through sales to larger markets.

The Ithaka Report

The 2007 Ithaka Report (**ithaka.org**) reviewed the state of university presses (Brown et al., 2007). The report concluded that universities need to be more involved in publishing scholarship and that university presses need to partner more closely with their institutions. University presses should help more in the digitization and management of their universities' information assets. Most imperatively, according to the Ithaka Report, university presses need to both publish and distribute more online, both commercially and not-for-profit at the same time. This report reflects the radical Internet-based changes taking place today in the knowledge business.

Still, the university presses may be in more trouble than these measures can remedy. In August 2007, for example, The American Anthropological Association withdrew from its university press (University of California) to be published commercially by Wiley-Blackwell, a move that worries many scholars, academic librarians, and publishers. According to an *Inside Higher Education* report (**insidehighered.com/news/2007/08/22/anthro**, Publishing and Values, August 22, 2007):

Some object to the move from a university press to a commercial entity and fear a lessening of commitment to important scholarship that may not make money. Others see this as a sign that the anthropology association—which has won praise for the online offerings of its journals—is taking a hard line against the open access movement embraced by many of its members (and the library world). Still others see the move as a sign that scholarly societies are facing tough decisions about their missions—without good mechanisms for involving the academic rank and file in making decisions.

Scholarly Publishing

Some examples of large and small academic or scholarly presses are National Academy Press (a government publisher), F. A. Davis Company, Cold Spring Harbor Laboratory Press, Laurence Erlbaum, M. E. Sharpe, Slack Incorporated, and I. B. Taurus. Many of these, along with many university presses, are members of the Society for Scholarly Publishing (**sspnet.org**).

Scholarly publishers, like university presses, have faced a growing crisis due mainly to three ongoing trends affecting the academic publishing industry and its markets: the revolt against journal pricing, a shift away from publishing pure scholarship, and the open access movement.

1. Libraries increasingly have refused to pay the high prices requested for scholarly and scientific journals and databases. Library consortia now routinely reduce costs by sharing these resources. As a result, companies whose journals account for much of their business have had difficulty resisting acquisition to remain independent. In 2006, for example, John Wiley & Sons acquired Blackwell Publishing for £572 million, along with Blackwell's 825 journals and a publishing list of 600 books a year (Munroe, 2007).

Project Gutenberg (**gutenberg.org**) was an early leader in making literature and scholarship in the public domain freely available in an online library. Well-known collaborations between libraries and publishers to provide broader access to scholarly journals—by putting back issues online—include, for example, Project Muse (Johns Hopkins University Press, **muse.jhu.edu**), JSTOR (Journal Storage, Andrew W. Mellon Foundation, **jstor.org**), and Science Direct (**science-direct.com**). Scholarly journals remain big moneymakers, however, despite this trend. In July 2007, with an eye to revenues, *Science* withdrew from JSTOR to manage its own online subscription services on a commercial basis.

2. Successful small academic presses continue to be gobbled up by large conglomerates that require higher profit margins from their companies. Commercially successful acquired products are rebranded and the rest are soon ditched or repurposed as "content." Even larger academic presses have struggled to remain profitable, however, as demand for academic and scholarly titles has fluctuated, plateaued, or fallen.

Other than market specialization, solutions have focused on shifting more acquisitions from scholarly manuscripts and monographs to either trade book or textbook manuscripts, both of which have larger markets and therefore are more lucrative. Publishers such as Sage, Palgrave, Springer, Routledge, and Taylor & Francis, for example, publish proportionally more college textbooks today than in the past. These and similar companies often seek to fill demand for second- and third-tier textbooks (or intermediate and graduate level), leaving the introductory markets to the bigger players.

3. The open access movement, along with the spread of the wiki phenomenon and the concept of Creative Commons, has detoured many scholarly works that otherwise might have found their way into acquisitions for the academic and scholarly publishing business. Open access works (peer-reviewed or not) have been made available for free online—potentially a great boon to students, librarians, researchers, and practitioners globally—and a foretaste of even more radical changes to come in the Information Age. This movement is discussed in more detail later in the chapter.

In 2006, sales of professional and scholarly books amounted to $50.8 million (AAP, 2007). Despite the crisis in scholarly publishing, this figure still represents only a slight decline from previous years. Meanwhile, the online publication of scholarly content is exploding through publishers such as Google Scholar (**scholar.google.com**), the MIT Press Cognet (**cognet.mit.edu/library**), DSpace projects such as MIT's (**dspace.mit.edu**), and new initiatives such as High Wire Press (**highwire.stanford.edu**).

Professional Books

Publishers of professional books publish how-to books for practitioners, training manuals, preparations for certification or licensure, guides to practice, desk references, readers or contributed volumes, surveys of literature and research on practices in a particular field, point-of-view books for colleagues and practitioners, and books on theory and research for graduate and postgraduate students. Acquisitions are by affiliation and field or profession. Publishers of professional books often also publish reference books in their fields.

Two distinct markets for professional books are referred to as PTR (Professional-Technical-Reference) and STM (Scientific-Technical-Medical). A range of PTR publishers includes, for example, Prentice Hall PTR, Thomson Course Technology, Sams Publishing (a computer book publisher owned by Pearson Education), and independents such as technical and computer book publisher O'Reilly. STM publishers include medical, legal, engineering, and scientific publishers such as Reed Elsevier, Wolters Kluwer Health, and associations such as the American Academy of Pediatrics. Other STM publishers are listed at **stm-assoc.org**.

PTR-STM markets, like other academic markets, are changing significantly as they become more webcentric, open access, and wiki-oriented. Examples are ChemWeb (**chemweb.com**), SPARC (Scholarly Publishing and Academic Resources Coalition, **arl.org/sparc**), and the Public Library of Science (**PLoS.org**). This trend is reinforced as many U.S. government agencies mandate that their information services be managed independently online. Examples are the web portals of the NTIS (National Technical Information Services, **ntis.gov**) and ERIC (Education Resources Information Center, **eric.ed.gov**).

Reference Books

Publishers of library and reference works publish annotated bibliographies, topical dictionaries and encyclopedias, foreign language dictionaries, subject area anthologies and handbooks, travel and college guides, data and databases (such as the Yellow Pages), and maps and atlases. Acquisitions are both general and by subject. Academic reference book divisions often are contained within larger parent companies, such as Oxford University Press, Houghton Mifflin, Rowman & Littlefield, Bowker, Merriam-Webster, St. Martins Press, and Thomson Gale. Thomson Gale, for example, maintains more than 600 databases; its imprints include Macmillan Reference, Charles Scribner's Sons, Scholarly Resources Inc., and online products such as InfoTrac College Edition.

Reference book publishers and divisions tend to specialize. Thomson West, for example, which incorporates the old West Publishing Company, Westlaw, Foundation Press, The Rutter Group, and FindLaw.com, publishes legal reference works exclusively. Thieme publishes highly targeted reference books in neurosurgery, radiology, otolaryngology, orthopedics, opthamology, audiology, and other medical sub-specialties. Reference book publishers include smaller and mid-size presses as well, which often succeed in niche markets.

Many standard reference works are now available by subscription online and offer limited free access. As in other parts of the industry, many proprietary reference book publishers see the open access movement as a threat to their business. For example, online dictionaries such as Microsoft's Encarta (**encarta.com**), the Merriam-Webster Dictionary (**m-w.com**), and Houghton Mifflin's American Heritage Dictionary (**yourdictionary.com**) all are offered for free online.

Commercial advertising increasingly supports free web-based reference works. With the current massive growth of online advertising, digitization projects ultimately may benefit the reference book business, which otherwise is one of the costliest to maintain for both producers and consumers. At risk, however, may be quality of content. According to lexicographers, for example, the free dictionaries obscure the existence of other dictionaries and may be (1) technically or editorially inferior to others, and (2) not the best choices for all users (Kirkpatrick, 2000). On this case, the jury is still out.

Trade Book Publishers

If you would like members of the general public to read your book, rather than students in a course or colleagues, then you may have written a trade book (certainly not a textbook or professional book). Trade books are sold or made available in brick-and-mortar and online bookshops and chain stores (such as Barnes & Noble or Borders), in mass-market outlets (such as Wal-mart or Costco), in public libraries, and in places such as gift shops, museums, and airports.

Trade book publishers publish children's, young adult, and adult fiction and nonfiction in various genres (e.g., self-help, humor, inspirational, career, and biography). For a complete list of genres, see the Book Industry Study Group's (BISG) subject listing at **bisg.org/standards/bisac_subject/major_subjects.html**. Another leading source of detailed information about trade book publishing is **simbanet.com**.

Trade book acquisitions are based on author reputation (or notoriety) and the sensationality, timeliness, trendiness, or mass-market appeal of the subject. Books by literati and other celebrities, Pulitzer Prize winners, politicians and political pundits, social critics, Nobel Laureates, and rogue scientists populate the lists of bestselling hardcover and paperback nonfiction. Academics have famously published their professional memoirs as trade books (for example, Mary Leakey's autobiography, *Disclosing the Past*, by Doubleday, and Jane Goodall's *My Life with the Chimpanzees*, by Aladdin). Scholars and scientists also have published popularizations of academic subjects for entertainment and enlightenment (and sometimes for Oprah interviews, television rights, and film adaptations—e.g., Carl Sagan's *Cosmos*, by Random, and Stephen Hawking's *A Brief History of Time*, by Bantam).

Trade book publishers (some of which have sibling textbook divisions) include, for example, Simon & Schuster (Isacson's *Einstein*), Penguin (Philbrick's *Mayflower*), Norton (Diamond's *Guns, Germs and Steel*), Houghton Mifflin (Dawkins's *The God Delusion*), Farrar, Straus and Giroux (Friedman's *The World Is Flat*), and others such as Harper Collins and Rodale—along with tens of thousands of small presses, such as those listed at **pma-online.org** (Independent Book Publishers Association).

Educational Publishers

Educational publishing is sometimes referred to as El-Hi Publishing, referring to preK-12 textbooks, readers, and other instructional materials for preschool, elementary school, and high school students and their teachers. Examples of commercial educational publishers are Benchmark, Corwin, Harcourt, Jostens, McGraw-Hill, Scholastic, and Scott Foresman (Pearson). The top three are Pearson, McGraw-Hill, and Houghton Mifflin. In 2007, Houghton Mifflin Riverdeep Group PLC began purchasing units of Harcourt (Harcourt Education, Harcourt Trade, and Greenwood-Heinemann) from Reed Elsevier for around $4 billion (CNNMoney.com, July 16, 2007). Those units include Harcourt's K-12 and higher education publishing assets.

Non-profit publishers outnumber the commercial houses in the K-12 field, however, and include, for example, the California Teacher's Association, George Lucas Educational Foundation, International Reading Association, National Endowment for the Humanities, National Science Teachers Association, and so on. For more examples, see the Association of Educational Publishers at **aepweb.org**.

Trade book authors and publishers often try to cross-market to education channels. This can work, especially when the product is tied in explicitly to curriculum and instruction, refers to state or national education standards, makes the recommended reading lists of school districts and state adoption committees, and instructs school teachers and school librarians in their use. Books for pre-service teachers are college textbooks or course supplements for the teacher education market, while books for in-service teachers usually are published as professional books.

The El-Hi basal and supplemental K-12 publishing industry posted decreased sales (by 5.9%) for 2006, totaling $6.2 billion (AAP, 2007). Educational publishing is in a different business than trade book publishers or even higher education textbook publishers. El-Hi market acceptance is more restrictive and regulated, their publishing and sales cycles are more long-term, and their marketing and distribution channels are more specialized—a subject for another book.

College Textbook Publishers

Commercial publishers of college textbooks publish introductory and intermediate textbooks and supplements for undergraduate students and graduate students enrolled in titled college courses. These courses include surveys and introductions to fields of study and their history and philosophy, theory and methods, and applications. Acquisitions are based on academic department or course name and author reputation.

The appendix at the end of this chapter presents a sampling of selected commercial college houses by subject area specialties, including the top 10 higher education publishers in the nation. The sample includes some small, highly specialized companies that publish in only one subject, as well as giant companies with many imprints that publish in all subjects taught at the college level.

The list, taken from the 2006 LMP and other sources, is incomplete and is not intended to provide specific recommendations. It emphasizes textbook publishers over scholarly and academic publishers but includes some academic publishers who identify themselves as suppliers to the market for college textbook supplements. Acqweb (**acqweb.org/pubr/text.html**) and the Literary Market Place (**literarymarketplace.com**) have more listings. Also, the sample may no longer be accurate, as mergers, consolidations, and divestitures are common in the publishing industry, with the effect of moving lists and imprints around and reducing the number of big players worldwide.

Thus, both the number and diversity of large textbook publishers change often in this highly competitive, merger-driven industry. In 2002 Vivendi sold Houghton Mifflin to private investors after less than two years of ownership, for example, and in 2003 Bertelsmann sold the science publisher BertelsmannSpringer (with more than 700 journals, 70 publishing houses, and 4,000 new books a year) to private equity firms. Previously Bertelsmann acquired Springer-Verlag, from which BertelsmannSpringer was created. After the sale, the latter was merged with another acquisition, Kluwer Academic Publishers (Poynder, 2003). And so it goes.

Corporations also are quick to divest themselves of units that show weakness or compete less well. A case in point is Thomson Learning, which, along with Nelson Canada, was sold in 2007 to two private equity investment firms for $7.75 billion (Quint, 2007). Thomson Learning imprints include (among others) Wadsworth, Delmar, Heinle, Brooks/Cole, Prometric, South-Western, West, and the Gale Group, which publishes reference books, databases, and news feeds, e.g., to Dialog, Factiva, and LexisNexis. The Thomson Corporation promptly put the proceeds of the sale of Thomson Learning toward acquiring the business news agency Reuters for over $17 billion (TheStreet.com, 2007).

One might well ask, why publish commercially? Good question, but in reality publishing commercially can be seen as an investment in your future as an expert and as a hedge against the cost of retirement. Such an investment may well be worth making in relation to (1) the impact you may have on future generations of workers in your field, and (2) the level of risk you are willing to undertake—the risks inherent in the textbook business today as well as the risks implicit in author-publisher relations (the subject of another chapter).

Despite the time and effort involved and the harsh realities and uncertainties, commercial publishing may give you—in addition to greater satisfaction professionally—larger advances, bigger royalties, broader exposure, more publicity, and greater influence on people in or entering your field. Quoting N. Gregory Mankiw, Professor of Economics at Harvard University and renowned textbook author in his field, "Writing a textbook is a lot of work, and I am sometimes asked why I choose to spend my time this way. So let me explain."

> Textbook writing is a form of teaching. As such, it has all the pluses and minuses of teaching. The major minus is that it takes time. And time is an academic's most valuable resource.
>
> Despite the cost, I view textbook writing, like classroom teaching, as a good use of my time. One benefit is pecuniary. Few people in the world earn a living just creating knowledge. Most academics spend some of their time imparting knowledge as well. Giving lectures is one way of imparting knowledge; writing textbooks is another. So far, I have been able to make enough money imparting knowledge to students that I have not had to spend time on other activities, such as paid consulting, to put food on the table. (Greg Mankiw's Blog, posted March 4, 2007)

At the same time, there are other alternatives.

Publishing Alternatives

Unlike trade books, textbooks normally are not agented, nor are they sold at auction to publishers. As Chapter 3 attempts to show, in the textbook market, getting published is not difficult if you meet certain conditions and talk to the right editor. Some authors have a strong preference to avoid the traditional commercial route, however. There are some good reasons for this, philosophical and practical, not least that publishing for profit on a national scale requires a huge outlay of time and some negotiation of the content and organization of your text. One alternative to commercial publishing is publishing a course supplement with a not-for-profit publisher, such as a professional association or society or, if you are positioned properly, the government. See for example, the National Academy Press at **nap.edu**. Two other alternatives are custom publishing and self-publishing.

Custom Publishing

Most large college houses have custom publishing units in which your syllabus, bibliography, and unique course materials can be bound together (or digitally assembled) with chapters you select from publishers' textbooks. Pearson Education has a custom publishing unit (**pearsoncustom.com**); also McGraw-Hill (**mhhe.com/primis**), Thomson (**thomsoncustom.com**), which partners with Atomic Dog Publishing (**atomicdogpublishing.com**), and Houghton Mifflin (**college.hmco.com/instructors/ins_custompub_home**). Smaller independent presses also offer custom publishing services to college instructors and academic authors. See, for example, **senatehall.com** and **cjp.com**.

Custom publishing is done both in print and electronically. At an institutional or departmental level, branded or proprietary course management software, such as Blackboard (**blackboard.com**), WebCT (**webct.com**), or CourseCompass (**coursecompass.com**), offer opportunities to customize online courses by selecting course modules, readings, learning objects, and interactivities, and adding specific, unique course information and instructional materials. Customization options also include compiling relevant current articles and images from database companies such as EBSCO (**epnet.com**), OVID (**ovid.com**), or H. W. Wilson (**hwwilson.com**).

Large copy centers, such as Kinko's (**kinkos.com**), and myriad desktop publishing enterprises also do custom publishing from camera-ready copy, from disk, or from digital archives. Usually, the author-instructor arranges for the college bookstore to sell the custom text to his or her students at cost plus the bookstore's markup. Colleges and universities have policies prohibiting the direct sale of course materials to students by instructors. However, vendors operating independently of publishing houses, such as Xanedu (**xanedu.com**) and Etext.net (**etext.net**) may broker print publishing services or offer custom electronic textbooks online. Distribution services usually include online direct sales to students. To face this challenge, many larger college stores manage custom publishing operations of their own. There are many examples, such as Indiana University's ClassPak Custom Publishing unit at **iubookstore.com/custom_pub**.

Custom publishing costs includes permissions fees, for permissions must be scrupulously compiled. Custom publishers will not produce a book until all permissions are cleared. Some providers offer the paid service of querying copyright clearance centers for you. Chapter 15 of this book provides more information about intellectual property rights and the permissioning process.

Self-Publishing

A registry for free and for-sale self-published online textbooks is maintained at **connectext.com**. However, most academic self-publishing is done on a small scale to meet specific instructional or career needs. For example, one form of self-publishing is self-archiving materials in online repositories, which then also serve as resources for citation or for custom publishing by others. Online self-publishing of dissertations is commonplace among students, as is online self-publication of preprints (and now postprints as well), among scholars and researchers. This kind of self-publishing, which some institutions now even require, has led to the development of online directories of these resources, especially in mathematics and the sciences. See, for example, **mathnet.preprints.org** or **hep.net/references/preprints**. Most colleges and universities and many associations archive dissertations for online access, such as the American Historical Association's (AHA) directory, **historians.org/pubs/dissertations**.

In addition, instructors can develop and self-publish multimedia courses or e-texts using for-sale or open access learning objects maintained, for example, at MERLOT (**merlot.org**). Finally, as noted previously, many fee-for-service companies, such as **brownwalker.com**, exist to assist instructors and academics in self-publishing and marketing their work.

Academic authors seeking to self-publish must be aware that publishing through a vanity or subsidy press (you pay them money to publish your book under their imprint) will make your book unmarketable to the trade. That is, with few exceptions your book will be rejected for review and bookstore and library buyers will not purchase it, because it is self-published with a subsidy press as the publisher of record. It is easy for authors to be misled. Vanity presses do not refer to themselves as such and go to some lengths to dispel authors' misgivings. They may even call themselves co-publishers. Their industry has evolved to reflect new printing technologies, especially print-on-demand (POD) publishing, in which books are printed on a sheet-fed press or output printer one copy at a time at a comparatively much higher per-unit cost. This kind of publishing is suitable if you plan to distribute or sell a small number of copies (say, a hundred or so), do not need to recover your printing costs, do not hope to distribute the book widely, and do not intend to cite the work in your bid for tenure.

In contrast, true self-publishing involves starting a business as an independent publisher and purchasing a block of ISBN numbers for your books, which you write, register, produce, promote, advertise, market, sell, and, often, ship by yourself. You pay the printer for the print run, the freight company, the phone company, and other operating and overhead costs. In time and money, the cost of marketing is easily three to five times greater than the cost of publishing. You call all the shots, but to break even or turn a profit—even with POD technology—textbook authors who self-publish need more than their own students to buy the book.

Examples of self-publishing textbook authors may be found in the ranks of small publishers, who collectively account for a significant percentage of industry revenues. Their role is to serve specialized markets—local or regional markets, esoteric subjects, and courses with enrollments too small to be profitable for the giants to enter or serve well. Some of these small companies then grow by publishing in other genres or by publishing the works of other authors. A range of examples of such companies may be seen at **amhistpress.com, paradigmpublishers.com, teaching-point.com**, and **orchardpublications.com.** Large publishers mine the small independents for acquisitions. An example may be seen at **larsontexts.com**, a self-publisher turned small publisher announcing that Houghton Mifflin now publishes its college textbooks. In addition, self-published authors often attract traditional commercial publishers for their second editions or subsequent titles.

If you are interested in being a publisher, you may find the information and inspiration you need in the following selected resources.

Byron, D. L. and Steve Broback. *Publish & Prosper: Blogging for Your Business*. New Riders Press, 2006.

Cardoza, Avery, *Complete Guide to Successful Publishing.* Cardoza Publishing, 2002.

Cole, David. *Complete Guide to Book Marketing*. Allworth Press, 2004.

Epstein, Jason. *Book Business: Publishing Past, Present, and Future*. W. W. Norton, 2002.

Kenley, Eric and Beach, Mark. *Getting It Printed: How to Work with Printers and Graphic Imaging*, 4th ed. F&W Publications Inc., 2004.

Kremer, John. *1001 Ways to Market Your Books*, 6th ed. Open Horizons, 2006.

Hupalo, Peter. I. *How to Start and Run a Small Book Publishing Company*. HCM Publishing, 2002.

Poynter, Dan. *The Self-Publishing Manual: How to Write, Print and Sell Your Own Book*, 16th ed. Para Publishing, 2007.

Rosenthal, Morris. *Print-on-Demand Book Publishing*. Foner Books, 2004.

Ross, Tom, and Marilyn H. Ross. *The Complete Guide to Self-Publishing*, 4th ed. Writer's Digest Books, 2002.

Shepard, Aaron. Perfect Pages: *Self-Publishing with Microsoft Word*. Shepard Publications, 2006.

_____. *Aiming at Amazon: The NEW Business of Self-Publishing*. Shepard Publications, 2007.

Silverman, Franklin H. *Self-Publishing Textbooks and Instructional Materials*. Atlantic Path Publishing, 2004.

Woll, Thomas. *Publishing for Profit*, 3rd rev. ed. Chicago Review Press, 2006.

Some links:

Academic Small Publishers Listserv: **finance.groups.yahoo.com/group/Academic-Education**

Para Publishing: **parapublishing.com**

Publishers Marketing Association: **pma-online.org**

Small Publishers Association of North America: **spannet.org**
Self-Publishing Listserv: **finance.groups.yahoo.com/group/Self-Publishing**

A key issue with self-publishing is the credibility and authority of authorship and content, and perhaps the only way to deal with this for a self-published textbook is to invest in a rigorous process of peer review and professional endorsement. One way to do this is on sites that organize online conferences and permit you to publish documents and invite reviewers to comment on them. See, for example, **oxford-abstracts.com** and **conferencereview.com.** Another possibility is custom survey sites, such as Survey Monkey (**surveymonkey.com**) or Zoomerand (**info.zoomerang.com**).

The Open Access Movement

Self-archiving is a form of self-publishing that has grown rapidly in popularity. See, for example, 2,795 or more open access STM (scientific, technical and medical) journals listed at **doaj.org**, the Directory of Open Access Journals. The Open Access movement actually began in the mid-1960s with the Open Archive Initiative (OAI) and establishment of the first digital libraries. (The related open source movement in software development began even earlier, in the 1950s.) The open access movement was (and is) born of idealism and based on principles of information sharing for the common good. For a fascinating historical perspective on this movement see Peter Suber's annotated timeline at **earlham.edu/~peters/fos/timeline**. Suber is a well-known leader and researcher in open access and SPARC (Scholarly Publishing and Academic Resources Coalition).

Some academics argue that information is an inalienable human right and that all knowledge should be free to all. My answer to this is absolutely yes, but where will my income come from? As a writer, editor, or publisher of information, how will I pay my bills? I would hate to think of us all becoming part of a government entitlement program, or of institutional control replacing free market forces in determining content and demand. I also would hate to publish my online chemistry textbook, say, with ads for Dow, Monsanto, Pfizer, and other chemical companies on the pages. For these reasons, along with the fact that we live in a world driven by capitalism, open access cannot replace commercial publishing at this time (or any time soon, barring economic apocalypse).

Many publishers are threatened by the open access movement nevertheless, even as they move more toward digital delivery of textbooks and instructional materials. Digital publishing presently is not as profitable as print. For participants in the open access movement, however, profitability simply is not an issue. Typically, the participants are scholars, scientists, researchers, and educators with funding from grants, endowed chairs, philanthropic organizations, institutional salaries, and the like. Publishing or self-archiving in an open access journal or repository is already paid for—that is, paying the bills does not depend on publishing revenues but on attracting funding from other sources.

Research has hinted that the chief attraction of open access for academics (aside from the philosophical) is (1) the easy searchability of content through keywords and metatags, (2) the far greater number of "hits" one gets than from readership through library patronage or paid journal subscriptions, and (3) the resulting increase in citations, which boosts visibility, credibility, and standing in the grant-getting world as well as with one's academic department, tenure committee, or institution. Scholarship criteria for promotion and tenure will have to change to reflect the new publishing model of open access. Also see Open Content Alliance at **opencontentalliance.org**.

Other new publishing models include blogs—chronological personal writings, including researchers' field notes; wikis—collaborative websites that anyone can edit; and crowdsourcing—online publishing of content to which readers are invited to contribute. For better or worse, some social science researchers already are using crowdsourcing as a way to collect qualitative data. For a perspective on the Open Education Resource movement in higher education, explore the database and pages at **oedb.org**, especially **oedb.org/library/features/80-oer-tools**.

Wikipedia, the online anyone-can-edit encyclopedia, gets better as time goes on, but at the same time its problems grow. Articles in *The Independent* (Verkaik, August 18, 2007) and *The New York Times* (Hafner, August 19, 2007) reported that censorship is rampant, especially on the part of large corporations, industry advocacy organizations, and the government. Companies can simply redact or remove facts unfavorable to their industries, products, policies, business dealings, or environmental impacts. Instructors hoping to use wiki software to build collaborative textbooks with their students must be vigilant against dishonest uses and rogue content, and must themselves be prepared to defend against charges of censorship.

Having difficulty imagining a textbook as a wiki? Just see **en.wikibooks.org/wiki**, where you will find over 26,000 open-content modules and whole textbooks written by instructors and their students on subjects ranging from Spanish to sociology, European history, paleoanthropology, and nuclear medicine. Many educators decry the trend toward wiki textbooks. As the famous librarian Michael Gorman points out, it's essentially an issue of content authorship:

> [In] essence, we are asked to believe two things—first that an authoritative work can be the result of the aggregation of the opinions of self-selected anonymous "experts" with or without

credentials and, second, that the collective wisdom of the cyberswarm will correct errors and ensure authority. (**blogs.britannica.com/blog/main/2007/06/jabberwiki-the-educational-response-part-ii**)

Let us assume for the moment that you want to write and develop a textbook (without the cyberswarm) that initially will be delivered in print. As you will see, finding the right publishing venue and the right publisher, making contact with the right editor, and signing the right contract are half the battle in publishing your textbook. This book assumes that you rightly wish to publish a college textbook (rather than some other type of product) and that you most likely will be dealing with a comparatively large commercial publisher. On this basis, after an overview of the publishing process in Chapter 2, Chapters 3 and 4 offer basic advice on how to interest a publisher in your book idea or manuscript and how to negotiate your publishing agreement.

APPENDIX
College Textbook Publishers: A Sample By List Subjects

Note that listings also sample publishers of academic works intended as textbook supplements. Imprints are grouped under the names of parent companies at the time of this printing.

Brill (brill.nl)
Netherlands company specializing in academic and scholarly books in ancient history, Asian and Islamic studies, medieval and early modern studies, classics, religion, and social sciences. Imprints include Martinus Nijhoff (international law and human rights), VSP (materials science, chemistry, physics, engineering), IDC (rare and archival books), and Hotei Publishing (Japan studies).

Broadview Press (broadviewpress.com)
Canadian independent, publishing academic books and textbook supplements in the arts, history, and social sciences.

Cold Spring Harbor Laboratory Press (cshlpress.com)
Molecular and cell biology, genetics, cancer, microbiology, development, neuroscience.

F. A. Davis Publishing Co. (fadavis.com)
Medical, nursing, allied health.

Focus (R. Pullins) (pullins.com)
Classics, languages, philosophy, theater, film.

Franklin, Beedle and Associates (fbeedle.com)
Computer sciences, computers in education, computer engineering.

Guilford Press (guilford.com)
Professional and trade books in psychology, research methods, economics and business, politics and philosophy, communication, education, geography.

Holtzbrinck LLC is now Macmillan (macmillan.com)
German company owning around 40 imprints, including Macmillan (**macmillan.com**)—academic and scholarly monographs, textbooks and references books, literature, science, technology, medicine; Palgrave (**palgrave.com; palgravemacmillan.com.au**)—mainly humanities, social sciences, business. Holtzbrinck publishers also include Farrar, Straus and Giroux, Henry Holt, St. Martins Press, the Bedford, Freeman & Worth Publishing Group, and others. Bedford, Freeman, & Worth

Publishing Group (**bfwpub.com**) publishes mainly in corporate training, career education, trade/vocational training, business, government, military, distance learning. BFW imprints include Bedford/St. Martins (**bedfordstmartins.com**)—English, history, communications, philosophy, religion, humanities; W. H. Freeman & Co. (**whfreeman.com**)—science and math; and Worth Publishers Inc. (**worthpublishers.com**)—psychology, political science, economics, sociology, anthropology, biochemistry.

Houghton Mifflin Co. (hmco.com/divisions/college_division.html)
The college division focuses mainly on math, chemistry, business, history, developmental reading and writing, modern languages, and college study skills. Purchased Harcourt in 2007.

Hunter Textbooks (huntertextbooks.com)
Geology, physical education, biology, humanities.

I. B. Taurus (ibtaurus.com)
Academic books in the humanities, social sciences, Middle East and Islamic studies, religion, international relations, history, political studies, film and visual culture.

John Wiley & Sons Inc. (wiley.com)
The higher education division (**he-cda.wiley.com/WileyCDA/**) publishes core texts in architecture and design, business, modern languages, mathematics and statistics, science, public health, social and behavioral science, engineering and computer science, hospitality and culinary arts, and technical trades. Imprints include **Wrox** (**wrox.com**) and **Sybex** (**sybex.com**) computer books and the famous CliffsNotes and Dummies series. In 1999, Wiley acquired **JosseyBass** (**josseybass.com**) from Pearson—business, psychology, health management, education, biology and anatomy, engineering, math, economics and finance, and teacher education. In 2007 Wiley created **Wiley-Blackwell** (**blackwellpublishing.com**) through acquisition of Blackwell Publishers and Blackwell Science—arts, business, economics, finance, accounting, construction, engineering, technology, humanities, law, criminology, mathematics, statistics, medicine, nursing, health, dentistry, science, social and behavioral sciences, veterinary medicine, agriculture, aquaculture.

Jones & Bartlett Publishing Inc. (jbpub.com)
Allied health, biological sciences, computer science and CIS, criminal justice and law enforcement, electrical, emergency care and EMS, fire, health sciences and nutrition, health administration, mathematics, medicine, nursing, physical sciences, public health, and public administration. Chemistry, physics, life sciences, health, nursing,

math, computer science, earth science, philosophy, emergency care. Recently acquired companies are **Aspen** (health care) and **Management Concepts**.

Laurence King (laurenceking.com; laurenceking.co.uk)
Art, art history, architecture, design, fashion, typography, interior design.

Lyceum Books Inc. (lyceumbooks.com)
Social work, history.

McCutchan Publishing Corp. (mccutchanpublishing.com)
Education, food service management, law enforcement, police officer training.

McGraw-Hill Higher Education (mhhe.com)
All subjects. Catalogs include college prep, business, economics and CIT, careers, education, engineering and computer science, humanities, social studies and world languages, science and math. Acquisitions have included **Dushkin** (anthologies now called McGraw-Hill contemporary Learning Series); **William C. Brown**—conservation, geography, cartography, statitics; **Mayfield**—education, dance, physical education, anthropology, theater, psychology, sociology, humanities, journalism, English, speech and communication; and information companies such as *Standard and Poor's* and *Business Week*. **McGraw-Hill Professional** (**mhprofessional.com**) publishes upper level textbooks and course supplements in all subjects. **Irwin/McGraw-Hill** (**auth.mhhe.com/Irwin**) publishes books in accounting, business, finance, CIT-MIS, economics, and marketing.

M. E. Sharpe Inc. (mesharpe.com)
Social sciences and humanities, economics, political science, management and public administration, history, and literature. Also publishes original works and translations in Asian and East European studies.

O'Reilly Media (oreilly.com)
Textbooks and reference books in artificial intelligence, computer science, software development, e-business, and applied science and mathematics.

Oxford University Press (oup.co.uk)
College textbooks in all subjects, especially legal, business, economics, politics, social science, chemistry, biosciences, medicine, dentistry, and the humanities.

Paradigm Publishers (paradigmpublishers.com)
Textbooks and academic books in anthropology, communication, media, cultural studies, composition and rhetoric, literature, education, gender studies, women's studies, history, international studies, legal studies, Native American studies, philosophy, political science, psychology, race and ethnic studies, religious studies, sociology, and sports.

Pearson Publishing (pearsoned.com/higher-ed)
UK company publishing in all subjects. Imprints include **Addison-Wesley (aw-bc.com)**—computing, economics, finance, mathematics, statistics; **Longman (ablongman.com)**—English, history, philosophy, political science, religion; **Longman ESL (longmanusahome.com)**; **Allyn and Bacon (ablongman.com)**—education, psychology, sociology, social work communication, anthropology, criminal justice; **Benjamin Cummings (aw-bc.com)**—anatomy and physiology, biology, chemistry, health, kinesiology, microbiology, astronomy, physics; **Prentice Hall (vig.prenhall.com)**—all subjects; **National Evaluation Systems (nesinc.com)**—educational assessment; **Merrill Professional (allynbacon merrill.com)**—professional development in education. Other than Pearson Education, Pearson's other major properties include Scott Foresman, Family Education Network, Financial Times, and Penguin. In 2007 Pearson bought **Harcourt Assessment (harcourtassessment.com)** and **Harcourt Education International** CliffsNotes (**harcourt.co.uk**) from Reed Elsevier, which included, e.g., Heinemann.

Perseus Books Group (perseusbooksgroup.com)
Alternative textbooks and textbook supplements through participating publishers, e.g., **Basic Books**—politics, journalism; **Basic Civitas**—African and African American studies; **Westview**—social sciences and humanities; **DaCapo**—popular culture; **Nation Books (nationbooks.org)**; **Seal Press**—women's studies; and **Public Affairs (publicaffairsbookd.com)**.

Peter Lang (peterlang.com)
European publisher of academic books in all subjects.

Reed Elsevier Inc. (reedelsevier.com)
Business, law, education, medicine, science. Imprints include K-12 educational publishers such as **Boynton/Cook (boyntoncook.com)**; **Morgan Kaufman (mkp.com)**—computer science; **Elsevier (elsevier.com)**, which includes Mosby Inc., Saunders, Churchill Livingstone, and Butterworth and focuses on the health sciences, including dentistry and veterinary science; **LexisNexis**—business; and **Harcourt General**, which includes **Academic Press (academicpress.com)**, **Holt Rinehart & Winston (hrw.com)**, **Steck-Vaughn (harcourtachieve.com)**, **Harcourt**

Education (**harcourt.com**), **Classroom Connect** (**classroomconnect.com**), and others, such as academic books for college classroom use at **Harcourt Trade** (**harcourtbooks.com/tradebooks/academics.asp**). Reed Elsevier recently acquired the **Greenwood Publishing Group** (**greenwood.com**), which, in turn, includes **Praeger**—mostly academic and scholarly works in education, humanities, social and behavioral sciences, business, and law; and **Heinemann USA**—careers. In 2007, Houghton Mifflin purchased Harcourt General, Harcourt Education, and Harcourt Trade inclusive of all the units listed above.

Rowman & Littlefield (**rowmanlittlefield.com**)
Scholarly books for college courses. Imprints include **AltaMira Press** (**altamirapress.com**)—anthropology, archaeology, museum studies, philanthropy and nonprofit management; **Lexington Books** (**lexingtonbooks.com**)—academic monographs; and **R&L Education** (**rowmaneducation.com**)—education. Has many institutional co-publishers, and distributes for **Smithsonian Institution Scholarly Press**—American history and related subjects; **Cowley Publications** and **Sheed and Ward**—religion; the **National Film Network**, and the **University Press of America**—monographs in humanities and social sciences.

Sage Publishers Inc. (**sagepub.com**)
Textbooks, academic books, journals, databases, and reference books in social and behavioral sciences, including African studies, business, communication, counseling, criminology and criminal justice, education, geography, gerontology, health, human development, family studies, political science, psychology, research methods, social work, sociology, and women's studies. Imprints: **Pine Forge Press** (**pine forge.com**)—sociological theory; **Corwin Press** (**corwinpress.com**)—education; **Paul Chapman Publishing** (**paulchapmanpublishing.co.uk**)—education.

Sinauer Associates Inc. (**sinauer.com**)
Textbooks and educational multimedia in biology, psychology, neuroscience, and allied subjects. World distribution through Macmillan and Palgrave.

Springer (**springer.com**)
Architecture, design, biomedicine, life sciences, biosciences, neuroscience, clinical medicine, pharmacology, physical sciences, geosciences, history of science, scientists' biographies, engineering, mathematics, physics, statistics, computer science, human sciences, economics. Imprints include **Birkhauser Boston** (**springer.com**),

Humana (**humanapress.com**), **CMG** (Current Medicine Group) (**currentmedicinegroup.com**), and others.

Springer Publishing (springerpub.com)
Nursing, psychology, gerontology, geriatrics, social work, counseling, public health, rehabilitation, medical education.

Taylor and Francis Group (taylorandfrancis.com)
All subjects, traditionally social sciences and social studies.

Imprints include **Lawrence Erlbaum Associates** (**erlbaum.com**)—behavioral sciences, communications, communication disorders, education; **Psychology Press** (**psypress.com**)—academic psychology; **The Analytic Press** (**the analyticpress.com**)—psychoanalysis; **Garland Science** (**garlandscience.com**)—molecular biology, cell biology, genetics, immunology; **CRC Press** (**crcpress.com**)—biomedical sciences, chemical engineering, computer science, environmental science, food science, health care, life sciences, math, nutrition, physics, business and management, chemistry, engineering, ergonomics, forensic science, IT, material science, medicine, pharmaceutical science, statistics; **Routledge** (**routledge.com**)—architecture, art, Asian studies, British and American studies, business and management, classics, criminology economics, education, English, environmental sciences, gender studies, geological sciences, history, literature, media and film, modern languages, music, nursing and health care, philosophy, politics, international relations, psychotherapy, clinical psychology, religion, Russian studies, sociology, sport and leisure, strategic studies, theater and performance, tourism, translation, urban studies.

Thomson Information (thomsonedu.com)
Professional, business, medical, and legal. College imprints of Thomson Learning, all sold in 2007, include: **Brooks/Cole** (**thomsonedu.com/brookscole**)—counseling, social work, psychology, health, helping professions, mathematics, physical sciences, chemistry, physics, statistics, career development; **Delmar** (**thomsonedu.com/delmar**)—mainly health care, also business, industry, government, education, retail and fashion, electronics, technology, nursing, allied health, child care, agriculture, math, vocational studies, automotive, travel and tourism, engineering, paralegal, building trades, multimedia, graphic arts, distance learning; **Heinle** (**heinle.com**)—ESL and ELT, foreign and second language textbooks; **South-Western** (**thomsonedu.com/south-western**)—economics, accounting, business, education, social sciences, math, science, career education; **West** (**west.thomson.com/westlaw**)—law; **Wadsworth** (**thomsonedu.com/wadsworth**)—sociology, psychology, education. **Course Technology** (**course.com**)—computer

science, graphic design, MIS, music technology, programming; **Gale Group (galegroup.com)**—reference works and databases; **Nelson Canada (nelson.com)**—textbooks in all subjects, including Canadian editions of Thomson projects.

Thieme (thieme.com)
Texts and reference works in medicine and chemistry.

Waveland Press, Inc.: (waveland.com)
Ethnographies and anthropological monographs. Also publishes textbooks and textbook supplements in all core college subjects.

Wolters Kluwer (wolterskluwer.com)
Imprints include **Walters Kluwer Health (wkhealth.com)**—professional books and textbooks in medicine, nursing, allied health, and pharmacy; and **Aspen Publishers (aspenpublishers.com)**—business and law.

W. W. Norton and Co. Inc. (wwnorton.com/college.htm)
College textbooks and academic and trade books in all subjects, especially English, literature, humanities, history, and social sciences; including, e.g., African American studies, anthropology, astronomy, biology, chemistry, economics, English, environmental studies, film studies, geology, history, mathematics, computational science, music, philosophy, physics, political science, psychology, sociology, women's studies.

2

How College Textbooks Get Published

DEMAND FOR COLLEGE TEXTBOOKS is based on course enrollments on campuses worldwide, and the authors of college textbooks often are instructors dissatisfied with existing course offerings. Perhaps you are one of these and have picked up this book to learn more about higher education publishing. Authoring a college textbook can be immensely satisfying personally, professionally, and financially—but it is a lot of work.

The Publishing Process

The publishing process has five basic, equally important phases. The first is the acquisition phase, in which you submit a portion of your manuscript and sign a contract, while your editor prepares a publishing plan for your proposed textbook. The next phase is development, in which you draft and revise your manuscript in response to editorial input and

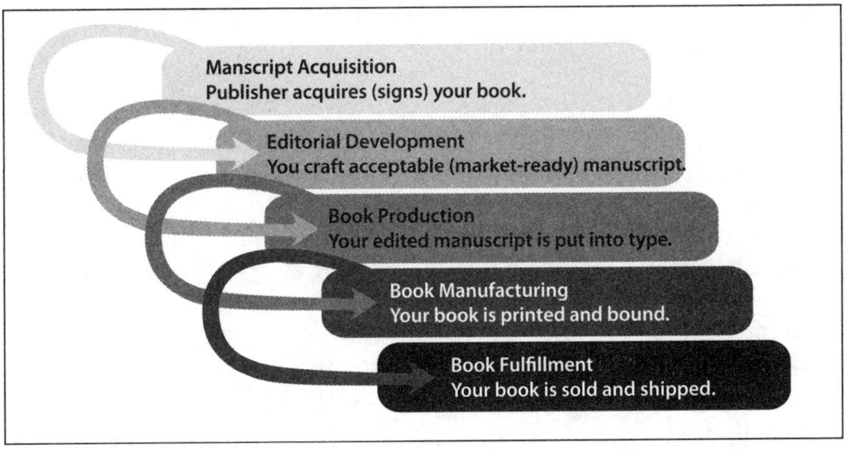

Figure 2-1. Five Phases of the Publishing Process

peer reviews, while your publisher prepares a marketing strategy. Your complete and final manuscript with all its components then enters the production phase, which ends when your copyedited, typeset manuscript is sent to the printer for manufacture. The manufacturing phase ends when your bound books are shipped to the warehouse, or the product is otherwise provided for distribution. Meanwhile, your publisher has arranged for the advertising, stocking, sampling, sales, and delivery of your book and its supplements to customers through college stores, sales catalogs, and commercial websites.

This book is chiefly about development, but this chapter is to acquaint you briefly with the publishing process and the publishing cycle.

Manuscript Acquisition

Publishing houses have editors whose job is to acquire manuscripts. Depending on the company's mission and size, this position is usually termed "acquisitions editor," or alternatively sponsoring editor, series editor, managing editor, associate editor, executive editor, or publisher. Acquisitions editors choose book projects and acquire manuscripts mainly through networking and recommendations from sales representatives in the field. They also attend professional meetings, survey professional literature, cultivate the colleagues of their current authors, and work at conventions, where product displays and company-sponsored events are staged to attract prospective authors as well as new customers. Your signing might take place in a meeting room at one of these conferences, or the company might pay your expenses to travel to their corporate headquarters. Today, however, many "signings" are done by mail and you may never have the opportunity to meet the editor or publisher. However, a high-quality acquisition almost always involves a face-to-face meeting at some point. The subject of publishing contracts is taken up in detail in Chapter 3.

Publishers' Lists

Acquisitions editors manage the publishers' book lists. A list covers a particular subject area and includes formerly published titles (its backlist), the current year's titles (its front list), and forthcoming signed books. Lists may be organized by field of study or academic department. Large lists might be divided among different editors according to finer distinctions within a subject area. For example, a history list might have different editors for American history and world history. In addition, books for graduate students and professional colleagues or practitioners in your field might be managed by one editor and books for undergraduates by another.

Publishers specialize in particular fields; therefore, their lists pertain only to certain subject areas or academic departments or even to particular courses. You cannot assume, therefore, that a publisher of textbooks on organic chemistry and polymer chemistry would be interested in one on biochemistry or molecular genetics, however related those subjects may be. Even very large houses specialize, usually according to the books they have sold most successfully in the past and their areas of strength as a result of list acquisitions, trades, or sales negotiated with other publishers as part of a larger corporate plan. The right publisher for your textbook may turn out to be a department within a subsidiary (a publishing unit) or an imprint (a publishing name or brand) within a much larger parent company.

Levels of Investment

During the acquisition phase, publishing executives plan the level of investment in your project. Levels of investment are expressed in a ranking system that reflects the book's market and projected sales. Ranking systems vary from publisher to publisher. Typically an "A-book" or a double- or triple-A is a four-color (full-color) product with an art and photo program, a package of print and electronic supplements for students and faculty, and possibly an instructor's edition. In the trade, an A-book often is referred to as a "major market book." A "B-book" is usually a two-color product with black and white photos, an instructor's manual, and a test bank and study guide; and a "C-book" is usually a one-color product, often without photos or supplements.

Rankings are not intended to reflect the quality or worth of a textbook, only the cost of investing in it, insofar as that cost is justified by the size of the market, the projected sales, and the competition. For example, your first-edition text probably will be designated as a C-book if the publisher expects to sell only 4,000 copies because only 8,000 people currently enroll in that course annually nationwide and competitors are already in this market with other C-book offerings.

Editorial Development

Depending on your publisher, the development phase of the textbook publishing process is the most variable. At one extreme, this phase might consist simply of you revising your manuscript without outside input from reviewers or market analysts, without editorial assistance, and without any special fulfillment planning on the part of your publisher. Your book sinks or swims with little investment and no guarantees. At the other extreme, your publisher calls and manages your book, everything in it, and everything connected with it for maximum commercial success.

Development is a complex recursive process. Editors and authors collaborate to bring a manuscript and its ancillaries and supplements to market level and prepare them for production. Major college houses usually have development editors on staff; they may also hire the services of development editors either directly on a freelance basis or indirectly through development houses or packaging firms that exist to serve publishers. On the other hand, small academic publishing houses, universities, and special presses rarely use development editors, and may not even provide the services of a copyeditor.

As a consequence of development, your textbook manuscript (say, a student edition of the main text for an undergraduate course) ultimately will contain the following components.

- Parts and chapters with pedagogical features
- Figures and tables with source notes and captions
- Chapter appendices, notes, and references
- Photo and art specifications and captions
- Permissions logs and grants
- Half-title, title, copyright, and dedication pages
- Brief and full tables of contents
- Instructor's preface with acknowledgments
- Student preface or advertisement
- Text appendices, notes, references, bibliography
- Glossary
- Name index and subject index

Chapter 5 of this book explains in more detail what is involved in textbook development, describes the roles of development editors, and offers advice on how to do your own planning and development. Chapters 6 through 12 elaborate on the critical authoring tasks involved in developing a textbook.

Book Marketing

In commercial textbook publishing, marketing actually begins during the acquisitions phase and continues during manuscript development and production. A marketing manager or assistant may be assigned to the project and may even attend your signing. This person may help determine the budget for your book based on market research and will develop a marketing plan based on a competition analysis. How will your textbook compare with others of its kind for that market, and how will it take away market share? The marketer advises on how many copies will sell and in what schools where the publisher already has customers.

Seeding Adoptions

An important function of the marketing department is to offer leads for reviewers to read and comment on your manuscript. Reviewing is a proven way to seed adoptions. Another strategy is to coordinate and lead focus groups to have instructors or students evaluate your book's plan, content, pedagogy, or presentation. Yet another strategy is to ask instructors to class-test your textbook in its prepublication form or to offer various premiums or incentives for instructors to try it out.

Marketing also has a public relations function; that is, to make the world aware that your book is coming and to pre-sell as many copies as possible. With input from editors, the marketing department may write marketing materials and help coach the sales force on how to sell your book when they visit faculty offices. They also may conduct or outsource a promotional campaign to prospective customers; for example, through telemarketing or direct mail. Any advertising, including publication of the company's catalogs, typically happens through the marketing department.

Self-Marketing

Authors have important roles in marketing. You likely will be asked for contact information for all your colleagues, who then will go into the database as potential reviewers, endorsers, contributors, and adopters, along with your ideas for publicity and potential sales. You would be wise to give full, high-quality responses on the form the publisher will provide for your marketing input. The company also may ask you to attend a sales meeting to talk to the people who will sell your book, and otherwise will expect you to promote your book formally or informally, for example, at professional or institutional meetings and conferences.

The publisher will commit only limited resources to marketing your book, and probably will not take initiative to seek special sales. Publishers rarely stray from their usual customers, sometimes even when new prospects are likely to prove profitable. Like most bureaucratic organizations, publishing houses have systems, channels, and limited flexibility. Also, the company's sales force, however large, cannot possibly visit every school where your textbook might be used. Thus, for your book to become massively successful, you will have to conduct your own marketing campaign.

New authors often naively fault publishers for failing for promote their books adequately. Your book might get only one direct mail piece, for example, and, along with online listings, a place in the print catalog that is mailed only to the company's customers. (Note that the bigger the company, the longer its mailing list of prospective customers who will receive this catalog.) Yet, universally in the book publishing industry, marketing is technically the author's responsibility. Some or all of the marketing expenses for your book may be charged against your royalties as plant costs. The publisher's responsibility is to produce and manufacture products and to communicate their availability for sale. Publishers

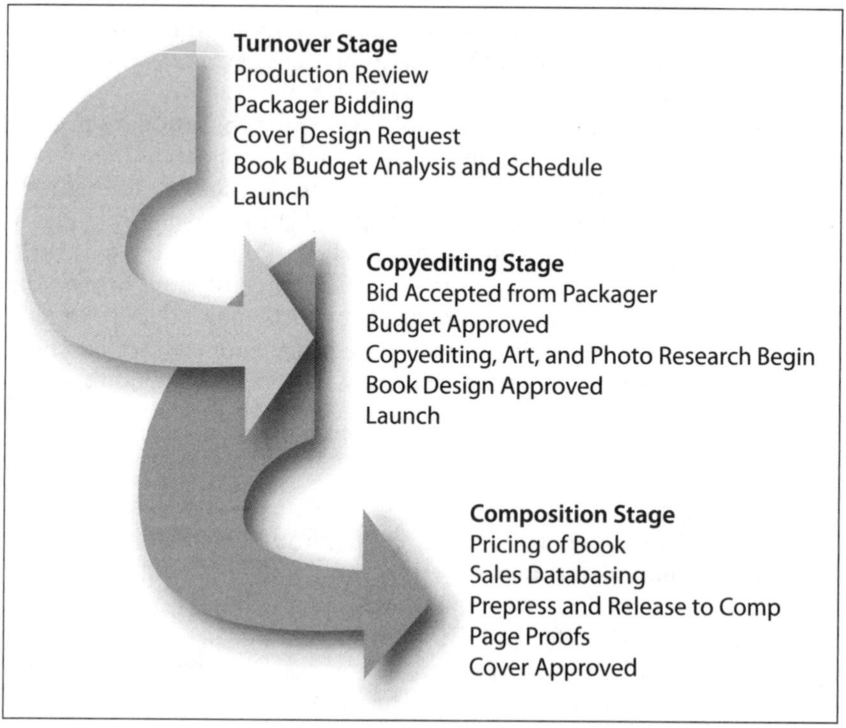

Figure 2-2. General Stages of Book Production

focus not on blanketing the market for your textbook but on channeling their marketing dollars into the highest sales volume they can muster. You, therefore, are your book's best chance of achieving its full potential in the marketplace. In light of this, and before even discussing how to write a good textbook, the chapter appendix offers suggestions for academic self-marketing.

Book Production

Assuming you bring your manuscript to completion successfully and on time and your publisher deems it acceptable, book production—the process by which an edited and developed manuscript becomes a book—can take up to another whole year. You and your editor usually remain involved during this time. Work also may begin on any supplements intended to accompany your text.

Each publishing house has its own unique systems for assigning bookmaking responsibilities and producing a book. After editors turn over a final manuscript to the production department, typical stages of book production might include the tasks shown in the figure. The "turnover stage" gets the manuscript into the hands of production editors and officially launches the book. The "copyediting stage" puts the book together and into the hands of book designers, and the "composition stage" gets the book into type and into the hands of printers.

Book Design

Many textbook authors have strong ideas about the way they want their textbook to look. They are the bane of publishers. This is why contracts are worded so strongly, reserving all rights regarding the physical appearance and characteristics of their product for the publishers. Design-conscious authors may chafe at this restriction, but experience repeatedly proves its necessity, for the simple reason that authors usually are not experts in text design, cover design, typesetting, or bookmaking.

Left to their own devices most authors choose the wrong kinds and number of fonts, type sizes, basal text margins, heading styles, and so on. However versed they may become in desktop publishing, they don't know the rules for making up pages in Quark or InDesign. They don't read pica rulers or know about line leading, base aligning, or sizing photos and art for the printed page. They don't know about choosing PMS (Pantone Matching System) colors to contain printing costs or even how to evaluate photos and art for reproducibility. They may not realize the make-or-break importance of book covers and chapter opening pages, in which a cover is or is not competitive in its market, or in which a single inferior or offending image can cost sales. It's likely, in other words, that you cannot design a textbook, and your snapshots and favorite color schemes will not do.

If you have strong opinions about the way your book should look, your best strategy is to write the production coordinator a memo stating your ideas. Submit the memo with your completed final draft. Most publishers will consider your ideas or will forward them to the book designer for his or her consideration. Make your comments general rather than prescriptive, pointing out how you think the book's concept and mission could be aided through design. The designer's job is to make the book look right for its audience, concept, mission, and competition, and in many cases they must work to the publisher's existing design templates and system preferences. Larger publishers often show authors the interior and cover designs under consideration, in which case you would have a chance to respond before press time.

Book Production Processes

In many larger commercial houses, the book production process typically goes something like this: Your manuscript in hard copy and on disk is turned over from editorial (acquisition and development editors) to production, and another whole group of people comes into play. A production administrator or coordinator might assign your book to an in-house production editor but more likely to a packager. A packager is an outside firm that secures talent and production services depending on what your book needs. These are services that you have not provided yourself or are not contractually obligated to provide. For example, your book might or might not need an artist, a permissions researcher, photo researcher, copyeditor, indexer, proofreader, book designer, page formatter, or others.

Production Editors

Editors might release sample chapters of your manuscript to the production department in advance of your manuscript so that your book can be designed. While the production administrator or packager is having a book design, art samples, and sample pages prepared, the company's composition buyer (or manufacturing buyer) might be sending out for bids on the paper, printing, and binding for your book.

In commercial publishing, if all is well, your book is officially launched in a series of meetings and paperwork distributions involving people in corporate management, editorial, marketing, production, and manufacturing. The budget is approved. The marketing strategy is approved. The design is approved. The schedule is approved. Composition is assigned to a vendor, and initial pricing—the cover price and what college bookstores will pay for it—is approved.

During production, a copyeditor marks your manuscript and sends it back to you, or to your editor first, for corrections. You respond to the copyeditor's or editor's queries and turn manuscript around, while the packager reviews what editorial says about the state and status of your manuscript. It is possible that your manuscript may go over budget or be delayed during production or even be pulled from production if things are not working out. Disasters sometimes happen if authors have not followed the agreed-upon plan, have omitted components, have gone over length, or have not attended to permissions (the subjects of Chapters 14 and 15 of this book).

However, the more time and money that go into your book, the greater the publisher's desire to see it into print. Your book has already become part of a larger publishing plan that aims to cover all bases in the publisher's chosen market with a carefully planned array of new titles and revisions for each copyright year.

Composition

Your copyedited manuscript with all its components is then released to composition (comp)—an old-fashioned term from the days when book pages were set (composed) from trays of inked hot lead type. Today, "composition" usually refers to electronic page make-up and printing "cold comp" from disk or film.

The compositor may estimate the length of your work in book pages (known as a "cast-off"), based on word count. Ideally, the cast-off takes into account the fonts, type sizes, and design elements chosen for your book. Assuming that your manuscript is not discovered to be too long at this late date, it is "poured" into its coded design or, in the old days, it was "typeset." Today, electronically produced manuscripts first appear in page proof rather than galleys. The page proof is proofread in production and sent to you for your review. The "compositor" checks all your changes and generates a corrected, usually final, page proof. Final page proof shows numbered pages and the actual placement of art, photos, and captions.

While your book is going back and forth among you, the editors, other company agents, and the compositor, your art and "art caption manuscript" might be with an artist or computer graphics specialist, and your photo specifications and "photo caption manuscript" might be with a photo researcher. On the other hand, depending on the market and level of investment, you may be responsible for supplying photos and photo releases, which the publisher then scans into the book. Today, digitized art and photos are the norm.

Author's Alterations

Usually, two or more rounds of page proof are needed before your book is right. However, changes during page proof require costly extra outlays of money for page formatters and proofreaders. Your changes, referred to as AAs or ACs (for "Author's Alterations" or "Author's Corrections") may be charged against your royalties. Thus, your role and responsibility as author is to make as few changes as possible during the production phase. Another reason relates to accuracy. Because page proof indicates the specific page numbers on which your index, table of contents, text cross-references, and supplements correlations are based, any changes you make have a ripple effect that may lead to factual errors.

For the people whose job it is to make your book come out right in time, the ripple effect can achieve nightmarish proportions. If you have ever felt disgusted by "sloppy" books in which page references did not lead you to the information you were seeking, now you know why this happens: The author's late changes required extra stages of page proof. The page layout affected the imposition (numbering sequence) of pages as a result. The author, production editor, and indexer could not reconcile the page references or afford to fix them all in time. When it comes to time, in textbook publishing the publishing process is unforgiving, such that your publisher will draw the line on changes even if doing so results in an imperfect product.

Book Manufacturing

All the decisions about the physical characteristics of your book—such as trim size, number of signatures, and type of binding—will have been made by the publisher before the manufacturing stage. Manufacturing begins after final page proof has been achieved, which includes all front matter, end matter, art, and photos in addition to the body of the manuscript. The technical processes by which all the elements are successfully put together in bookmaking are very complex and well beyond the scope of this book. Basically, your book goes to the printer, who puts it "on press" and runs proofs. You may hear some proofs referred to literally as "blues" or "cromalins" or other terms. After printer's proofs are OK'd, your first printing commences, consisting perhaps of 5,000 or 10,000 or 50,000 copies or more (or fewer if your company is printing on demand).

Today, because of technological developments in web offset, sheet fed, photographic, and digital printing, manufacturing may be done on a short run or print-on-demand basis, especially for reprints. Print-on-demand, in which copies are printed to order, has a higher per-unit cost but greatly reduces warehouse and inventory costs. Other benefits include the possibility of comparatively frequent and inexpensive corrections and revisions. In addition, the digitization of content allows for multiple reuses in diverse media, including online courses.

When books are made from film, the publisher's agents check the quality of each piece of film and mark for correction any instances of poor registration, alignment, or typesetting errors. As noted, however, innovations in printing and allied industries have caused sweeping changes in book manufacture. Your entire manuscript may go directly from disk to printing plate or from vacuum frame to output printer, never at all existing as film. Highly paid computer experts will have made up the pages and entered corrections on screen.

The new technology has major implications for authoring. For one thing, the manuscript you release to production has to be complete and final. Only minor corrections can be entertained in page proof, and books go from final proof directly into their print runs. The publisher's production administrators or manufacturing managers might travel with your book to the printing plant and to the bindery, overseeing the press run and checking that the cover is put on right-side up and that your name is spelled correctly.

There are always some badly trimmed or mangled copies, ones whose covers are manufactured without enough grinding or glue, or ones with upside down pages, etc., that must be destroyed. The whole process of book publishing is so complex that a perfect book does not exist. In addition to having inevitably less-than-perfect content, every book contains typographic or formatting errors, something missing or something that shouldn't be in there, and visible and "invisible" (to non-experts) physical flaws. Egregious, correctable, found flaws can be fixed in second printings. ("Errata" usually are reserved for scholarly books.) Although everyone feels indignant about technical errors in textbooks, we should all appreciate that publishing professionals strive for beauty and perfection. In recognition of bookmaking as both art and science, the industry hosts numerous annual awards for excellence. See, for example, Bookbuilders of Boston (**bbboston.org**).

Book Fulfillment

"Fulfillment" is publisher talk for getting the product to the customer. Your bound book is shipped to the company's warehouse, where it is inventoried. It is also sent to the warehouses of distributors and wholesalers with whom the company does business. Advance copies go to you and to the publisher's marketers and sales representatives for sampling among potential customers.

Sampling involves sending complimentary copies to people who might adopt the text for their course. This is a speculative marketing activity entailing significant expense, but sending comp copies is seen as necessary. Mailing lists, to which you will be asked to contribute, are carefully drawn to try to maximize sell-through. Larger publishers use special covers on giveaway "comp copies" to distinguish them, prominently marking the covers "Not for Sale." This tactic does not prevent used textbook brokers from buying and reselling them, however. Many examination copies find their way onto eBay, prompting publishers to make examination copies available as read-only "Look inside the Book"-type samples on their websites.

Your Sales Reps

As noted previously, the company already has sent out promotional material, bought advertising, and/or begun direct mail marketing campaigns. The road to fulfillment actually begins well before your book even exists as a product and may include your presentation to the company's sales force about why they should make every effort to sell your textbook out of the dozens or hundreds of books they must field each year. The sales reps must understand and believe in your product, and it would be a mistake to think that this happens automatically.

Dedicated sales forces are a major expense for publishing houses, and smaller houses do not have them. Your book may be fielded by freelance salespersons or sold through catalog distribution alone. Sales forces have proven effectiveness in the textbook publishing industry. However, publishing with a house that has a dedicated sales force does not guarantee that your book will get sold. This is because sales representatives maximize their earnings by selling the most popular books or the ones they have been able to sell most successfully in the past. If they are already selling another textbook for your market, in other words, they may have little incentive to spend time switching their customers to your new product. Publishers have various incentive schemes for getting their sales forces to back their frontlist titles each year. Nevertheless, awareness of the publisher's other directly competing titles and their sales records should be a part of your discussions during the acquisitions phase.

College Stores

Near the end of the fulfillment phase, on campuses across the country, faculty members place or post orders for your textbook. The company's field reps and a home office sales support staff take those orders, and the warehouse or distributor ships your book to college bookstores in time for students to purchase them at the store's markup price before the start of the first term of your copyright year.

College stores mark up textbooks by 25 to 35% on average and buy back the books at the end of the term. Nationally, the campus stores' average margin is 22 to 25% for new textbooks and 33 to 35% for used textbooks (NACS, 2007). However, because of the high volumes involved in distribution to chains, chain store markups on new textbooks may be as much as 45 to 70%, with the result that publishers must deeply discount books sold through that channel. These deep discounts in turn reduce your author royalties, which are calculated on the basis of net sales after any discount.

College and campus stores may be private, institutionally affiliated, independent, or run by a chain that specializes in bookstore management. The chains are affiliated with prominent book wholesalers and distributors who become exclusive suppliers. The Follett Higher Education Group (**fheg.follett.com**), including Follett of Canada, for example, supplies textbooks to 580 or so stores. Barnes & Noble College Booksellers Inc. (**bkstore.com**) manages and supplies 575 stores nationwide. The Nebraska Book Company (**nebook.com**) supplies more than 660 independently run college stores through its Connect2One (**connect2one.com**) division.

More than 3,000 stores of all kinds are members of the National Association of College Stores (**nacs.org**), an advocate for retailers that also serves as a book distributor through its NACSCORP (**nacscorp.com**) division. The Independent College Bookstore Association (**icbainc.**

com) represents another 150 independents, mainly at community and state colleges.

As in all other parts of the industry, college store indies struggle to keep their doors open. For example, the American Booksellers Association (**bookweb.org**) champions around 1,900 independent trade book stores today, down from more than 5,000 members in the 1990s. Independents have difficulty competing if they do not offer online retailing (see **eCampus.com**), cannot access the economies of scale that the chains enjoy, and cannot afford to offer the crowd-pleasing amenities that one will find at Borders (including Waldenbooks), Barnes & Noble (including B. Dalton), and Chapters (**chapters.indigo.ca**), Canada's biggest bookstore chain.

Textbook Wholesalers and Distributors

Bookstores order your textbook from your publisher or through your publisher's distributor and preferred wholesalers. For instance, Ingram Book Company (**ingrambook.com**) distributes approximately 2.3 million textbooks each year, and Baker & Taylor (**btol.com**), a library wholesaler, channels college textbooks and academic books through its J. A. Majors and Yankee Book Peddler units. Smaller companies specialize in textbooks alone, such as MBS Textbook Exchange (**mbsbooks.com**), or specialize in certain markets. The virtual distributor, Varsity Books (**varsitybooks.com**), for example, supplies off-campus stores that serve college preparatory schools, parochial schools, and Christian academies. As another example, Rittenhouse (**rittenhouse.com**) distributes healthcare and medical books to universities.

Used Textbooks

Traditionally, students bought textbooks and kept them until sometime after graduation. You may still have some of your old textbooks in your bookshelves. Today, many students avoid buying textbooks; they often buy used ones, share or rent copies, find older, foreign, or pirated versions online, and sell books back for cash at the end of the term. The college stores and other used book brokers advertise attractive buyback deals. Some also buy and sell advance reading copies (ARCs), examination copies, complimentary (comp) copies, and review copies, along with textbooks in which students have used colored highlighting pens and have written answers or comments. A whole new e-commerce industry has sprung up to serve the used textbook market, such as **directtextbook.com, buyusedtextbooks.com**, and **collegeswapshop.com.**

Unless they were distributed on a "no returns" basis, new unsold copies of your textbook are returned to the publisher for a loss, and in the following semester, store buybacks are sold to students first, reducing your second-term sales (again reducing your royalties). This dynamic is behind the tendency for publishers to ask authors for two-year revisions, as an earlier edition is put out of print automatically when a new edition comes out. In the past, another, even less popular, strategy—discussed in Chapter 1—was to make up for second-year revenue shortfalls by bundling cheap supplements into higher-priced textbook packages.

The Textbook Package

Publisher investment in your textbook includes print and non-print supplements, many of which the publisher must provide to customers for free in order to remain competitive. Their cost—such as payment to a work-for-hire test bank author—is charged against your book or written off as a loss. Supplements and ancillaries are seen as sales incentives, however, and as value-added products. Ancillaries are separate publications essential for using the textbook, such as a lab manual or student workbook without which the textbook is incomplete. Supplements are separate products that stand alone, such as test item files, readers, or Internet guides, although these often are regarded as essential to the book's success in the marketplace.

College publishers continually produce an array of print and non-print supplements for both instructors and students. These products may be for the general subject area as well as for specific titles. Print supplements include any matter that is typeset or printed photographically, while non-print supplements or teaching aids include physical models—such as a double helix, fossils, or a scale model pyramid—and any content on either film or digital or magnetic media. "Supplements" also may include special texts and alternative texts, such as instructors' annotated editions, interactive editions with CDs or DVDs, web editions or e-texts, Blackboard cartridges or Web CT conversions, and online courses. The following are the most common types of print and non-print textbook supplements.

Print Supplements

- Instructor's manual
- Transparency masters or acetate transparencies
- Test bank or alternate test banks
- Student workbook, lab manual, or practice tests
- Student study guide
- Companion reader or magazine
- User's guides to supplements
- Maps or posters

Non-Print Supplements

- Computerized test bank and study guide
- Tutorial, application, or simulation software

- Video or audio disks or DVDs
- Electronic slides for course presentation
- Customized course management software
- Digital image or digital media archives
- Models or manipulatives
- Companion website

Typically, only larger commercial publishing houses are in a position to publish this range of print and non-print supplements. Textbook packages are complex and costly to produce. In this context, digitization is a boon to publishers. The cost of an electronic slide set, for example, is a tiny fraction of the cost of a set of acetate transparencies.

As author, your role in any of the package components is determined during the acquisition phase of the publishing process. You would be wise to discuss supplements in detail at the time of your contract negotiations with the publisher. In particular, you should consider how many and what kinds of supplements to have, if any will be for sale, who will provide them, how they will be paid for, and how they will affect pricing and sales revenue.

If you author or edit key supplements yourself, you retain more control of the content and quality of the materials that will accompany your textbook. Thus, the more you are involved in planning, creating, or editing supplements, the better. Your involvement also encourages increased publisher investment in supplements, which, even with debundling mandates, significantly aid sales. A companion volume to this one, *Writing and Developing College Textbook Supplements, 2nd Edition*, explores in detail the development of textbook package components.

The Publishing Cycle

When your textbook and its ancillaries and supplements are all in the fulfillment stage of publishing, you will have completed one turn of the publishing cycle. This is typically a two-year enterprise that then, after a brief hiatus, repeats. Another turn of the wheel represents the life of your second edition, assuming it has been successful enough to be revised, and so on. Release from this cycle of revision comes when your last edition is declared OOP (out of print).

The publishing cycle places the phases of the publishing process into a time frame. This time frame is similar for all college houses, and it is much longer than you might think, typically (for the first edition) two to four years from start (concept) to finish (customer), plus two to four years between revised editions. Timing is crucial in the textbook publishing industry. That is, your textbook is doomed to failure commercially if it does not come out in time. At the same time, the publishing cycle is continuous.

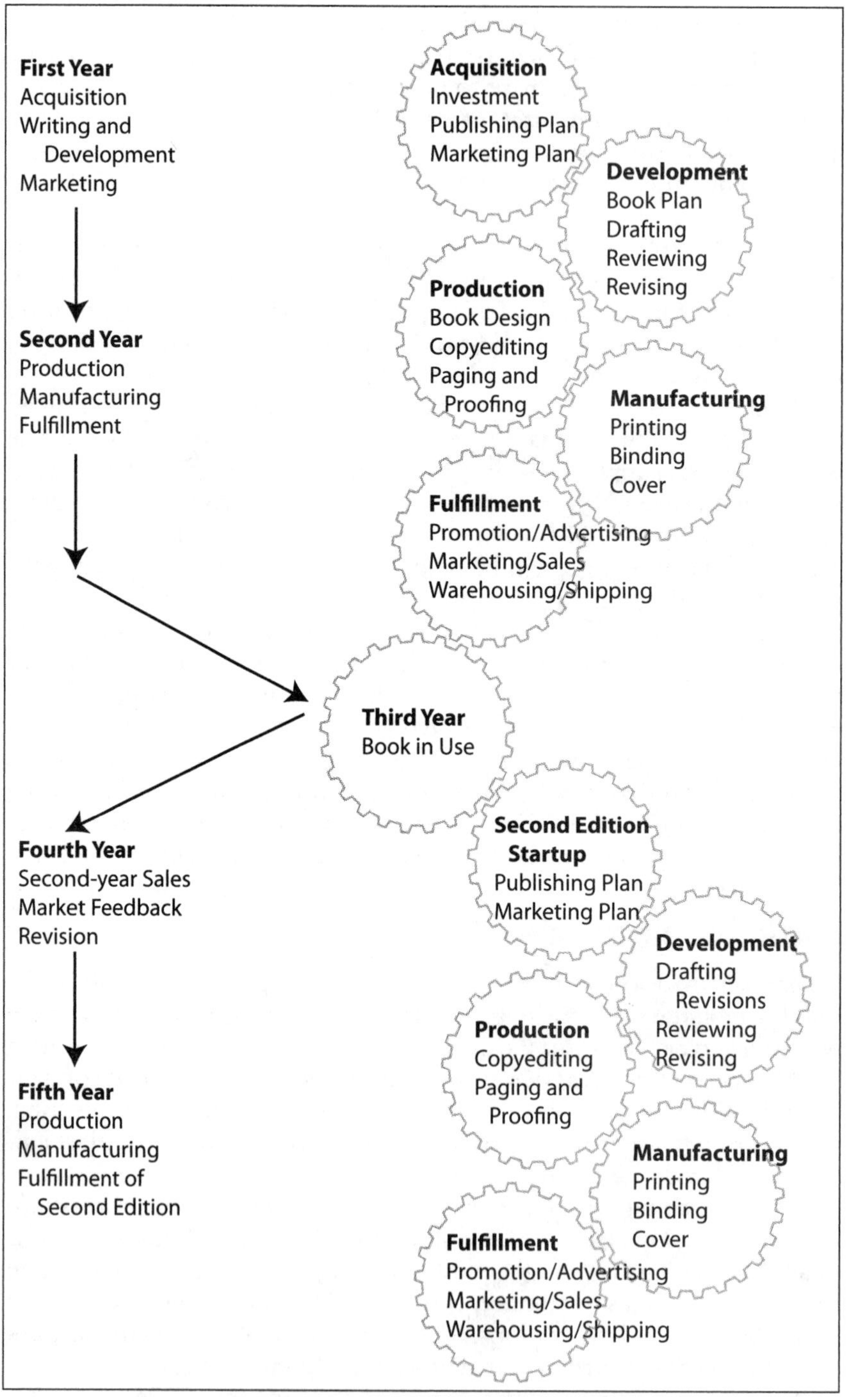

Figure 2-3. Phases of the Publishing Cycle

Acquisitions editors sign authors at all times during the year, but the peak signing periods are in the mid-fall and mid-spring. Books are signed one to three years prior to the planned publication date, depending on the state of existence of your manuscript; your availability to complete the work; the publisher's list needs, projected investment, and existing print queue for other products; and perceived competitive market forces.

Manuscript development and drafting optimally take place during the six months to a year following signing. This time period includes summer, when you might have more time to devote to writing projects. Reviewing, additional development, and revising continue into the fall. First, second, and final drafts are not unusual for a first edition. If you author a first edition starting from scratch, unless you can devote full time to the project, you would be wise to insist on a two-year drafting and revising schedule. The figure shows the publishing process in relation to the phases of the publishing cycle for a first edition book on a two-year revision schedule.

Your final manuscript is released from the manuscript acquisition and editorial development phases to the production phase by the end of a calendar year, preferably in mid-fall. Production and manufacturing take up all the remaining time—another six months to a year depending on the type of product, the level of investment, the technology in use, and other factors—before your book is ready for warehousing. Books inevitably are out of date by the time they reach customers, although online supplements now make it possible to update books on company websites during the life of an edition.

New authors typically do not understand why they must submit their manuscripts so early—often more than a year in advance of the copyright year. This is not arbitrary. The reason is that finished books must be in stock in time for instructors to (1) sample them well *before* the copyright year, (2) order and receive them through campus bookstores in time for students (3) to buy them *before* the start of the copyright year. It's a logistics problem.

As noted previously, in sampling, your publisher sends out up to hundreds of free desk copies of your textbook in advance to your potential customers: individual instructors and departmental textbook adoption committees. Adopters and committees usually must place their textbook orders a full semester or more *in advance* of the semester in which it will be used. So, a long lead time really is needed.

The hope is that after looking at your book, the people who have been sampled will order it for their students. However, if there is no time for this sampling process to happen (because your book did not come out in time) then your book will lose at least one semester's worth of potential sales nationwide. The customers had to choose the other company's text that was timed to compete with yours, which will make it much harder for your publisher to switch them to yours when it does become available. This adds up to a lot of lost revenue (as well as dashed hopes for future sales), which is very discouraging for both publisher and author. A consequence may be that your sales numbers are not good enough for the publisher to risk investing in a revision. Then that's the end of it.

The publishing cycle for textbooks explains why editors become so obsessive about due dates. Academic and scholarly presses are less concerned about market timing because they invest less, are not committed to matching course offerings in college catalogues, are not wedded to academic timetables for course scheduling, do not need to send out comp copies for advance sales, and do not need to depend on specific brokers such as college stores. If you sign with a large commercial textbook publisher, therefore, you will be under some pressure to attend to the realities of timing in the textbook publishing cycle.

Ideally, your manuscript goes into production in time to succeed, and your book hits its market. All the time and effort you spent on development begin to pay off as your book does well. Most of the cost of producing and manufacturing your book is recovered in the first year of sales, and you begin receiving royalty checks. Perhaps you begin to see results for sales of subsidiary rights also, and you learn that your textbook is being adapted for a Canadian or an American edition or a foreign market. In no time at all, it seems, your editor calls to discuss starting a revised edition and has some ideas for increasing your market share. Thus, the publishing cycle begins again. Your major market textbook may see a dozen or more editions and in the course of your lifetime never go out of print. You may even be able to retire earlier on your earnings.

APPENDIX
Suggestions for Self-Marketing Your Textbook

Prepublication Strategies

- Help your publisher choose well-known or authoritative reviewers for your textbook—as many as possible. Cite them and their institutional affiliations in your preface and acknowledgements sections, which also functions as a sales tool.
- Collect positive statements about your textbook from peer reviews, user testimonials, and private correspondences, and request permission to use the quotes in marketing literature. When your book is in production, give this list to your publisher to use in promotion.
- List all your relevant institutional affiliations and professional memberships, past and present, along with complete contact information, including street addresses and URLs. Include listservs in your field in which you lurk or participate. Include your alumni magazines, professional journals to which you subscribe, and any other news media that might have any interest at all in you or your textbook. Your publication announcement should go to them all, and it probably will be up to you to send it.
- Draft a publication announcement. Ask your publisher to approve it before sending it out, as publication dates are kept secret until later in the publishing process (to prevent the competition from benefiting in any way from the market timing or product foreknowledge).

Spreading the Word

- Send out your publication announcement by e-mail and/or surface mail. Include information about where and when to order.
- Have a press release written (preferably by a professional PR person) and sent out to media, including RSS feeds.
- Ask the publisher for a high-resolution cover image file and have a 4-color postcard made with your announcement on the back. Having a quantity of postcards made is a small investment (although mailing them will cost you). Send them out to your contact list (or have the postcard company send them), or see if the publisher will send them to their contact lists as well as to yours.
- Consider renting a mailing list of instructors who teach the course for which you wrote your textbook. You can rent such targeted addresses for one-time use for around $100 per

1,000 names from companies such as Market Data Retrieval (**schooldata.com**) or Quality Education Data (**qeddata.com**). These companies will also do the mailing for you.
- Add the title of your book to your signature so that it goes out with every e-mail and letter you send—e.g., "Author of *Invitation to College Algebra* (Textbook Press, 2009)."

Clueing in Your Publisher

- Create a tip sheet for your publisher's sales reps on how to present your book. For example, identify what you think are the three most significant benefits of adopting your book over others and the three most attractive features.
- Mark up a copy of your book with self-stick notes identifying examples of each of the main benefits and features outlined in your book plan. For example, if a selling point of your book is your coverage of globalization, what should a sales rep actually show to the customer to highlight or prove this? A marked copy is a useful tool for the marketing and sales department.
- Present your publisher with a personal marketing plan listing all the things you are doing to promote your textbook. The publisher can help with activities that require a publisher's aegis, such as registering to exhibit at association book shows.

Postpublication Strategies

- Purchase extra copies of your book from the publisher at discount (in addition to the author copies enumerated in your contract). Reward your prepublication reviewers and use the extra copies to solicit post-production reviews. This encourages sales and gives you feedback for the next edition.
- Donate copies of your book to your institution's academic library and student study skills center or department library, and give a copy to your department chair (or dean or provost).
- Ask your publisher to list your book with a library wholesaler. Textbook publishers usually are interested only in quantity sales for course adoption and may miss the academic library market. Some authors address this market directly themselves, for example, through members of the Association of Research and College Libraries (ACRL, **ala.org/ala/acrl**).
- Exhibit your textbook at professional meetings in your field. If your publisher does not customarily rent booths at your meetings, ask the publisher to register your title to be displayed through an exhibiting service. See, for example, Association Book Exhibit (**bookexhibit.com**) and Combined Book Exhibit

(**combinedbook.com**). You also may be able to do this on your own.

- Consider displaying or advertising your book at a professional meeting in which you give a talk or presentation on teaching your subject.

Increasing Visibility

- Where should your textbook be listed? Gather the information and ask your publisher to submit listings for your book in key directories or references for your field or pertaining to higher education.
- Add a reference to your new textbook on your website. Include a description and the table of contents and a picture of the cover. If possible, include a link to your publisher's ordering address. Some authors arrange to take and fill orders directly from their websites.
- Purchase a domain name for your title and have a website for your book. Keep the page active by having a blog, perhaps about teaching the course, or a discussion forum, e.g., about using your textbook. Your publisher may buy such a domain name for you and host the site.
- Offer a virtual author tour, teleseminar, podcast, webcast, or webinar for instructors and/or students using your textbook.

3

Interest a Publisher in Your Manuscript

FICTION OR TRADE BOOK PUBLISHING houses are notorious for rejecting manuscripts that later become bestsellers or posthumous classics. Textbook publishing, however, is not like that. Acquisitions editors in college houses are always looking for books to sign. In larger companies, editors' performance evaluations and bonuses are based in part on their number of signings each year. In addition, college textbook markets are constantly expanding as enrollments increase and new courses routinely are added to the curriculum. And as educational publishing moves toward electronic archiving and delivery systems, industry demand for books to pour into multimedia platforms is growing exponentially. So, if you and your textbook meet certain basic criteria, you should have no difficulty finding a publisher. What are these basic criteria?

Basic criteria for publishing a college textbook include: (1) having a market for your book, (2) having institutional affiliation and a professional track record, (3) knowing publishers' existing products, and (4) intending to provide an intellectually and pedagogically sound work in a well-written and otherwise acceptable form.

A Market for Your Book

Your manuscript is on a subject or area in your field that is or will be in demand in courses on campuses nationwide. It corresponds to known departmental course offerings listed in college catalogues and contains at least the basics of what is generally expected and taught in those courses. Publishers refer to this as a "mainstream" text.

A mainstream text addresses a clearly identifiable audience, such as all undergraduates taking organic chemistry. The larger the audience, the better. A large market has many potential customers among faculty members whose course assignments give them control over a large number of textbook adoptions. Thus, large markets are the most competitive and the most lucrative for publishers and authors. Small, or niche, markets are served, especially in technical fields and at the graduate level, but they attract fewer investment dollars from the publisher and usually—but not always—smaller earnings.

The largest markets are for introductory textbooks, and despite rumors of market saturation there usually is room for a new introductory text in any field. The reason is that a good intro—one that your students can read and like and learn from, that covers adequately material you regard as important, and that is revised often enough to remain current—is hard to find. Many instructors switch texts from semester to semester in search of the right one or resort to photocopied customized tomes. Your motivation for writing a textbook possibly stems from dissatisfaction with existing offerings for a course you teach. In addition, college textbook marketing practices encourage frequent changes in adoptions, such that new intros are marketed successfully each year. The intro market, often with four-color books and large supplement packages, is big business.

Do Your Homework

"The market" consists of customers' wants and needs as reflected in companies' competing products and instructors' course syllabi. Textbook publishing involves satisfying rather than creating demand. Fully understanding that demand is what it means to know your market. Begin by making it your business to know the companies' products. Before making contact with a publisher about your manuscript, acquire and study the publisher's catalogue of books in your field, and order examination copies of any books that seem like the one you want to write or are in the same market.

Do not be concerned if the publisher already has a similar book or one that is pitched to the same audience. Large houses, especially in this era of corporate mergers, often have several directly competing titles that are marketed successfully in successive copyright years. The sales base for each book is protected (1) by clearly differentiating it as a product, and (2) by putting it on a two-, three-, or four-year revision cycle. Whichever title comes out as a new or revised edition for any given year is supposed to be the one that is emphasized in sales efforts, or "gets sold." While this scheme does not always work and sometimes even backfires, the presence of at least one competing title guarantees that the sales force is going to the places where your book can be sold.

It is also important to study other companies' textbooks intended for your book's course. Those books are your real competition, and your publisher will want to know how you think your textbook will attract market share away from competitors' titles.

Strategies for Conducting Market Research

The best sources of information about external competition are publishers' websites. Find them directly or via online publisher directories. See, the higher education division of the AAP (**publishers.org/main/Higher-Education**) or a directory of academic publishers' catalogs, such as the one found at **brockport.edu/~library2/ubcats.htm**. An excellent source of textbook reviews is Monument Information Resource (MIR), which provides (free to faculty members) detailed market information on leading college textbooks (see Faculty Online at **facultyonline.com**).

In addition to studying publishers' catalogs and reading textbook reviews, use higher education directories (such as "U.S. Universities, by State," **utexas.edu/world/univ/state**) to locate colleges and departments where your course is taught. Survey their course syllabi, especially at top schools for your subject. A sample of syllabi will give you a perspective on how the course is being taught currently, a matter of great interest to publishers. You also will find interesting instructional materials developed by faculty members for classroom use and distance learning (but remember that unless otherwise stated, everything you see online is copyright-protected).

Survey textbooks in your campus store, noting who publishes them, and check out textbooks on Amazon or other online retailers. In addition to helping you identify the market for your textbook, your market survey will help you identify specific companies to contact and also will give you ideas for explaining to a publisher how your book will be competitive.

Your published colleagues can be a valuable resource. Ask them about their publishers. Contact colleagues via e-mail to discuss your project or solicit feedback. Consider writing a blog or starting an online discussion group as a forum for developing your textbook. Also critically survey sites that serve as advocates for textbook authors, such as the Text and Academic Authors Association (**TAAonline.net**) and the Society for Academic Authors (**SA2.info**), hosted by textbook author John Vivian.

Finally, visit the websites of professional organizations and publications in your discipline and survey their indexes for information and contacts you can use. It will be useful to you to have an overview of the latest news, developments, and trends in your subject as well as in textbook publishing. A prospective publisher will want to know how your textbook will reflect these developments and trends. For general perspectives, see, for example, the *Chronicle of Higher Education* (**chronicle.com**) and *Inside Higher Education* (**insidehighered.com**).

The publisher's marketing department uses these same strategies to develop publishing proposals. By discovering the market for your book in these ways you will (1) identify what your customers want and need, (2) make useful contacts, (3) learn what to tell a publisher about your book, (4) come to appreciate the marketplace challenges your book will face, and (5) become a "market savvy" author, which will not fail to impress the publisher. Last but not least, your research will help you commit (or not) to your project.

A Track Record

In most fields, authors are recruited on the basis of rank and reputation, and books are sold on the basis of market impact and name recognition or loyalty. Optimally you are a full or associate professor in a four-year college or university; have tenure or are firmly on tenure track; and your curriculum vitae is laden with accomplishments. For example, you have published articles, conducted research, reviewed works in your field, and/or presented at conferences or symposia. In some practice-oriented subject areas (such as psychiatry, criminology, or finance), however, administrative responsibilities, classroom experience, commercial success, and specialized knowledge or technical expertise may matter more than academic credentials. The main concern of publishers is that a textbook will have authority and credibility with its adopters.

It is a plus to have already published, because it shows that you can write acceptable, publishable material and therefore can match the publisher's author profile perfectly. However, if you can't write (or can't write for students), you are not desirable as a textbook author. Of all the factors involved in making a textbook, your authorial voice and audience-appropriate writing quality comprise the single greatest determinant of success. Thus, engendering confidence in your authorship is one of the prerequisites for interesting a publisher in your textbook proposal. It is for this reason that you should submit carefully crafted sample chapters with your proposal. But no cheating! Prospective authors have been known to hire professional writers to help draft (or ghost) winning samples for their proposals, only to prove themselves incompetent as authors later on. Ultimately, unpublishable manuscripts waste everyone's time.

The Author Profile

Publishers establish guidelines for acquisitions editors to follow when finding authors. These guidelines include an "author profile"—a description of the qualities and characteristics the company desires in an author. These vary from company to company, but generally publishers are looking for mid-career academics with institutional affiliation at a four-year school and a track record. As in all profiling, injustices sometimes result. Retired professors emeriti, junior or adjunct faculty, community college instructors, and transplanted or unknown scholars with exotic names, for example, may find themselves disadvantaged in the competition for textbook authorship (though not necessarily for other kinds of books). Selection (or discrimination) is based solely on perceived risk factors for achieving salability and sustainable profitability in relation to the cost of investment.

If you do not fit the author profile, you need a strategy for presenting yourself to a prospective publisher. The strategy I have seen work most often is the author team. That is, in lieu of a desirable author profile or track record, you nevertheless can qualify by being part of an author team. For example, if you are a junior faculty member with a good book idea and are seeking to publish for the first time, consider presenting your book ideas to one or two carefully selected colleagues, discussing the mutual potential benefits of collaborating, and building trust.

The Author Team

Publishers like author teams that include individuals who have solid reputations in their field or specialty and who offer balance or perspective in authorship, including women and men and members of culturally diverse groups. Author teams whose ranks swell to four or more members may not be so desirable, however. A large group of authors may (in addition to challenging cover designers) be more prone to contractual complications, royalty dilution, author collaboration problems, and inconsistencies in style.

On the other hand, working with co-authors has many benefits. As textbook author N. Gregory Mankiw notes on his blog (March 4, 2007), having coauthors permits specialization, thereby raising productivity, and reduces loneliness:

> The third reason I work with co-authors is the most important: a good co-author improves you forever. In the most successful collaborations, both co-authors learn from the experience. A co-author can help you expand your knowledge, improve your skills, and expose your biases. Even after the collaboration is over, you take these benefits with you to future projects.

Key decisions in forging an author team revolve around answers to the questions below, to which everyone on the team must be able to make an equal commitment. Author teams that settle these questions right at the beginning of their collaboration have the greatest success.

- What will be the rationale, assumptions, principles, goals, and mission of the book?
- What will be the scope and sequence of content and organization?
- Who will be the audience?
- What will be the writing style and tone?
- What will be the long-term availability of each member of the author team?
- How will authoring tasks be divided?
- By what dates will each phase of the work be completed?

- Who will be responsible for ensuring that the book has a consistent overall voice and style?
- By what means, how often, and how extensively will the authors communicate with each other to collaborate?
- Who will be listed as the principal author?
- In what order will author names appear on the title page?
- How will advances and royalties be divided?

Publishers sometimes suggest author teams. They might propose a coauthor if they think the combination will result in a stronger, more secure, or more salable product, or to cover more adequately the entire course content. Bringing in new coauthors also is a time-honored way of keeping a book-in-use alive as the original authors cease contributing for any reason. In this case, royalty splits are recalibrated proportionally, although the name of a deceased original author usually remains on the cover through a certain number of subsequent editions.

Reviewing

Another strategy for overcoming author profile and track record concerns that I have seen work is to provide services to the publisher in the form of reviews and contributions. Many acquisitions editors look for prospective authors from among lists of reviewers of their textbooks and those of competitors.

A publisher may contact you to review a manuscript, especially if you respond to their market survey. To become a reviewer, simply send publishers in your field your curriculum vitae and a letter of interest in reviewing. In the letter to the editor, refer to titles of theirs that you use or have used in the past, and state your areas of expertise. Report the number of adoptions you control by noting the number of courses or sections you teach annually and the size of enrollments in those courses. Editors tend to give priority to reviewers through whom they feel they can seed future adoptions.

Types of Reviews

College textbook publishers are always looking for reviewers to provide the following kinds of assistance with first and revised editions.

User Review: You use their textbook in your course and know its strengths and weaknesses through direct experience.

Comparative Review: You use their textbook and have an interest in how it is revised. You would like to compare the revised draft with the edition in use, report on improvements, and suggest ways to further strengthen the revision.

Nonuser Review: You looked at their book but chose a competitor's offering instead. You know why their book failed to persuade you to order it and why the other company's book was better for you and your students.

Competitive Review: You have looked at several leading textbooks for your course and have an interest in comparing their strengths and weaknesses in whole or in part.

Expert Review: You are an acknowledged expert in your field but not necessarily an instructor. You have published professional articles or books on your specialty or have served on panels or as a consultant. You are interested in reviewing selected chapters on your area of expertise to check mainly for soundness, currency, completeness, and accuracy.

Developmental Review: You are familiar with the strengths and weaknesses of all the leading textbooks for your course. You would like to review manuscript with a view to seeing how well it fulfills the publisher's stated market needs. You would also like to contribute your ideas to the book plan.

Supplements Review: You have used the supplements package with their book, such as the test item file or the website, and have found it wanting. You are interested in providing a critical content review with specific suggestions for improvement.

Unsolicited reviews are welcome and often lead to agreements for further reviewing or other contributions. College houses sometimes offer good reviewers assignments as supplements authors, and sometimes offer book contracts to proven supplements authors, a route to publishing that benefits junior faculty.

Characeristics of Good Reviewing

Here are the characteristics of good reviewing that editors prize.

Reliability: The reviewer is available for assignments, readily accepts them, and turns them around on time.

Legibility: The review is keyboarded or typed.

Efficiency: The review is neither too long nor too short. Four or five pages is standard for chapter reviews, ten or more pages for whole book reviews; but each publisher has its own criteria.

Completeness: The reviewer answers all the general and specific reviewing questions that the publisher has asked and fills out the reviewer profile sheet, including social security number, which is needed to cut checks, and gives permission to acknowledge the reviewer in the preface.

Conceptual Balance: The reviewer avoids too broad or too narrow a focus, neither giving blanket approval or condemnation nor merely correcting typographical errors and errors of spelling and grammar—the job of a paid professional copyeditor.

Soundness: Comments are logical and coherent. They reflect valid concerns and accepted interpretations or trends in the field, not solely the reviewer's personal preferences or idiosyncratic views.

Substantiveness or specificity: The review is detailed and includes specific suggestions with some documentation. For example, the reviewer cites manuscript page references in support of evaluative statements and explains the basis for his or her professional judgments.

Fairness: Comments respect the authors and their effort. The reviewer objectively notes both the strengths and the weaknesses of their draft and uses appropriate language.

Reasonableness: The review realistically guides revision in relation to the book's aims; that is, the reviewer resists wholesale restructuring and radical reconceptualization of the content.

Why You Should Submit a Careful Review

Some faculty members see reviewing as an unpleasant, unrewarding chore. Honoraria often are pitifully low—as little as $25 per chapter, though an expert review in some subject areas can command $200 to $400 per chapter. Companies and editors vary considerably in what they will pay. In addition, reviewing schedules may be inconvenient. Editors may send chapters later than promised and then ask for your response within the week.

Some faculty members feel exploited by the reviewing system and reject assignments when asked. Others feel justified in doing a hasty or mediocre job. In addition to the latter, among the least helpful reviewers are those who lavishly praise a manuscript in the most general terms, thinking this is what the publisher wants to hear. Savvy editors do not call on unhelpful reviewers again, however, and a record of their undesirable performance might go into the files or database to warn off other editors.

From the publisher's standpoint, the purpose of reviews is to determine market fit, to vet the manuscript, and especially to attract potential customers. As noted previously, asking faculty members with high enrollments to serve as reviewers is known as "seeding adoptions," because reviewers who become invested in improving a manuscript often adopt the product that results.

From the author's standpoint, the purpose of reviews (if truth be told) usually is to glean positive feedback and avoid embarrassment. For editors, however, reviews aid in crafting a sound and successful product.

Reviewers' contributions also play a significant role in marketing. With the authors' thanks, reviewers' names appear in print in the acknowledgments section of a textbook. With permission, laudatory quotes from reviews are used extensively in materials for promotion and sales.

Contributing

Another route to establishing credibility as a prospective royaltied textbook author is to contribute chapters or pedagogical features to a textbook already under contract. Work-for-hire contributions may include other original writing for a book, such as chapter vignettes, case studies, research briefs, content applications, first-person accounts, articles, figures, or topical features (often called "boxes"). Publishers are always on the lookout for professors who would like to share their original course materials, such as presentation slides, preferably for free, but they routinely purchase ready-made ancillaries and supplements for their textbook packages.

You also can become a contributor by proposing yourself as a supplement author to the publisher of a text you use in your courses. Work-for-hire supplements may include, for example, study guides, test banks, instructor's manuals, or online learning objects for a companion website. Payment for writing supplements is low, reflecting the publisher's need to invest as little as possible in supplements to keep the price down. Publishers routinely absorb losses on them, and it is rare for a supplement to carry a royalty unless it is for sale and is expected to do well.

In reality most of the cost of "free" supplements is added to the plant costs for your textbook as well as to the price of the student text. One consequence of this dynamic is that the supplement author's income is less than desired in relation to the time and effort it takes to cover a course and do good work. Mediocre and poor supplements abound as a result.

Partly for that reason, many student supplements go unsold, such that publishers increasingly print them on demand (POD) rather than tie up inventory space. If instructors do not require students to buy supplements for a course, the college bookstores do not order them. Even if instructors assign supplements, there is no guarantee that students will purchase them.

You no doubt have had direct experience with bad supplements. Your motivation for becoming a supplement author may stem from your experience with supplements in courses you have taught. Providing high-quality, content-rich supplements in the service of a course, an academic discipline, or student learning is a strong motivation for becoming a supplements author.

Authoring Contributed Material

Contributors and supplement authors rarely work directly with the authors of the textbooks for which they write. Your primary roles as a supplement author are (1) to be faithful to the textbook author's mission and content, (2) to help customers use the textbook conveniently and beneficially, and (3) to give the publisher what it needs to field the textbook successfully. Only then can you (4) enrich or remediate the teaching or learning experiences of the people who will use your supplement and the textbook it supports.

A surprising number of supplement authors write at cross-purposes with the textbook they have been assigned. They have their own philosophy, messages, or data to convey, or they detect omissions or faults in the textbook, for which they then attempt to compensate. Results can undermine the product and baffle end users. You should promptly disclose discovered faults to the editor or publisher, therefore, rather than try to remedy them secretly in a supplement. Your editor might or might not welcome your innovative solutions for improving exposition, achieving better topical balance, citing more current sources, or overcoming perceived bias. If there is time for it, and if your input on a supplement will improve the textbook's salability, good editors will reward your vigilance. Editors also may recognize in you the characteristics of a good textbook author.

Characteristics of Good Contributors

Publishers in higher education are always searching for supplement authors, as turnover tends to be high because of low investment. Publishers also tend to rely on their proven contributors and supplement authors on a long-term basis. Thus, your work could easily lead to steady demand or to a lucrative larger-scale publishing contract. Publishers look for contributing authors who are available, reliable, reasonable, cooperative, and on time, and who can provide work that is solid, savvy, and sound.

Available: Readily accepts assignments when needed.
Reliable: Maintains contact, works consistently and independently, and can be trusted to fulfill the contract appropriately.
Reasonable: Gives accurate estimates, charges standard fees, works quickly and efficiently, and avoids surprise cost overruns.
Cooperative: Readily accepts and applies editorial and marketing input.
On time: Delivers complete manuscript in acceptable form according to schedule.
Solid: Provides substantive, comprehensive, and complete content per agreed plan.
Savvy: Provides work that does not infringe on copyrights, draw complaints from textbook authors or customers, or cost sales.
Sound: Provides accurate, current, and valid content.

As with reviewing, the best way to become a contributor or supplement author is to send a letter of background and interest to editors who acquire manuscripts in your field. Editors look for authors who teach the course and understand content standards. For example, there are right and wrong ways to compose test items, right and wrong ways to construct websites, and so on.

Supplements seldom are reviewed and there may be little editorial or marketing input. Ask the publisher or editor to provide you with some or all of the following resources for authoring a textbook supplement.

- A development plan and models on which to base your work. In some cases you may be asked to create such a plan and models
- Copy of the textbook in near-final or final form (or a copy of the previous edition if a light revision is planned)
- Copies of comparable supplements from top competing textbook packages
- Copies of any relevant reviews or marketing surveys
- Summary of any correspondence between the textbook author and the editor regarding supplement content
- Detailed description of what is wanted; e.g., specifying the types and numbers of elements and items to include in the supplement
- Guidelines for manuscript preparation, style, length, and permissions
- Access to downloadable authoring software, as needed
- Contact information and a schedule for submitting and revising the supplement manuscript
- A work-for-hire agreement formally specifying all the above

Making Contact

After you have attended to the prerequisites—have ascertained the existence and nature of the market for your book, have established your credibility or reputation as a prospective author, have done your homework to gain familiarity with competing books and the courses in which they are used, and possibly have done some reviewing or contributing—you are ready to locate the right publisher and make contact. This is assuming you are ready to write a manuscript proposal. The right publisher is on your shortlist of houses that publish textbooks at your level in your field (see the Chapter 1 Appendix).

Whom To Contact

As explained in Chapter 2, the person to contact is the acquisitions or sponsoring editor or the publisher. Often, the quickest way to gain the attention of an acquisitions or sponsoring editor is through the sales representative who comes to your campus office to interest you in new titles. Tell the sales rep that you have written or are writing a textbook and are looking for a publisher. Identify the subject of your text and the academic level or course for which it is intended (introductory, undergraduate, graduate, or professional). Then ask the sales rep for the name and phone number, voicemail, or e-mail address of the appropriate contact editor, or ask to be contacted. As an alternative, try publishers' contact phone numbers and e-mail addresses found on their websites or the back covers of their textbooks.

Reaching the right editor is important. As mentioned previously, lists may be divided among different editors. Signings of introductory economics or introductory psychology, for example, may be controlled by individuals other than those who sign textbooks on macroeconomics or abnormal psychology. Additionally, books for professional colleagues rather than for students are usually managed separately. Editors typically are too busy or too competitive among themselves to share prospects or even to re-refer. At times staff turnover may be high, and projects seldom carry over from one editor to the next unless they are already under contract. Nothing will happen, therefore, if you do not make the right connection.

As noted, published colleagues also are good sources for leads. Another way to make contact is at professional meetings where publishers have booths displaying their products and where sponsoring editors network among convention participants. Simply point out the books you use, have used, or are considering for adoption, and announce the existence of your manuscript or your intention to draft one. Ask to be contacted or whom to call.

Note that, unlike unsolicited reviews, unsolicited manuscripts are not welcome. Always query to determine interest in seeing your proposal. With commercial publishers especially, it is best not to attempt a "cold call" or submit an unsolicited manuscript. Nobody has the time for these, however brilliant they may be.

When To Call

Because of the general publishing cycle, explained at the end of Chapter 2, the best time to make contact is in the early fall or early spring. At those times of the year, sales forces are canvassing campuses, and editors and marketing managers are presenting products at professional meetings and looking for prospective authors. In large houses, other times of the year are busy with meetings. Companies' national sales meetings typically are conducted in mid-winter and in late summer when schools are in intersession. Thus, attempts to make contact during these times are likely to fail.

When you call the acquisitions editor, expect to leave a voicemail message. Typically in a publishing house, no one actually answers, unless you are calling for sales support (and sometimes not even then). For most editors today, e-mail is the preferred medium of communication.

What To Say

When the editor gets back to you, which may take some time if the editor is on the road or preparing for sales meetings, you might find the following communication sequence helpful.

1. Give your name and institutional affiliation and the name of the referring sales representative or colleague or other contact. Identify any of the company's titles you order or have used (by name of author) and the size of the enrollments you cover—the number of students you teach and thus the number of copies of a textbook (number of units) that you control by ordering a particular title for your course. The editor might ask you about your degree of satisfaction with the titles and service, or about competitors' titles you have used. The editor also might ask you on the spot if you are interested in being a reviewer or contributor.
2. Express an interest in reviewing, noting, however, that you are busy writing a textbook. Then identify the subject, grade level, and course, audience, or customer base that you are writing for. Briefly explain why you are writing this book. For example, perhaps you have identified a segment of the market that is not being served (such as a new course), or perhaps you are addressing important new concerns, discoveries, trends, or developments in your field. Name the courses in which your book might be used.
3. Briefly identify any potentially or partially competing book that the company already publishes, and describe in general terms how yours will be different (based on your review of the book). For example, perhaps your book is aimed at a different segment of the market, such as anatomy and physiology for nursing school students, educational psychology for education majors, or finite mathematics for non-majors in mathematics. Your book might have a different approach (e.g., constructivist, micro, macro, multicultural, research-based, applied, theoretical, historical, analytical, case-based, interdisciplinary, etc.) or compelling features and a value-adding supplement (e.g., primary source material, models, application activities, casebook, manual, Internet activities, software, video, etc.).

What Not To Say

This is not the time to ask editors if they would like to publish your book, nor to open any discussion about policies concerning advances, grants, or royalties. Decisions to publish are complex, involve a lot of money, involve other people in the company, and take considerable time. Instead, offer to send your curriculum vitae, a prospectus of your proposed textbook, a preliminary book outline, and one or two sample chapters. Editors will say no only if they feel the book you describe is a complete mismatch with the lists they have been assigned to manage. As explained in Chapter 2, publishers specialize. The worthiness and excellence of your book is irrelevant if the company's sales force does not happen to visit the academic departments in which your book might be adopted.

What To Submit

The most important part of your quest after making contact is submitting a curriculum vitae, book plan prospectus and outline, and a writing sample in the form of sample chapters. Assuming that you meet the basic pre-qualifying criteria described earlier in this chapter and that your book idea fits the publisher's needs, the decision to sign you on as an author will be based on these artifacts.

What to Send to the Editor, At-a-Glance

- Full curriculum vitae
- Prospectus
- The story, rationale, goal
- Topic, scope, theme
- Audience, level
- Planned apparatus, pedagogy, art, and presentation
- Analysis of primary and secondary markets
- Competition analysis and unique features
- Preliminary, working, whole book drafting outline
- Complete sample chapters
- Cover letter
- Present status of the manuscript
- Planned length and estimated completion date
- Contact information

Your Prospectus

Each company has its own requirements for a prospectus and might send you guidelines or a preprinted form. Typically the prospectus is a two- or three-page explanation of what you are doing, for whom you are doing it, and why. That is, the prospectus states your topic, scope and sequence, and theme; identifies your market and audience; and sets forth your rationale or main goal. This is the "story" of your book.

In commercial publishing, a book's story is critically important. Editors usually are teamed with marketing and advertising managers, who use the story (1) to determine if the company thinks it can sell your book profitably, (2) to identify specific potential customers, (3) to launch marketing and advertising campaigns, and (4) to educate and win the commitment of the sales force. The story also guides the book designer and others whose job it is to make sure your book looks right for what it is trying to do.

Telling The Story

Because your book is one of dozens or even hundreds presented by editorial teams to the publisher and ultimately to the sales force, its story should be stated briefly. The brief statement is like an abstract containing a working title and the key words that define and sell the book idea. The prospectus should start with this story abstract and then go on to elaborate. Examples of book stories follow.

Social Work will be an introductory text for entry-level courses in programs leading to licensure in social work and will integrate theory and practice using a problem-solving casebook approach.

Technology and the Environment is a thematic, multidisciplinary treatment of the global impacts of technology on human environments from prehistoric times to the present and supports courses in earth science and cultural ecology.

Principles of Scientific Research will be a comprehensive general -purpose handbook with guidelines for observing, measuring, describing, and reporting research in the physical and social sciences.

History Then and Now: Historiography in Perspective is a topical survey of the history of history for graduate students taking Historiography I and Historiography II, with an emphasis on the role of culture in the selection and interpretation of evidence.

In the First Instance will reexamine theories of the origins of the universe in light of new discoveries in quantum mechanics, radiotelemetry, and particle physics, and will complement general introductory textbooks in physics.

Introduction to Technical Writing surveys all aspects of professional practice in technical writing and features authentic models of excellent writing in both technological and non-technological fields.

Biology and the Life Sciences: An Introduction is an introductory text for undergraduate survey courses in biology or the life sciences. Genomic research and its applications and implications is the unifying central theme of the book, and a whole chapter is devoted to the implications of recombinant DNA for reproductive technologies and gene therapies in the treatment of disease.

Education and Diversity will focus on the social foundations of education in the United States with an emphasis on the social contexts of issues concerning multicultural education, bilingual education, and inclusion.

Note that your title is only a working title. Try not to become wedded to it, because titles are the products of market research, and the publisher has final say on titles and subtitles and anything else that appears on a book's cover.

Planned Contents

The prospectus next walks the editor through the nuts and bolts of the book by describing its organization and what elements and features it will include—its apparatus and pedagogy, the subjects of later chapters of this book. How will chapters open and close, for example, and what regular features will appear in each chapter? Will there be figures and tables? Photos? How many of each? Will there be a glossary? An instructor's manual? And so on.

Many new textbook authors naively fail to plan enough in advance. This work is necessary, though, even if, inevitably, the plan later changes. In reality, almost everything about a textbook is decided before drafting even begins. The plan then is re-decided or adjusted as the work progresses. A working table of contents for all the chapters is prepared up front, for example, and if you cannot create such a document then you are not ready to write your book.

Markets

The prospectus should go on to identify the likely primary and secondary markets for the book. Who will buy it? Who will read it? Your primary market is where you expect to sell the most copies, while the secondary market includes others who might be interested in using your textbook. For instance, the primary market for this book is prospective textbook authors and their editors, the people for whom I have written it, the people who will buy it directly from the publisher or from retailers such as Amazon. Secondary markets include institutions of higher education, academic libraries, faculty development centers, and college textbook publishers, who will order the book through a wholesaler or distributor.

Identify your primary market as the instructors who teach the course, not the students, because it is the instructors who will order the book. Thus, it is the instructors and their tastes that interest the publisher, just as mothers and their tastes interest a manufacturer of baby food. In both cases the end user must be nourished and not poisoned, but the end user is not the one who makes the decision to buy. Students figure in as an estimate of what the total annual enrollments might be in the course for which you are writing your textbook.

Competition

Your prospectus should include your analysis of the competition. Briefly list and evaluate each competing text you have identified, explaining how your book will be similar to and different from it in goals, structure, and content. This discussion should lead to an explanation of what you believe is outstanding and different or unique about your book. Also report if your book idea or chapters have been field tested or class tested in your own or others' courses.

Chapter 5 contains more information about performing a competition analysis. A sample prospectus—the one for this book, which was accepted by a major publisher (I declined because of low royalties and passive marketing and established my own company)—is presented in the chapter appendix. While this book is not a college textbook, and the prospectus is unusually brief, the same elements of a good prospectus are there.

Your Preliminary Book Outline

An outline functions as both a writing guide and an organizational scheme. Each part or unit and each chapter is identified by number and title, followed by topics and subtopics in the order you plan to write. Observing the formal rules for outlining rather than merely listing topics will help you establish a structure for the book.

Preliminary book outlines typically undergo changes as a result of the publisher's market analyses, analyses of competing books, and feedback from editors and peer reviewers, not to mention needed changes that authors themselves usually discover during drafting. In addition, if your undergraduate textbook involves a large investment, the publisher might propose changes to your outline to ensure any of the following outcomes, based on customer wants and needs.

- Chapters generally have consistent and appropriate lengths.
- The book includes timely topics and topics that customers generally expect, and foregoes topics that customers insist they do not want or need.
- To a reasonable extent the book organization works according to known ways in which the course is taught.
- The content is appropriate for the intended course level or for the reading or intellectual level of the intended audience.
- The book can compete successfully with market leaders in its field.

The writing outline is the basis for a table of contents (TOC), which is perhaps the most important tool for marketing and selling the book. If you are developing your book in collaboration with editors, you may receive specific informed suggestions for converting your outline into the system of headings and subheadings that will become your TOC. Otherwise, you will need to do this yourself in an informed way. Chapter 9 of this book is devoted to the art and science of creating a proper heading structure for your book.

Some prospective authors feel it is unreasonable to expect a whole-book outline prior to drafting, but they are wrong. As noted earlier, if you do not have a working whole-book outline, you are not ready to draft. Textbooks—indeed all nonfiction—are written to spec.

Your Sample Chapters

If possible, include two or three sample chapters with your prospectus and drafting outline, or establish when you will send sample chapters. A sample chapter should be double-spaced with pages numbered consecutively and should have all its components in place, including any apparatus and pedagogical features you have planned, figures and tables, and references. It is assumed that you are working on a computer, availing yourself of the spell-checker, and saving to hard drive or disk.

Aside from giving the editor an example of how far your planning has gone and what you have to say, sample chapters present your voice and show off your ability to express yourself in writing and maintain a consistent writing style and format. Take care to submit clean, revised, and corrected or edited chapter manuscripts. From those pages, reviewers gain an impression of you and your offering. And I have seen reviewers trash manuscripts on the basis of typos and composition errors alone. Reviewers' responses will weigh heavily in the editor's decision to offer a contract or decline the project.

Your Cover Letter

The cover letter recalls your previous contact with the editor, briefly reiterates that you have a manuscript or book idea for the publisher's consideration, and identifies all your enclosures. You also provide detailed information about your availability for your project and where, when, and how the editor can reach you. The editor will need practical information as well, such as the present status of the manuscript, your timetable for submitting sample chapters and for completing the work, the estimated length, and even the word processing program you are using.

In your cover letter, you may indicate if you are making a multiple submission—submitting a prospectus to more than one publisher simultaneously—although you are not obligated to do so. Publishers naturally discourage simultaneous submissions to more than one publisher at a time, and some will reject a multiple submission outright. Because of the extreme competitiveness of the textbook industry and the amounts of money involved, publishers are sensitive about product secrecy and competitive advantage. Authors have used the multiple submission strategy to their advantage, however, as it facilitates an earlier response from the publisher.

Waiting is next and often takes longer than one would like. Acquisitions editors may be on the road, traveling to conventions and campuses, and unable to attend to your submission immediately. Few acquisitions editors are capable of evaluating your materials themselves. They typically send out your prospectus and sample chapters for professional peer review, which also can take considerable time. Finally, the sponsoring editor may need to present your book plan to other tiers of corporate management before an offer can be made. Regardless, as a prospective author, you are justified in re-contacting the editor in a month or two if there has been no response.

Sometimes editors will offer you a contract on the basis of positive peer reviews, but they more typically request additional information or sample chapters or your response to the peer reviews. Let us say, for instance, that reviewers unanimously feel that your sample chapter on law enforcement is too long, overemphasizes federal law enforcement over local and state law enforcement, and omits any mention of special law enforcement units such as border patrol, tribal police, and campus police. The editor might ask you to address these concerns by revising and resubmitting the chapter. As well as addressing real market concerns, such a request is a test of your desirability as an author. The decision to make you an offer will rest on your response. Inexperienced or arrogant prospects who do not respond well or refuse to make changes, perhaps in the belief that their work is a fait accompli, do not get signed.

Consider your attitudes in this context. For example, what if you don't know anything about border police or tribal police? Then you would find out, because your customers want this information, or perhaps a colleague would contribute on those topics. And what if you believe that federal law enforcement *should* be emphasized over other jurisdictions? Then you would say so. You have an obligation to let buyers and readers know that a conscious choice has been made about emphasizing or omitting selected content. But will your emphasis alienate customers? Then you should reconsider. How much would it compromise your intellectual integrity to provide more balanced coverage? If you think you would find such compromises too great or troubling, then you probably should not seek to publish commercially an undergraduate textbook.

Let us assume, however, that you offer a thorough, timely, and thoughtful response to the editorial suggestions, and that, as the next chapter suggests, the editor offers you a contract to sign with the publisher of your choice.

Appendix
A Simple Sample Prospectus

Dear Suzanne,

Thank you for sending me your submission guidelines and inviting me to submit my book proposal and sample chapters. As we discussed, I am writing a professional reference for authors and editors on WRITING AND DEVELOPING YOUR COLLEGE TEXTBOOK. Enclosed please find my résumé, a working TOC, and three sample chapters of my manuscript.

The work is based on my many years of experience as a development editor in secondary and higher education publishing. As you will see from my résumé, I have developed textbooks and textbook packages, including many first editions, for Allyn and Bacon, Prentice-Hall, Houghton Mifflin, Little Brown, McGraw-Hill, Sage Inc., John Wiley & Sons, and several other educational publishers. I also have taught at both the secondary and college levels.

The main audience for my book is current and prospective authors of textbooks for college courses in all academic disciplines, especially introductory textbooks for undergraduates. Direct mail marketing, campus bookstores and libraries, professional meetings, and the Internet seem suitable avenues for reaching this target audience.

Although writing and editing advice and self-help books for authors and academics abound, I know of no title that addresses textbook development for college markets specifically and in detail, although I have seen articles on the subject by members of the Text and Academic Authors Association. My book seeks to inform on standard practices and best practices in commercial textbook publishing and will be the first of its kind in the marketplace.

A secondary market for my book, other than academic libraries, is editors and publishers of college textbooks, who may wish to use it in whole or in part as instructional material for their authors or as professional development material for their editors. The work is easily adaptable to publishers' unique needs and also is appropriate for site-based professional workshops or campus seminars, which I am interested in conducting. I am presently developing an online course in textbook development for schools that offer certificate programs in publishing. I also have drafts of two companion titles for authors and editors respectively, WRITING AND DEVELOPING COLLEGE TEXTBOOK SUPPLEMENTS and MANAGING YOUR AUTHORS.

I think you will agree that there is a clear need for the kind of book I am proposing. In commercial higher education publishing today, development tends to be reserved for a small number of high-projection titles. I wrote WRITING AND DEVELOPING YOUR COLLEGE TEXTBOOK to help improve the quality and shelf life of instructional materials for college students by teaching authors how to craft a commercially successful textbook on their own through self-managed product development.

I visualize this project as a 14-chapter handbook under 300 pages in length. Style and tone are succinct, no-nonsense, and highly practical. My research- and experience-based insider advice tends to be both encouraging and outspoken, which may serve to entertain as well. The initial draft has approximately 110,000 words, 8 rendered figures, several matrices, and at least 14 chapter appendices.

I chose your company because of similar titles you publish on writing and scholarly publishing. I am working on the book part time and expect to achieve a completed revised draft by June 1, 2002. If my project fits your list needs, I will be glad to send you more manuscript for review. This query is not part of a multiple submission, however, so I would appreciate your letting me know within 30 days of receipt if you remain interested in talking with me further about publishing and marketing possibilities. My contact information appears below.

Thank you very much for your consideration.

Sincerely,

4

Sign a Mutually Lucrative Contract

WHEN THE ACQUISITIONS or sponsoring editor receives your prospectus and enclosures, he or she will read it and decide whether to reject it outright or to send it for peer review. In some smaller houses, an in-house editorial board or panel decides. This is what is happening during the weeks or months that you receive no response. A considerate editor will let you know the status of your submission.

Steps to Getting an Offer

On receiving generally positive reviews, the editor will call you to discuss the project further. Before discussing contracts and royalties, however, the editor will want to get to know you a little and feel you out on the following questions. These are questions you should also answer for yourself before you proceed.

Ten Things Your Sponsor Wants to Know About You before Signing

1. Are you and your book a good choice for the company and for the market?
2. How committed are you to the project and do you have the self-management skills to accomplish it?
3, Can you put aside enough time for this monumental task?
4. What resources do you have for getting help with your project and completing it on time?
5. How knowledgeable are you about what is involved in textbook publishing?
6. How responsive are you to market issues and company needs?
7. How responsive are you to professional peer review and to editorial input?
8. How willing are you to consider suggested changes?
9. Do you seem to have good interaction and collaboration skills?
10. Do you seem to have positive attitudes toward the editor's and the publisher's roles?

The sponsoring editor has compelling reasons to try to gauge your ability to deliver. Publishing a textbook involves a major commitment of time and resources. Ask anyone who has done it. The publishing process, like the writing process, is complex, ongoing, and recursive. Also, in most large commercial houses, publishing schedules have decision points, points of no return, and only minor flexibility.

If authors cannot fulfill all their authoring tasks in time, it is expected that they will be able to delegate or let the publisher do so. If scheduling does not work out for any reason, a book can miss its intended copyright year, thus upsetting the company's publishing plan. The book could then be bumped one to three years depending on other titles already in the pipeline. Delayed books usually need further revision before they are ready again for production, and some delayed books never see print. The editor has a stake in seeing that this does not happen, which is why he or she must try to develop a relationship with you before deciding to make an offer.

In the company's eyes, your commitment is not only to your book but also to its market—the customers your book serves. As suggested at the end of Chapter 3, it is expected that you will be responsive to reviewer concerns and proven customer needs. Further, author commitment may not end with publication, especially if the company is handling your book as a major-market offering. You might be called upon to contribute material for advertising and promotion, talk to potential customers, provide signed copies of your book, or conduct a forum on a companion website. The sponsoring editor therefore has strong reasons to gauge your market savvy and sensitivity and interest in helping make your book a commercial success.

Establishing a Positive Relationship

A prospective author's attitudes and ability to work well with other professionals are important factors for the success of a project. In addition to teaming with an acquisitions editor and possibly a coauthor or two, you also might be working with a development editor or managing editor, production coordinator, copyeditor, photo researcher, packager, marketing manager, supplements authors, and others. Through interpersonal conflicts and misunderstandings about the roles of all the players, projects can fail to meet their potential or can altogether crash. Legendary cases involve lawsuits. Your sponsoring editor therefore has a stake in establishing friendly rapport with you and gauging your cooperative spirit. Unproductive author attitudes toward publishers and editors usually relate to issues of trust, power, and control.

Trust

Mistrust about contracts and the publisher as capitalist are common. It is true that publishers try to cut themselves the best possible deal and some are not above misrepresentation. So-called standard contracts definitely favor the publisher. You should be aware, however, that there are industry standards regarding ethical practices, and reputable publishers take those standards seriously. Normally, it is not in a reputable publisher's long-term interests to be underhanded with authors.

In abnormal situations, however, such as small subsidiaries being squeezed for profits, things can change. Also, in giant mergers large numbers of books on the same subjects change hands, and publishers routinely discontinue less profitable titles by putting them out of print. Discontinued authors justifiably feel abused, although, as mentioned previously, all rights are reassigned to them eventually and they can seek another publisher. In the balance, authors should be wary of potential ruthlessness but should not assume that author-publisher relations are predicated on opportunities for exploitation.

Trust issues may also arise over the role of publishing in society. Some see the publishing industry is a threat to academic freedom, not to mention democracy, and portray publishing conglomerates as bastions of thought control. The reasoning seems to be that by determining or censoring what gets published, unscrupulous plutocratic monopolists can amass wealth and global political power and influence through the control of information. Certainly the control of information is a crucial concern of the twenty-first century, but in mass media such control is more a by-product of business than the goal, even for a Rupert Murdoch. The goal is, simply, profit. As in all media, it's the ratings that count, and this dynamic more profoundly affects the quality of information than the control of it.

Power

This is not to say that publishers in higher education only follow market trends. They innovate to create demand, sometimes making it difficult for customers to stick with tried and true ways. For example, the revolution in electronically delivered instruction, which instructors certainly never asked for, was spearheaded by publishers. Nevertheless, some academics are insulted or disappointed to discover that textbooks are products and obey the dictates of a market economy. As suggested in Chapter 3, they may treat requests for changes to their manuscripts as Faustian confrontations in which making any amendment is selling out.

It is true that publishing companies have market-derived power over content. A common misperception, however, is that marketability requires textbooks to be dumbed down and that publishers are to blame for this. Actually, textbooks need to address their true readers—students for whom the book is intended, those whose learning is at stake. These students need to be addressed where they *are*. That is, textbooks need to be brought to market level, wherever that level is, and if instructors demand low-level textbooks, publishers will supply them. Bringing readers to your intellectual level is a different problem. For most introductory college courses, the reader is an 18- or 19-year-old person in late adolescence with little or no prior exposure to your field. If you do not wish to write for this audience, but prefer to maintain the language and style of discourse you use in journal articles, monographs, and graduate seminars, you should not attempt to write an undergraduate textbook.

Another common misperception is that books must be made into clones of all the other books on the market. On the contrary, publishers know that each title needs to be unique or special or innovative in some way to distinguish itself among competitors. At the same time, they know that textbooks that are too different or too far before their time, even great ones, like other great ideas for which the world is not ready, will fail.

Control

Many control issues concern the manuscript. Some authors believe strongly that their words should not be subject to outside forces. They tend to think like this: I am the expert and no one can tell me what to write. Reviewers have their own axes to grind or cancel each other out and thus can be ignored. Customers should have the good sense to want what I am providing. These authors also tend to see their editors as adversaries and treat every editorial request as an issue of ownership and control. If you tend to hold strongly Orwellian views, consider the following reasons other than thought control that editors might have for asking you to revise, add, or delete material.

Chief Reasons Editors Ask for Changes to Organization or Content

- The book is too long for its intended market or its budget and has to be cut.
- Undocumented opinion is presented as fact.
- Undocumented facts seem inaccurate or misleading.
- Information seems outdated or lacks currency.
- Topical coverage seems unbalanced or biased.
- Material is judged to be strongly offensive to some or all readers.
- Abstractions or conclusions are insufficiently supported by concrete examples.
- Language or expression seems inappropriate to the subject, course, or audience.
- Digressions, redundancy, or lack of transitions compromise meaning or coherence.
- There are errors of grammar, punctuation, spelling, or usage.
- The manuscript departs significantly from the agreed-upon book plan.
- New intelligence about the market or competition suggests changes.

Editors, too, are experts. They can save you from yourself and help you craft a successful book—the editor's true purpose. Reviewers and customers also are experts. Authors uninterested in satisfying the people who will order, buy, and read their textbook should consider self-publishing or custom publishing instead. Positive author-editor relations are built on mutual respect, benefit-of-the-doubt trust, power-sharing, and rationally negotiated control over content.

Know How to Negotiate Your Agreement

Let us assume, on the basis of your response to peer reviews and editorial input on your sample chapters, the sponsoring editor wants to get you under contract to do the book and is satisfied that the company can work with you amicably, productively, and profitably. Now, finally, comes the discussion of mutual contractual obligations and royalties and advances.

First, here are ten questions you should ask a publisher before signing a contract.

Ten Things You Want to Know from Your Publisher before Signing

1. Why should you publish with them rather than with another publisher?
2. What will be the publisher's investment in your book and its package?
3. How will your book be marketed, promoted, advertised, and sold?
4. How many copies of your book can the publisher expect to sell and to whom?
5. What will be your royalty percentage and how will royalties be paid?
6. Will you receive a grant and/or advances on royalties, how much, and when?
7. What are all your rights and responsibilities regarding your manuscript? What are all the publisher's rights and responsibilities?
8. How many chapters, pages, or words will you be expected to provide, and when will the manuscript be due?
9. By what process and criteria will the publisher determine that your manuscript is "acceptable?" How extensively and by whom will your manuscript be reviewed?
10. Will you have the assistance of a development editor? How will you be rewarded if you undertake development on your own?

In commercial publishing, contracts favor the publisher, read like you are signing your life away, and make you wonder if you should retain a famous lawyer. Having the contract reviewed and amended by an attorney who knows publishing (an intellectual property rights lawyer) certainly is a very good idea. After all, you are signing a legally binding document. You cannot count on your acquisitions editor to act in your interests or even to refrain from taking advantage of your naivety. Intellectual property rights lawyers are expensive but really worth it if you first figure out as much as possible on your own. Pro bono advice for authors also is available.

All publishing contracts are negotiable to some degree. According to Michael Lennie, an attorney specializing in author-publisher contracts (**lennieliterary.com**):

> An offer is an invitation to dicker. A contract is an agreement. An agreement takes two persons. Publishers do not expect you to sign their standard contract as is. Everything in the contract is negotiable. It is merely their wish list.

Publishers usually are willing to negotiate more in contracts for high-projection textbooks than for scholarly books that are more likely to become loss leaders for them. To allow wiggle room in negotiation, you would be wise to prioritize the amendments you want. Which clauses, if any, are so important to you that you would walk away if the publisher did not agree to change them? Please note, however that the suggestions in this chapter cannot substitute for proper legal advice. Selected resources for legal advice are listed in the chapter appendix.

Understand the Language in Your Contract

What are those clauses? The formidable boilerplate in an agreement reflects the fact that publishers—in addition to being under pressure for profits from their parent company and stockholders—routinely take losses on a percentage of their titles each year or are burned by authors who drop out. Publishers also are sued regularly. Even suits without merit are costly. The larger the company, the greater the need for profit protection and legal safeguards. Hence, awesome-looking Nazi-sounding contracts.

The clauses in a standard contract that may prove most negotiable include the following.

- Confidentiality Clause
- Non-Compete Clause
- Satisfactory Manuscript Clause
- Termination (Walk Away) Clause
- Out of Print Clause

Confidentiality Clause
A typical confidentiality clause might read:

> The author shall keep confidential and shall not disclose the terms of this agreement except to the author's authorized legal and financial representative and then only for purposes of representing the author's interests hereunder.

The clause functions as a kind of gag order to prevent you from discussing the terms with others, including colleagues and other publishers. From a marketing perspective, the publisher's desire to keep your project a secret is understandable, but the clause is not enforceable and probably can be deleted.

Non-Compete Clause
This clause seeks to prevent you from writing a directly competing book for another publisher. For example:

> The Author will not publish or participate in the publication of a Book to be marketed in competition with the Book in this contract.

Although this may sound reasonable from a publisher's perspective, a narrow interpretation of it could bar you from any form of publication in your field with any other publisher. Although no sane publisher would take such a narrow view, this clause should be amended. According to textbook author John Vivian, the best way to fix it is to specify duration of time, a specific discipline, a specific type of writing, and a specific academic level (**sa2.info**). For example:

> During the four (4) years following publication of this book, the Author will not publish or participate in the publication of any other business management textbook to be marketed at the introductory college level.

Such an amendment essentially frees you to publish other kinds of works for other publishers and other books in your field for other markets. At the same time, it still protects the publisher from potentially unfair, simultaneous, direct competition.

Satisfactory Manuscript Clause
Contracts are worded to allow publishers to terminate a project and recover advances that have been paid if the author's manuscript is deemed unsatisfactory or unacceptable for any reason. For example:

> If any of such material, as delivered, is unsatisfactory to the publisher, then, upon the publisher's written request, the author will promptly repay all sums previously paid to the author by the publisher under this agreement, and the publisher upon receipt thereof will terminate this agreement.

Some publishers are not above threatening authors with the specter of owing the company money that the author has already spent. However, legal challenges concerning the definition of "satisfactory" often lead to court rulings favoring the author, stripping this clause of its power. It should be crossed out and replaced with a provision that allows either the author or the publisher to abandon the project. This is usually done through a termination or "walk away" clause.

Termination Clause

It is critical for a commercial publisher be able to "pull the plug" on an unsalable manuscript. It is equally important that an author be able to drop out without undue penalty. If you drop out *before* acceptance of final manuscript for any reason, you should return all advance money paid to you to that time, unless the publisher continues the project with another author. In that case, and in the case of your dropping out *after* acceptance of final manuscript, any return of advances should be prorated or reduced to reflect your time on task. In this case, partial retention of advances functions as a kind of "kill fee" for the author. Savvy authors do not spend their initial advance.

If, on the other hand, the publisher terminates the contract during manuscript preparation, you should be able to retain all advances against royalties paid up to that time. If the publisher terminates after accepting the final manuscript, giving the right to publish it, you should be able to retain all advances plus the projected royalties. It's a good idea to add that upon notice of termination you may seek another publisher for the work without any encumbrances from the contract.

Out of Print Clause

Most standard contracts say that provisions remain in effect until the publisher declares your book out of print. With print-on-demand technology, however, the publisher can keep your book in print indefinitely in very small numbers, even one at a time. This prevents you from getting back the rights, which is a prerequisite for signing with another publisher. The best way to amend this clause is to identify a sales number—say 50 or 500 copies in a year—below which the book will automatically go out of print and rights will be returned.

In addition, you could ask that language pertaining to the following points be included in the agreement (but beware, as publishers' tolerance for even discussing these points will vary):

- Restrictive language defining what is meant by the manuscript's "acceptability" to the publisher.
- Return of all rights to you if your book is not published within a specific agreed period of time.
- Right to review your contract with the new owners if the company is acquired by or merged with another.
- Divisions of income from the licensing of subsidiary rights.
- Right to negotiate a selected sub-right separately rather than granting all rights.
- Royalty rates based on payable (versus received) net sales to bookstores (in reality publishers cannot agree to this).

Your Royalties

Perhaps the issue of greatest concern to authors is the royalty schedule. Today, royalties can range from 2 to 20 percent depending on the following factors:

- Across-the-board ceilings decided at the corporate level
- How badly the company wants your book or you as an author
- How high the projected sales are for your book
- How much it will cost to develop, produce, manufacture, and sell your book

Royalties of 8 to 15 percent are typical for major market textbooks, but smaller houses may offer less. Academic and scholarly presses offer royalty splits as low as 5 percent on the net for the first 1,000 copies sold, 7.5 percent on the next 1,500 copies, and 9.5 percent above that. In large and small houses, royalty amounts commonly are split, with one percentage rate for an initial number of units (say, the first 2,000 copies), a higher rate for the next set of units (say copies 2,001 to 4,000), and so on. Companies cut their losses this way if your book does not sell as many copies as hoped.

Authors sometimes get shortchanged on royalties for sales of subsidiary rights. Some contracts specify 10 or 15 percent for foreign language rights, for example, when the industry standard for such sales is a 50-50 split between author and publisher. A lower percentage is justified if the publisher is underwriting the cost of translation. In any case, you would be wise to ask about projected sales of sub-rights in connection with your textbook.

Authors typically do not make much money with academic and scholarly presses or with small or niche textbook publishers. These publishers sometimes get away with outrageously one-sided contracts because of the "publish or perish" syndrome and the naivety of academics, especially those who spurn capitalism in connection with their intellectual mission and life's work. Authors who need to publish to win a place in their field or advance their career may be content simply to get into print. They sign with or without illusions of income and do not make good advocates for publisher responsibility and contractual fairness. Some acquisitions editors are not above taking advantage of these authors.

On the other hand, some authors do very well. Those with routinely revised best-selling introductory textbooks in popular undergraduate courses with large enrollments have been known to earn in excess of $100,000 a year in royalties, and more than one college instructor-author has been able to retire comfortably on royalty earnings.

Your share of the royalties will be affected by the number of coauthors or amount of material you contribute to the book. Coauthors agree among themselves on how to subdivide the pie further, and this decision is written into the contact. Royalties are then paid periodically—typically biannually or quarterly on the net of copies sold after returns. You should request to receive royalty statements at least twice a year, and you should make sure that "net sales" and all similar language is explicitly defined in the contract.

Advances and Grants

A grant is an outright cash payment to you to be spent on particular goods or services that you need to complete your textbook project. This money is yours and need not be returned if the project aborts for any reason. The publisher will be very reluctant to agree to a request for a grant. Some have a no-grant policy, because they have no way to recover these expenses. Advances against royalties are standard practice in larger commercial houses, but like cash grants, are becoming rarer. In smaller houses they are nonexistent. Companies and contracts vary widely in the allocation of assets and responsibilities and the flexibility for negotiating them.

Where advances exist—and they are common for textbooks—they are paid on a schedule that corresponds with benchmarks in the publishing process. For example, 25% of the advance may be paid upon signing, 25% on completion of the first third of the manuscript, another 25% on completion of the second third, and the last 25% on final completion. Another common schedule for textbooks is one-third on signing, one-third on completed draft, and one-third on release of final draft to production. Sometimes the schedule is further divided into fourths or fifths.

The amount of an advance is based on a formula that takes into account a conservative estimate of projected royalty earnings, usually over the book's first copyright year. The royalty percentage typically is applied to the wholesale price of your textbook, which averages to roughly half the "cover price." Advances must "earn out"—that is, your book must be profitable enough to afford the royalty amount on which advances are calculated. Publishers may tell you that if your book does not earn out, you will owe them the difference. Whether or not they can hold you to this, it shows that the size of the advance is directly tied to projected revenue. Thus, it would not be in your interest to campaign for unrealistically large advances against your unearned royalties. Textbook advances are nowhere near the amounts advertised for best-selling trade book authors.

Royalty Statements

Royalty payments kick in after a break-even number has been reached—that is, after the publisher has recovered a percentage of the plant costs, including all advances against royalties. Theoretically, as noted, if a book does not do well enough, the authors can end up earning no royalties or owing the company money. Traditionally, publishers underwrote this loss. In twenty-first-century publishing, however, as publishers continue to deflect costs and absorb losses of profit, authors increasingly are threatened with being billed for their books that fail to break even.

Royalty statements may be difficult to understand, rarely calculate arithmetically, and may conceal hidden costs, even improprieties. For instance, a publisher may deduct some legitimate costs of doing business from royalty statements, such as insurance, warehousing, and freight. Publishers also typically hold back some amounts as reserves against returns—the unsold new books that bookstores return to the publisher for credit at the end of each quarter or semester. Royalty statements also may omit some information about discount sales, special sales, or subsidiary sales.

Your acquisitions editor very likely will not know how to explain your royalty statements. Nevertheless, you have a legal right to review the publisher's books and records regarding sales of your textbook and reporting of royalties. If your contract does not have an audit clause, it would be a good to have one added. In any case, you could hire a royalty review service or an accountant specialist to help you understand your royalty statements. You also may need a knowledgeable tax preparer. Author royalty income is reported on Schedule C (not Schedule E) and is subject to self-employment tax.

If you wish to find a publisher and arrange your publishing contract through a literary agent—and only a handful of agencies represent textbook and academic authors—I recommend that you research them carefully. Depending on the complexity and value of your agreement, you can expect to pay an agent between 10% and 20% of your earnings.

Contractual Rights and Responsibilities

Check carefully the services your publisher intends to charge against your royalties, which should be made clear to you at the outset. In particular, ask who does the following, who pays for it (directly or indirectly), and for how much (in rate or percentage):

- Permissions research
- Permissions fees
- Photo research
- Photo use fees
- Art rendering
- Captioning
- Copyediting
- Proofreading
- Indexing
- Authors' Alterations (the changes you make during production after the book is set into type)
- Print and electronic supplements that are free to customers
- Print and electronic supplements that are sold to customers

The Boilerplate

All standard contracts, or "Agreements," identify "the Author," the nature of "the Work," the length of the Work (or the number of words), and the date the Work will be delivered. The Agreement further specifies what rights you are giving to the publisher, for example, all rights exclusively throughout the world in all languages for the life of the copyright including revised editions and derivative works, such as electronic editions. The publisher will want to retain all rights, but you should carefully consider each right you are granting. Some experienced authors or authors with agents may withhold some rights and assign them themselves. For instance, they might retain second serial rights and recording rights to create and sell other forms of their work themselves. You may wish to have subsidiary rights (such as publishing rights to British Commonwealth nations) returned to you if the publisher does not assign them within two or three years of publication of your textbook.

After specifying the rights being granted to the publisher, agreements then declare the royalty percentage and the manner in which it will be paid. Codicils to the Agreement present further conditions and iron out details. Details include what happens to your book if you cannot or will not provide a satisfactory revision (the company might want to get someone else to do it at your expense), or if not enough copies of your book get sold (the company might want to put it out of print and destroy all existing forms of it).

As mentioned earlier, all companies will seek to bar you from publishing a directly competing work with another company during the term of your contract and will shun all liability for any copyright infringements or instances of libel on your part. Indemnity clauses in some contracts specify that you will pay court costs for any claims against your book, but you should try to restrict this to only successful claims. Protecting yourself in view of copyright laws is the subject of Chapter 15 of this book.

Other contractual details specify exactly what you will provide in what form, including the authoring tasks you will perform, such as correcting proofs and furnishing various elements—a table of contents, index, illustrations, photos, instructor's manual, etc. The publisher's duties are similarly spelled out.

All companies reserve the right to edit your book so long as your meaning is not changed, and to manufacture and sell your book as they see fit, choosing the design, paper, binding, cover, and price. In addition, publishers usually reserve for themselves all decision-making rights concerning the quality of materials and visual presentation. If you feel strongly about having a say in your book's presentation, therefore, discuss this at the time of signing.

The Role of Internal Competition

Before you sign with a publisher, ask about the planned revision cycle if your book is successful. It would be in your interest to request or agree to the shortest revision cycle for which you have the time. It would also be in your interest to avoid having your book come out in the same copyright year as the publisher's other directly competing title(s).

In any case, it is a good idea to ask the editor about the impacts of recent mergers on his or her list, especially on titles that would compete with yours. An unpleasant outcome of grand-scale mergering is the killing of books, in which leading books from different acquired imprints are pitted against each other, and all but the top sellers are dropped. Although companies vary in the number of directly competing titles they will carry and sell successfully, many perfectly respectable textbooks may go out of print in a merger, along with "heirloom" titles that are no longer profitable despite their status as classics in the field. That a textbook was written by the founder of a key paradigm in the history of your field is no guarantee of immortality. In scholarly and trade book publishing, paperback and reprint rights might give classic books new leases on life. However, these rights normally are not sought for textbooks. Scholars interested in the history of ideas, as well as critics concerned with freedom of information, despise the loss of diversity that corporate libracide implies.

The Role of Company Investment

Considering all that you give up in a contract, what can you expect a commercial publisher to do for you? If your textbook is a C-book, your publisher may be investing at least $20K just to get it into print. If it is an A-book, the company is investing perhaps a half a million dollars or more. If the publisher is producing a videotape, CD, and website to license or to give away free to adopters of your book, then its direct investment is even higher.

Depending on company size, besides direct investment the publisher has other resources and networks for bringing your book to market that a small publisher or an author alone cannot easily match:

- Wholesale buyers
- Processes and vendors for mass production and manufacturing
- Nationwide marketing research
- Advertising and promotion budgets
- Direct mail and Internet marketing capabilities
- Professional sales force in the field and sales support staff
- Editors, book designers, photo researchers, artists, and a host of other specialists
- Systems for providing print and non-print supplements, such as transparencies, software, video, and so on
- Warehousing and distribution
- Access to foreign markets

The combined cost of direct and indirect investment can be quite high. An area of misunderstanding between authors and publishers stems from authors' ignorance about the hidden costs of publishing. As a result of escalating competition within the college textbook industry, commercial publishers try to outdo each other by giving away products and services free to adopters, although this practice is changing today as the cost of producing "freebies" becomes increasingly prohibitive.

Publishing Costs

Other examples of hidden costs of publishing are increases in postage rates, production and printing costs, the price of paper (especially green or recycled paper), warehouse leasing, salaries of IT and other experts, benefit packages and incentive plans for employees, and other overhead. The following examples of typical publishing costs in 2007 may give you an idea of the publisher's potential cost of investment in your book.

Editorial development: $200–$400 per day
Project coordination: $5–$15 per page
Copyediting and proofreading: $2–$4 per page
Book design and cover design: $500–$4,000
Page layout: $3–$5 per page
Art and photo coordination: $4–$6 per piece
Cost of production: $10–$30 per page
Plant costs (manufacturing): $25–$250 per page

Instructor's manual: $1,500–$5,000
Videotape: $5,000–$20,000
Website: $10,000–$50,000

Other hidden costs relate to the role of the brokers involved in the distribution of textbooks, including college stores and used book dealers. As an instructor, you already may have had the experience of being approached by used book dealers asking you to sell your old textbooks to them right off the shelves of the bookcase in your office. If you did so, you boosted the cost of new editions of that textbook and stole royalty earnings from the authors, and the same thing can happen to you. Returned copies of unsold new textbooks, meanwhile, must be remaindered or destroyed at publisher expense, as tax laws prevent publishers from writing off unsold inventory. Publishers also have been prohibited from buying back and reselling their own products.

Together with the high cost of personnel, overhead, vendor services, and technology, all the above conditions put a tight squeeze on companies' profit margins at the same time as corporate chiefs continue to demand double-digit growth in profits. Giant mergers are one response, along with dubious economies of scale. Publishing conglomerates' strategies for protecting profit margins, as in other industries in the twenty-first century, sometimes lead to over-standardization; overburdened or downsized in-house staffs; excessive outsourcing and the exporting of manufactory; products of lesser quality or lesser variety or with "loose bolts" as a result of cost-cutting measures; and profit-squeezing contracts, wholesaling practices, and fulfillment policies.

All these realities underlie publishing contracts. In the end, it must be acknowledged that, even with a killer contract, your publisher probably is not making a killing on your textbook. Publishers' problems should not discourage you as a prospective author, however. As noted at the beginning of this chapter, as formidable as contracts are as legal documents, they are negotiable. Many contracts have passages added or crossed out and initialed amendments modifying one detail or another. Savvy authors ask a lot of questions and return point-for-point memos requesting changes, clarifications, additions, or deletions in their contract. They also avoid signing with a publisher that treats its contract as nonnegotiable.

In commercial textbook publishing, mutually lucrative author-publisher agreements are more the rule than the exception, and this should be the principal goal of your negotiations during the signing process. Let your acquisitions editor know at the outset that this is what you expect.

APPENDIX
Resources for Legal and Expert Advice for Authors

On Contracts and Royalties

Society of Academic Authors: **sa2.info**
Contract Terms and Royalties: **fonerooks.com**
National Writers Union Contracts Glossary: **nwu.org/nwu**
Publishing Law Center: **publaw.com**
Author's Guild: **authorsguild.org**
Writer's Guild: **wga.org**
American Society of Journals and Authors: **asja.org**
The Authors Registry: **authorsregistry.org**
Royalty Review service: **royaltyreviewllc.com**
Ivan Hoffman: **ivanhoffman.com**
Lloyd J. Jassin: **copylaw.com**
Publishing Law: **www.answers.com/topic/publishing-law**

Textbook Agents (A Sample)

Michael Lennie: **lennieliterary.com**
The Rosenberg Group: **rosenberggroup.com**
The Susan Rabiner Literary Agency: **rabiner.net**

Selected References

Crawford, Tad. *Business and Legal Forms for Authors and Self-Publishers,* 3rd ed. Allworth Press, 2005.

Crawford, Tad, and Kay Murray. *The Writer's Legal Guide*, 3rd ed. Allworth Press, 2002.

DuBoff, Leonard. *The Law in Plain English for Writers.* 4th ed. Sphinx, 2005.

Evans, Tonya M., and Susan Gordon Evans. *Literary Law Guide for Authors: Copyrights, Trademarks and Contracts in Plain Language.* FYOS Entertainment/Legal Write Publications, 2005.

Jones, Hugh. *Publishing Law*, 3rd ed. Taylor & Francis Group, 2006.

5

Why Your Textbook Needs Development

NOW THAT YOU HAVE NEGOTIATED and signed your contract, you can get back to work on your textbook. Development should take place at this time. As defined in Chapter 2, *development* is a complex recursive process in which authors and editors collaborate to bring a manuscript and all its ancillary material to market level and prepare it for publication. If you already have a completed manuscript in hand, you might wonder why your book needs development. As one author recalls, anonymously:

> It was my magnum opus—brilliant, classroom-tested, as near perfect as I could make it, the fruit of long years of painstaking study and splendid revelation and long nights at the computer. It was a labor of love and professional fulfillment in a "publish or perish" world. I had said exactly what I meant to say in exactly the way I wanted to say it. My colleagues in my department, my students, and my spouse all said that they liked it. As far as I was concerned, it was done. This was it, take it or leave it. Then I met my development editor.

This author learned that every writer needs an editor and that most textbooks need development to succeed in a big way. With development, a textbook can double its sales in its first two editions, as this author's did.

Development Decisions

Development involves the following decisions, among others:

Market and Audience

What is the book's market? Whom specifically will the book be for?

What will be the intellectual level, style, and tone?

On what basis will the book be marketed and sold? How will it take away business from the competition?

Organization and Content

What topics will the book cover and in what order?
How many parts and chapters of what length will the book need?
How will content be organized in terms of headings and subheadings?
What figures and tables will be included, and how many?

Apparatus and Pedagogy

How will chapters consistently open and close?
What pedagogical features will be included and how frequently will they appear?
Will there be pedagogical captions? A glossary? Marginalia?
What will be in the front matter and end matter?

Authoring and Managing Tasks

How will each authoring task be accomplished?
Who will review the manuscript, how many reviewers will there be, and to what questions will they respond?
What will be the schedules for drafting, reviewing, and revising?
What will be the supplements, who will do them, what will be in them, how will they be done, and when?

Presentation

What photos and illustrations will be included and how many?
What will the book look like? What will be on the cover?
How will the book be promoted and advertised?

Domains of Development

These authoring decisions reflect the ten domains of development. Although many of the questions are in the publisher's purview, it is a good idea to keep the big picture in mind as you work on answering your authorship questions.

Ideally, development is done up front before manuscript even exists and certainly before you have polished a presumed final draft. As with technological applications, retrofitting a manuscript to match a later development plan can be a nightmare for all involved. Thus, plan early and well, and, if possible, get development help.

Negotiate for Development Help

Ask your publisher or sponsoring editor if you will have the help of a development editor (DE). It would be in your interests to ask for develop-

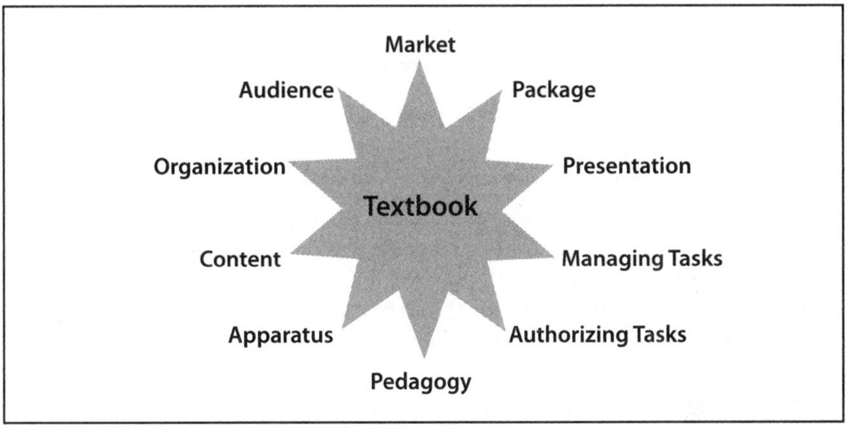

Figure 5-1. Ten Domains of Development

ment help as part of your contract negotiation. If your publisher declines to invest in development, ask what the sales projection will be and negotiate for development on the next edition if expectations are met. If your book is an untried first edition in an uncertain market, or is already in its eighth edition with declining sales, or serves a small, specialized readership, investment in development might not be forthcoming. If, however, the sales projection is, say, 5,000 units in a new market or 10,000 units in an established market, some professional development help might be warranted. Note, however, that publishers vary in the cut-off figures they use to determine if a book can afford development.

Levels of Development

Publishers vary in the way they define the DE's role and the levels of development. Typically, in *minor development* the DE:

- Responds to the book proposal and sample chapters
- Examines the top competing book for comparison
- Clarifies the story, market, and product fit
- Proposes chapter pedagogy and apparatus
- Includes the above in a development plan

In *moderate development* the DE additionally:

- Communicates with the author about the sample chapters
- Communicates with the author about the development plan
- Performs a competition analysis
- Proposes improvements to the table of contents

- Manages the reviewing process and analyzes the reviews
- Recommends on the basis of the competition and reviews

In *full development* the DE additionally:

- Communicates with the author about level, voice, and style
- Communicates with the author about organization and content
- Creates samples or models of pedagogical features
- Line edits the manuscript
- Acquires and manages contributors
- Develops the supplements plan

Publishing houses also specify different levels of development in relation to the level of investment. Minor development might involve only a few days of developmental review by an editor who writes a report but does not establish contact with you, while full development might involve having your project managed in every detail and your manuscript line edited by the DE. Thus, if your publisher is investing in development, ask what level of development is planned. If help is not forthcoming, however, negotiate for some consideration of your personal investment of time and resources for development, and announce your intention to develop the book yourself.

Realistically, unless your work is slated as a four-color introductory textbook, your chances of having development help are small. Development usually is reserved for products with high-volume sales projections and for promising new markets into which the company hopes to expand. In some companies, a portion of the staff development editor's annual salary is figured as part of the cost of a book, so only the books with the largest sales projections can afford a DE. The publisher might prorate the services of an in-house or freelance DE at $250 to $500 per day, charged to the plant costs for your book.

The Development Editor's Role

A development editor has a different role from the acquisitions editor and the copyeditor. As you have seen, the acquisitions editor sponsors your book, signs you on, proposes budget considerations for the project, often is responsible for arranging professional peer reviewing, and decides whether or not to invest in development. The copyeditor checks your writing style, spelling, punctuation, grammar, usage, sentence construction, paragraphing, and other mechanics. The development editor, on the other hand, analyzes your competition and reviewer feedback and collaborates with you to improve your organization and content; to create a heading system, a pedagogy plan, and a program of figures and tables; and to prepare your manuscript for release to production.

In some houses, development editors also are responsible for a variety of other tasks. They may be involved in commissioning reviewers, developing an art and photo program, assisting with permissions research, presenting your book to a book designer, checking stages of proof, developing the supplements and working with supplements authors, and tracking and routing all the paperwork for your project. In some instances, DEs might help you revise or rewrite. If they are content experts, DEs might even contribute original material for your book. Every house defines the role of a development editor differently, and development editors also vary among themselves in how they define their role as well as in expertise.

Whom Does the DE Work For?

The DE represents both the publisher and the customers for your textbook and in that capacity helps to answer the questions or make the decisions in the 10 domains of development (see page 88). For example, the DE addresses the domains of market and audience on behalf of both the reader and the company and reports or reconciles any discrepancies. The following hypothetical scenarios are examples.

> *What is the book's market? Whom specifically will the book be for?*
> The DE reconciles the audience addressed in the manuscript with the audience in the desired market placement.

> *What will be the intellectual level, style, and tone?*
> The DE champions the real reader and also tries to help you say what you really mean.

> *On what basis will the book be marketed and sold? How will it take away business from the competition?*
> The DE reconciles the manuscript with the publisher's ambitions for the book.

Now consider the domains of organization and content.

> *What topics will the book cover and in what order?*
> The DE serves the students taking the course, the instructors teaching the subject, and the company (by ensuring a competitive scope and sequence). The DE also tries to help you think and write clearly about what to include.

How many parts and chapters of what length will the book need? How will content be organized in terms of headings and subheadings?
The DE champions the reader as learner while giving the company a competitive TOC and a book that is the right length for its market.

What figures and tables will be included and how many?
The DE serves the learner while protecting the company's budget and market needs.

Inexperienced authors sometimes assume that development editors' only allegiance is to the publisher and that their job is solely to guarantee a salable product. Publishers, no doubt, would like to think so, too. As you have seen, however, the truth is that the professional development editor's chief allegiance probably is to your book and the people who will use it. For as little as a few days to as much as two years or more, the DE works for them as well as for you and the publisher. Making an excellent book that will achieve its purpose as well as its full market potential is the goal. And the process can be arduous, so much so that the metaphor of pregnancy and birth for publishing a book has entered the canon of cliché.

Establish a Good Working Relationship

Working with a development editor usually involves frequent contact, collaborative or consensual decision-making, and adherence to manuscript length requirements and schedules for submitting work. Working with a DE also involves trying to have a positive attitude and an appreciation for what the editor needs from you and what he or she can do for you and your book. This editor traditionally and normally is, above all, your ally, your champion, and should be treated accordingly.

Sources of Tension in Author-Editor Relations

For a variety of reasons, authors and editors typically experience some tension in their relationship. Author and editor need each other to achieve their goals but have differing agenda. When author-editor relationships are unsatisfying or stressful, their book is at risk, much as a child is at risk when parents bicker or separate. In addition to the issues of trust, power, and control in author-publisher relations described in Chapter 4, sources of tension between authors and editors range from issues of manuscript preparation to feelings of ownership, as suggested in the following examples.

Schedule, Length, and Mechanics

Editor has unrealistic expectations about schedule; nags about deadlines; asks for or dictates "impossible" cuts for length; requests nitpicking formatting changes.

Author cannot be reached or does not return calls promptly; sends manuscript late without notice; does not draft to length; does not attend to rules of manuscript preparation; does not attend to permissions correctly or in a timely way.

Effort and Commitment

Editor requests changes that involve too much time or effort; requests extra rounds of revision or causes more work by changing the book plan in midstream.

Author is too busy (or out of town) or insufficiently committed to get the job done; does not update sources sufficiently; submits manuscript with elements missing or treated inconsistently; avoids responsibility for pedagogical features.

Evaluation and Ego

Editor expects too much or too little, is overly critical, focuses on weaknesses; edits too heavily and is too heavy-handed or else fails to provide sufficient feedback.

Author cannot take valid criticism, is unresponsive to reviewer concerns and sound editorial suggestions, and accepts or insists on mediocre output.

Ownership and Control

Editor dictates cuts and changes but refuses to assist with (or to desist from performing) authoring tasks; acts like this is his or her book. Whose book is it anyway?

Author makes un-negotiated changes to text at the last minute without notice; expects the editor to perform the author's responsibilities or over-depends; has to be bailed out through unbudgeted help or unscheduled overtime.

Editors, like authors, vary greatly in their personalities, knowledge, abilities, professional commitments, standards, strengths, and needs. They vary greatly in education, subject area knowledge, and publishing experience, not to mention motivation and skill. In failing to deal with tensions, if and when they arise, authors and editors can become unmotivated, suspicious, antagonistic, or alienated. Straightforward communication and a spirit of cooperative problem solving are the antidotes. It helps to know something about the coded expressions that many editors commonly use.

Knowing the Code: Some Examples

Editor's Comment	Context	Meaning
Bring to market level	Evaluating content	Not good enough yet
See Reviewer A	Evaluating content	If possible, enable Reviewer A to adopt
Strongly suggest	Suggesting a change	Could affect sales
If at all possible	Requesting a change	Mandatory
Some length creep	Evaluating length	Cut to reduce length
A bit wordy	Evaluating style	Restate with fewer words
Watch voice	Evaluating style	Eliminate bad voice
Not clear (or "?")	Evaluating exposition	Rewrite for learner
Cite (?)	Requesting documentation	Are you infringing copyright?
Please cite	Requesting documentation	Mandatory

Rules of Thumb

Respect the editor's recommendations, as he or she understands the textbook publishing business. For every editorial request, however grand or trivial, normally there is a reason relating to publishing needs and realities. The first rule of thumb, therefore, is never to ignore an editorial request. Good development editors hesitate to confound authors routinely with the many technical details of publishing needs, but they will gladly explain reasons or argue a case. It is the editor's job to anticipate and address your questions and concerns—you need only ask.

The second rule of thumb is to carefully establish the boundaries and ground rules for your working relationship early on in a positive manner, starting with mutual appreciation for the many personal and professional sacrifices both author and editor may make in creating a textbook. Ask the DE precisely what his or her role on the project will be and what will be expected of you. Establish when and how your communications will take place.

The third rule of thumb is not to complain to the publisher about your development editor without confronting the editor directly first, because publishing houses, like academic departments, are political working environments. That is, if you have a grievance about the way development is going, the development editor has a right to know about it directly first and to have an opportunity to amend the process. Smart DEs ask their authors for feedback on their work to ensure mutual satisfaction with the manner in which development is done.

Do Your Own Development

Since the mid-1980s the role of the development editor has been changing—from that of author's alter ego, mentor, critic, muse, market analyst, creative consultant, advocate, and interpreter of the culture of publishing to that of product manager. Some publishers have found it in their interest to reduce the cost of development by having DEs handle as many books as possible, and the more titles they handle, the less time and care they can spend on each one. Correspondingly, publishers are placing a greater burden of responsibility for books on their authors. Costs that were once assumed by publishers or treated as author perks are being passed back to authors, along with tasks that restructured development editors may no longer have time to perform.

Even if you are assigned development help, in other words, you might find yourself pretty much on your own, which is the reason for this book. Lacking substantive collaboration with editors, you need to be able to do your own development. A major advantage of doing your own development is that you retain more control over your product and what goes into it. The disadvantage is that you need to devote more time and resources to planning your book with a view to commercial success.

This chapter offers guidelines for performing development tasks to ensure that success. If you are just starting out, these tasks will help you develop your prospectus, TOC, and sample chapters as described in Chapter 3. If you already have signed with a publisher, the information will guide you in further drafting and revising. And if you already have published and are working on a revision, the following practices will help you increase your market share. These practices include getting publisher input, charting the competition, professional networking, and working with reviews.

Get the Input You Need

Request information from the publisher about your book's market. How large is this market? What are the current top sellers? What percent of the market do they control? Who orders those books? Why are those books successful? What are customers looking for now? Acquisitions editors and marketing managers have their ears to the ground, constantly searching out market trends, consumer demand, and competitive edges. Ask them about their market research in your subject area and to send you the results of any pertinent marketing surveys. Also ask for information about competing texts.

Acquire examination copies of the current leading competing books and compare their contents. Or study the relevant product information on competing companies' websites. Then perform a competition analysis, including tallies of types of chapter elements. The aim is to ensure that your book will be competitive enough to succeed in the marketplace. The matrix in this chapter's Appendix A provides categories for a simple comparison grid.

Chart Your Competition

Some authors resist looking at their competition, for a variety of reasons: fear of being influenced unduly, fear of unconscious imitation, professional pride, professional jealousy, fear of invading turf, and fear of feeling outgunned. Natural fears such as these are worth overcoming, however, because a close examination of competing books will help you avoid spending a lot of time writing something that the publisher cannot sell because (a) it's a clone of all the other books out there, or (b) it's an alien from outer space—unlike any other book out there—that instructors can't use.

At the same time as they are unique, successful books also selectively match or top the characteristics that make competing books successful. These characteristics include the organization of the book, the length, the topical coverage, the pedagogical features, and so on. Also, anything you discover about the competition is ammunition for getting your publisher to invest more in your textbook, because textbooks must be competitive to sell. Perhaps you can make a good argument for going two-color, having more photos, or putting up a companion website.

Your Competition Analysis

So, how many chapters do other art history books have on the European Renaissance? Is it significant that all the other introductory psychology texts devote at least 40 pages to cognition? Should you also plan to have embedded calculus problems for students to solve as they read? In what primary context do the other health books discuss AIDS in detail? Do the other books in criminal justice cite Smith and Jones on their controversial new research? Should you consider adding maps showing frequency distributions in every chapter of your sociology text? Should engineering applications be treated in a separate chapter or integrated into every chapter? Should you think about converting some concepts in business law into flow charts or graphics? Does your social problems text have enough global and comparative coverage to be competitive?

To help organize your competition analysis and keep it from becoming overwhelming, try focusing on both the stock-in-trade and the hot buttons, buzzwords, sore points, and sticking points in your field for the course you are writing. Every subject area has these and they change fairly often, reflecting new trends and paradigms, as in the following example.

Example: Thinking about Competition Analysis
Looking at syllabi for Introduction to Earth Science, for example, I see that all the courses "must" include rocks and minerals, volcanoes and earthquakes, plate tectonics, the atmosphere and weather, and water and topography. Most are taught in one semester. Some courses crave a more big-picture approach and include a bit of planetary geology and earth history. Others are more lab-oriented and include a bit of chemistry or field trips to roadside exemplars of rock formations and landforms—travertine, breccia, flood plain, drumlin swarm.

Some courses insist on being called Earth *System* Science rather than Earth Science. The former are organized to survey the interactions and transformations of systems (e.g., lithosphere, atmosphere, biosphere, hydrosphere, etc.), while the latter are organized more concretely to survey materials near to far, granite to hurricanes to glaciers to stars.

Buzzwords in earth science today seem to include, for example, biodiversity, desertification, greenhouse effect. Global warming certainly is a hot button. Remote sensing and the role of El Niños may be sore points. And things like astrobiology no doubt are sticking points. In a competition analysis, textbooks for earth science could be compared on all these points and on the amount of coverage they have of each topic.

My point is that for each of these nuances there will be a textbook whose publisher or author has recognized the market need and has purposely set out to fill it. An important corollary is that no one textbook can be all things to all people. Typically, however, this truth does not prevent publishers from wanting you to write for the greatest mass of students taking Introduction to Earth History. Which earth history textbook would you write, and for whom? How would you highlight what you are doing?

Networking

Competition analysis also can be accomplished through networking. Use your own professional network, professional meetings, or resources such as the *Higher Education Directory* to contact instructors who teach the course for which you are writing your text. These people are potential adopters of your book. Select schools with large enrollments in the course you are writing for. Find out what books they are using, why they chose them, what they think the strengths and weaknesses of the books are, what pedagogical features they use or don't use, what they need in a book that existing ones lack, and what supplements they would like to have.

As you network, try out some of your ideas. Without giving away the whole show, ask them if they would be interested in a book that does what you are planning to do. Within reason, maintain strict confidentiality in your contacts. You are working on an introduction to African American literature, and that is all anyone really needs to know. More than one book has been scooped in its market because word of it reached rival publishers. If your book is a revision, keep the new copyright date to yourself. Keep a log of what you learn from your networking contacts and discuss the information with your sponsoring editor for additional feedback and follow-up.

Transform your informal mail or phone survey into an online search. The possibilities are limited only by your imagination. Browse websites and databases for information on your subject or field that might enhance your book's currency and appeal. Start or join a discussion group, asking colleagues about their courses and instructional concerns and about the books they use. This kind of information gathering gives you a broader insight into the instructional needs, hot topics, research developments, academic movements, patterns, and trends that your book might profitably reflect or represent.

Use information from the publisher, your competition analysis, and your networking to refine your TOC and to draft or revise your manuscript. Your final book plan should especially include the numbers and types of pedagogical features you plan to have for each chapter and samples of what they will look like. Chapters 8–12 guide you in the specifics of developing your TOC, apparatus, and pedagogy.

Get and Use Helpful Reviews

The next step in development is to send out revised chapters for professional peer review, a process that the publisher should manage for you. The acquisitions editor has already had your book prospectus, TOC, and sample chapters reviewed, and has available a ready database for selecting reviewers.

For each chapter of your manuscript, develop a list of specific questions you would like your reviewers to address. The editor can include these questions with the general reviewing guidelines that go out to cover the publisher's concerns. Your questions should reflect your informed concerns and should be worded neutrally—that is: no leading, loaded, or rhetorical questions. Would the reviewer assign this chapter for students to read? Why or why not? Does it cover all the topics it should? What should be added? Dropped? Is it current? Accurate? Balanced? Coherent? Clear? If your book is a revision, develop two sets of questions, one for past users of your book and one for nonusers—potential new customers.

A sample set of general reviewing guidelines and questions that you can adapt to your particular needs is provided in this chapter's Appendix B.

Also identify chapters that you think should go out for expert review. As defined in Chapter 3, expert reviews are critical reviews by specialists in a field. Especially in an introductory or survey text, you would be wise to select a chapter or two at the edge of your range of expertise that a specialist could check for you.

The Number of Reviews

Advocate for the publisher to have your book reviewed adequately and reviewers sufficiently remunerated. In some houses, skimping on reviewing is a solution to overstretched editorial budgets. Ask how many reviews are being commissioned and what the honorarium will be. As a rule of thumb, every chapter should have an absolute minimum of three generalist reviews, and selected chapters should have additional expert reviews. In large college houses, five to eight reviews per chapter are more typical. The more reviews you have to work with, the easier it is to identify areas of critical consensus, and the surer you can be of crafting a successful book. Your publisher usually pays the honorarium for each review and should not disclose to you the identities of reviewers until your book is in print.

Authors who are signed with university, scholarly, association, or academic presses sometimes are asked to arrange their own reviewing. These kinds of reviews function quite differently, however, as authors naturally ask friends and like-minded colleagues to review their work. The purpose is not so much to improve the manuscript as to collect positive testimonials for the publisher's promotional campaign. This focus is not appropriate for textbook publishing, however. If you are sincere about providing intellectual and educational value to instructors and students, you will want critical reviews.

For commercial textbook publishers, reviews are everything. Editors typically are not content experts, though they may become so. Most count on reviewers to give them an idea of whether or not to publish or revise a manuscript. You do want positive reviews, therefore, in addition to critical ones. Helpful reviewers both guide you in improving your manuscript and also make you look good in the eyes of the publisher, and finding and cultivating these reviewers is an art. You can help yourself best in the process by providing reviewers with complete manuscript—no missing pieces—that you have at least spell-checked.

Your Review Analysis

When the reviews come in, perform your own analysis of them as objectively as possible. Analyzing reviews can be difficult. It is natural to focus on laudatory remarks, tempting to dismiss criticism, easy to become defensive and to discard wholesale the comments of people who seem to disagree with you philosophically. Reviewers do sometimes have axes to grind and may not communicate in ways that are helpful or kind. Focusing too much on criticism also is a fault.

Review analysis also can be confusing. Positive and negative reviews have a way of canceling each other out, leaving you with no clear direction. However, your natural resistance must be balanced with openness to the possibility that the chapter is imperfect and can be improved, that improvements can be made without compromising your views or intellectual integrity, and that such improvements can lead to greater success for your book. At the same time, avoid joining the small minority of "knee-jerk" authors who attempt to accommodate every stray comment that every reviewer has to offer. Often, theirs are the books that critics call "vacillating and bland."

As with your competition analysis, you can use your analysis of reviews to further refine your book plan, beginning with issues of writing style and voice and moving on to issues of structure, organization, and content. If the publisher has conducted the reviewing for you, you should receive annotated copies of the reviews and a review summary or analysis. Your editors will use the reviews to request changes that they think will affect sales and to make final decisions about when and how to publish your book. Your final draft should accommodate proven publisher concerns and also should fairly address reviewer concerns. Chief among those concerns is whether you are reaching your true audience, and this is the subject of the next chapter.

APPENDIX A
Sample Competition Grid

	Competitor 1	Competitor 2	Competitor 3
Book Author, title, edition, publisher, year			
Market Authors' mission, text themes, unique features, special coverage			
Organization and Content Number of parts and chapters, number of pages per topic			
Apparatus and Pedagogy Chapter openers, chapter closers, pedagogical features			
Presentation Number of pages, number of colors, trim size and binding, number of figures/ tables, number of photos			
Supplements For instructors, for students			

APPENDIX B
Guidelines and Questions for Peer Reviews

Your critical review of this manuscript will greatly help us revise it for publication. Using the following questions as a guide, please comment in some detail.

Organization and Content

1. Does the manuscript organization match the way the course is taught in your department? How, if at all, would you change the sequence of parts and chapters? Are there chapters you could drop, add, or combine? Are there chapters you would not assign? Why?
2. Does topical coverage in the manuscript match syllabi for this course at your school? What topics, if any, would you drop or add? How, if at all, would you change topical emphasis or improve topical balance?
3. Is this manuscript current enough and accurate? What chapters and topics are most in need of updating? Does it cover appropriate research and trends in the field and provide appropriate examples? Is it sufficiently documented? What source citations or references do you think should be added?

Writing Style and Presentation

1. Is the manuscript written at an appropriate length and intellectual level for the students taking this course? Are the writing style and tone appropriate and motivating? Is the exposition clear? What sections, if any, may need to be revised for greater unity, clarity, or coherence? Which chapters and sections would hold the most and the least interest for students?
2. Are the figures and tables appropriate, clear, and useful to students? Which figures and tables in each chapter would you identify as the most and the least valuable to learners? Which, if any, would you drop or add?

Apparatus and Pedagogy

1. Are the chapter opening and chapter closing elements inviting to students and useful as learning tools? What, if anything, would you change about the way chapters open and close?
2. Are the features or boxes appropriate in themes, interesting to students, and useful as learning tools? What are some examples of features you regard as especially strong or weak? What, if anything, would you change about the feature strands? How else, if at all, would you improve the pedagogical value of each chapter for students?

Overall Assessment

1. What do you identify as the three greatest strengths of this manuscript? What, if any, weaknesses do you identify? How well

> does this manuscript compare with other texts you have used for this course? How well does this manuscript achieve its mission, as set out in the preface? Would you adopt this text for use in your course?

Thank you in advance for your help.

6

Write To Reach Your True Audience

IN WRITING, YOUR VOICE is the way you "speak" to your audience, and it includes your "tone" of voice. Style is the way you use words to express yourself in writing. A second meaning of style is the system of conventions you adopt to format your writing for your subject area, such as the APA, MLA, CBE, or Chicago A or B styles. These editorial styles are discussed further later in this chapter. Voice, the subject of Chapter 7, and style are important matters in textbook publishing. By themselves, your writing style and voice can make or break your book. Making decisions about style and voice involves reflecting on your mission, understanding your audience, choosing how you will represent yourself and your subject, and monitoring your tone. This chapter focuses on audience and intentions.

Reflect On Your Mission

A good way to ascertain if you are ready to write your textbook is to draft a working preface. The preface sets out your mission—the reason you wrote it, other than the potential status, security, and income—and what you hope it will accomplish. Textbook authors might have any of the following goals or a combination.

- Correct misconceptions, myths, and stereotypes.
- Expose students to the subject.
- Assist instructors teaching the course.
- Enable mastery of the subject.
- Fill a need for more, less, or different content coverage.
- Share love of subject and attract students to the field.
- Get students to think differently about the subject.
- Introduce new facts, ideas, models, or paradigms.
- Show students how to use or apply subject knowledge and skills.
- Share professional knowledge, skills, and experiences.

However, authors with the following mission or goals (intentional or latent) enter a shady or risky area, especially if they are writing an introductory text:

- Advance an argument.
- Expose falsehoods or misconduct.
- Discredit a person, theory, or point of view.
- Promote a particular paradigm or approach to the subject.
- Indoctrinate students.
- Discourage induction into the field.
- Change the way the course is taught.

Instructors teach to their venerable, perhaps decades-old, oft-revised course syllabi and lecture notes. They really do not want to overhaul the way they teach the course. Changing a course takes additional thought, time, and effort. While most instructors strive to improve their courses through minor changes, few will be up for massive changes or changes based on unknown or unwelcome paradigm shifts.

Your mission also should be grounded in the fact that textbooks are by nature expository. They should present facts, theories, research, analyses, comparisons, contrasts, examples, non-examples, applications, extensions, and interpretations in a balanced, objective way. Above all, textbooks should teach. Personal syntheses (everything you have learned so far), critical analyses of your field, and crusades (reforming the field or changing the way your subject is taught) unfortunately tend to be too idiosyncratic and difficult (hence inappropriate) for introductory undergraduate textbooks. In this sense, the concept of a "mainstream" text extends to the content as well as to the course or market.

Take a moment, then, to reflect on your mission. Frame a mission statement to keep before you as you draft. What will students come away with when they have finished reading your textbook? What of importance will they take with them (other than a grade) when they have finished the course? Who is your real reader anyway?

Identify Your Real Reader

What students will read your textbook? Identifying and successfully addressing your readership is a complex enterprise. Even then, many authors forget who their true audience is as they draft. Magnetic shifts occur in which the writer draws away from the student toward his or her peers: the faculty member, adoption committee, professional review board, journal editorial committee, colleague, doctoral student, reviewer, or critic. Authors writing for experts, on the other hand, by some reverse compulsion tend to creep toward treating the expert reader as a neophyte. Keeping the real reader firmly in mind requires mindfulness and self-discipline.

Who is your true audience? In the case of introductory college textbooks, the real reader might be eighteen or nineteen years old, semi-permanently away from home for the first time, heavily invested in peer culture, and not yet transformed from late adolescence into adulthood. This reader has not declared a major, is uncertain about career options, and is not, for now, planning to enter your field or follow in your footsteps. Probably your textbook is this student's first substantive exposure to your specialty. This reader also is naive in the sense that he or she has few assumptions about your subject and little direct experience with it; might harbor misconceptions; does not recognize the big names you cite; and is not aware of the in-group issues, controversies, histories, personalities, debates, agendas, and nuances that rivet the attention of professionals in your field.

This student brings few or many skills to the classroom, depending on background and preparation at the secondary level. He or she might be in a two-year college, a technical school, a small private four-year college, an adult education night school, or a large state university—wherever your course is taught. Regardless of preparation, your undergraduate readers are still developing reading comprehension skills and critical thinking skills. They are still learning to distinguish fact from opinion and to evaluate evidence. They still tend to treat constructs as real, and they are still concrete thinkers (Piaget aside), who need concrete examples to grasp abstractions. Most important, few of these students have learned to question what they read.

Thus, on unfamiliar ground, your undergraduate readers, however smart, often struggle to construct meaning from text. The majority will not recognize irony, for instance, at least not your idea of it. Nor will they distinguish well among irony, sarcasm, cynicism, humor, sexual innuendo, and opinion in a textbook on French composition, neurophysiology, sociolinguistics, or political science. Irony, sarcasm, cynicism, and sexual innuendo especially have no place in textbook writing. Authors of textbooks at any educational level need to provide straightforward, un-nuanced, expository prose.

Avoid Undeclared Bias

Your introductory audience also is diverse. Nationally, at least a third of your readership will be members of racial, ethnic, religious, and language minority groups. As many as ten percent will be students with disabilities and another ten percent will be senior citizens. As many as half will come from single-parent, blended, and low-income inner-city and rural families. And more than half will be women. Textbook authors, most often in the past white males in middle age from comparatively affluent suburban backgrounds, easily forget these facts about their readers, which is why editors remain constantly vigilant about political correctness.

Political Correctness

Political correctness is not about politics, nor is it necessarily about making books politically neutral. In textbook publishing, the term "politically correct" is a borrowed euphemism for language that does not offend readers who happen to be members of minority groups, to have disabilities, to be elderly, to come from economically disadvantaged environments, or to be female, etc. Condescension toward the young or inexperienced also is taboo. Some authors have disdain for publishers' concerns about political correctness. However, it makes a good deal of practical sense not to offend your intended reader if you can avoid it. An offended reader will stop reading—will not learn from you. In addition, your publisher will be handicapped in attempting to sell your book successfully.

Guidelines for making your textbook culture and gender fair are presented below, and there are many resources for writers on this subject. The classic source is *The Handbook of Nonsexist Writing: For Writers, Editors and Speakers*, 2nd edition (2001) by Casey Miller and Kate Swift. Be aware, however, that rules and labels are constantly changing in the world of political correctness. Check with your editor about this as well as about house style preferences in the naming of social aggregates, attributes, and groups. See also **apa.udel.edu/apa/publications/texts/nonsexist.html**, the American Psychological Association *Guidelines for Non-Sexist Use of Language* by Virginia L. Warren.

Guidelines for Making Your Textbook Culture and Gender Fair

- Balance your representation of people, places, and activities so that all your readers can identify with your textbook examples.
- Use examples that relate to the prior experience or future expectations of all your potential readers.
- Include ethnically diverse given names and both males and females in examples.
- Scrupulously avoid all stereotypes, unless stereotyping is itself the subject of discourse.
- Use nonsexist language, including occupational designations.
- Use "he or she" and "his or her," etc., rather than shortcuts such as "he/she," "s/he," or "him or herself." Alternating sexes in examples, such that an example about "Fred" is followed by an example about "Becky," and so on, as in the naming of hurricanes, may seem fair, but this strategy confuses readers.

- Use formally correct names and labels for categories or aggregates of people, especially racial and ethnic designations, and for groups and organizations.
- Use "people first" language for individuals with disabilities (e.g., "students with mental retardation," "child with hearing impairment," etc.)
- Refer to "low-income" vs. "poor" or "disadvantaged" people or groups, unless the subject of discourse is poverty or "the poor."

Unfortunately, political correctness sometimes can extend to matters involving (a) reality and (b) the truth, and in these matters, concerns about censorship can be quite valid. In textbooks the Vietnam War was for years not a "war" but a "police action," for instance. Publishers only recently gave up insisting on referring to "the United States" versus "America" on grounds of actual political geography; and after September 11, 2001, sympathetic or self-critical responses to international and domestic terrorism are, for better or worse, not especially welcome.

A survey of schoolbooks through time reveals racist moralizing in McGuffey's Readers of the 19th century and political chauvinism in early-twentieth-century editions of Muzzy's *American History*. There are countless other examples; they are global—and sometimes extreme. Maps in Saudi geography textbooks do not show Israel, for instance. Additionally, according to research reported in *The Washington Post* (Shea, May 21, 2006), Saudi schoolbooks explicitly teach hatred of Christians and Jews.

Textbooks enter an already made world that changes, and publishing as a social institution is no less influenced by political and economic factors than other social institutions, such as the family, education, or medicine. As a textbook author of your time and place, it is up to you, your editor, and your publisher to decide where to draw the line regarding political correctness.

Pitfalls of Unwarranted Assumptions

As simple and sensible as ideas about political correctness and the guidelines above may seem, authors frequently violate them, usually unintentionally. Instances of insensitivity are not always obvious. In the following examples from college textbooks, which shall remain anonymous, put yourself in the place of any intended reader. How might you feel about the passages? How might you feel if the passages described you (or did not describe you)? How might you feel toward learning the subjects of these passages?

> **Example A:** Suppose a person jumps from the top of the Sears Tower in Chicago. The scientific law of gravity leaves him little

choice: He will fall swiftly to the ground, most likely to his death. However, should he choose to equip himself with a parachute, he would foil the law of gravity by exploiting other laws of physics.

Example B: The essential characteristic of physical experience is the abstraction of the physical properties of objects encountered in the environment. For example, by setting a spinnaker, playing the oboe, or cultivating freesias, one comes to know that spinnakers are "billowy," oboes are "reedy," and freesias smell "sweet."

Example C: Restricted language codes are associated with short, simple, and grammatically uncomplicated sentences, which are usually devoted to actions and things in specific contexts. Language codes have a strong correlation with parenting styles, with restricted language codes being more characteristic of authoritarian, power-centered families or neglecting, ignoring families. In such families questions are rarely asked. Children from this type of language environment are behind when they enter school and their deficit grows as they continue through school. Elaborated language codes, on the other hand, are most often found in middle and upper class, educated families. Parents who exhibit elaborated language codes tend to socialize their children. Speech is used for communication and discussion when children are asked to comply with parental wishes, not as an element of control.

In Example A, personhood involves being male, knowledge of a specific cultural landmark is assumed, and the scenario evokes an image of suicide (or memories of the 2001 World Trade Center tragedy). In Example B, as lovely as it sounds, the assumption that readers have the kind of background and social environment that would have enabled them to experience spinnakers, oboes, and freesias is unwarranted. Example C is even more classist and by extension racist. Lower- and working-class families are authoritarian or neglecting; they do not have elaborated language and do not socialize their children! In addition, naive readers might not notice or understand the significance of the fact that passage C is undocumented. Source citations, in addition to their other functions, are important clues for readers' reasoned judgments about what you are saying and what you are telling them to think.

The Place of Ideology

Unlike different theoretical perspectives in your academic discipline, political ideologies have no place in introductory textbooks unless they are themselves the subject of discourse or are presented in a balanced way. Contrary to critics' complaints, this does not mean that authors must avoid taking a stand on issues, only that they must refrain from doing so secretly, claiming that theirs is the only stand, or misrepresenting other stands.

If your liberalism, conservatism, Marxism, feminism, deism, positivism, existentialism, or other "ism" unavoidably informs (or contaminates) your content, it is your duty to declare it. Depending on the level of investment in your textbook, your publisher may prevail upon you to eliminate the need for a declaration of this kind, because it inevitably shrinks the market for your book and reduces sales. Even with only a particular single-focus theoretical perspective, you risk becoming the author of a niche book, more so if you are authoring an introductory undergraduate textbook.

Niche books may not earn enough to be revised. To sales representatives, the label "niche" can be a kiss of death—realistically, they won't want to spend a lot of time trying to sell a niche book. Besides, how can readers taking their first college-level course in your subject possibly be in a position to detect your stance on their own, to compare and contrast it with other stances, and to evaluate critically what you are asking them to believe? On both mercantile and moral grounds, therefore, authors must be mindful of inappropriate ideological biases in instructional materials.

In many ways, then, understanding your readership and avoiding undeclared bias is more complex than you might expect. "Respect your audience and meet their needs as learners" is the prime directive. If you find you have difficulty remaining mindful of your readers and their needs, take a snapshot of your students or a class in which your book might become the assigned text. Mount the picture on your computer monitor and glance at it as you draft. See if you can develop a liking for those students and sympathy for their individual journeys to enlightenment. Write for them.

Write to Reading Level

Your vocabulary, sentence length, sentence construction, paragraph length, and level of conceptual abstraction determine the reading level of your book. Other commonly used terms for "reading level" are "cognitive level," "comprehension level," and "difficulty level." In elementary and secondary textbooks, various mathematical formulae are applied to determine reading levels, which are critical for successful adoption by state- and district-run textbook adoption committees. In college publishing, however, tests of reading level usually are commissioned only when the publisher needs to prove that a book is too far above or below reading level for the course for which it is intended. As a rule of thumb, introductory undergraduate textbooks should be written at a grade 12 or grade 13 level. The reader is a high school graduate.

Reading level and difficulty level are not the same thing, though they may be related. The level of difficulty of your textbook depends on the quality and integrity of your expository writing, your explanation of the language or vocabulary you use, and your progression of completed thought. The language you choose for exposition should have the following characteristics:

- Audience appropriate
- Content appropriate
- Level appropriate
- Readable (well written)
- Comprehensible (meaningful)
- Unbiased and inoffensive

Language that is not appropriate for any reason, not well defined, or not well integrated into narrative context automatically increases the difficulty level. The level of difficulty also depends on the following factors:

- Amount of prerequisite knowledge or skill
- Amount of new information
- Pace of instruction
- Assumptions about reading comprehension
- Expectation of reader prediction, application, or practice
- Expectation of reader expertise or innovation

The greater the number or salience of these factors, the greater the difficulty. A relevant comparison can be made to difficulty levels in video games, which increase as the following vectors increase.

- Number and speed of attacks
- Degree of chance, surprise, or unpredictability
- Degree of strength or resistance
- Degree of protection or immunity
- Degree of accuracy of response
- Amount of experience
- Amount of risk

Reading level, on the other hand, relates more to the ease with which people of different ages or levels of educational attainment can read for comprehension.

Readability

A system commonly used for checking post-secondary reading level is the Fry Readability Formula, which is readily available for free online. See **school.discovery.com/schrockguide/fry/fry.html**, for example. Your word processing program probably also will calculate readability based on the statistics it tracks on the number of pages, words, characters, paragraphs, and lines in your chapter files. This function usually is an option in the spelling and grammar check utility. Note, however, that word processing programs use different calculi, such as the Flesch scale (general) or the Flesch-Kincaid (reading ease and grade level). The Coleman-Liau and the Bormuth scales both use only word length and sentence length to determine a grade level and so are not optimal for calculating readability in college textbooks. You can check the readability of your text online using various scales at **readability.info**.

If you find that your reading level is too high, the following rules of thumb will help you improve readability without compromising content.

Rules of Thumb for Improving Readability

- Avoid strings of polysyllabic words.
- Reduce sentence length. (Using active voice automatically reduces the number of words in a sentence.)
- Avoid interrupting compound verb forms—including infinitive phrases—with adverbs.
- Keep the verb as near as possible to its subject. Keep the object as near as possible to its verb.
- Eliminate unnecessary prepositional and appositive phrases.
- Eliminate unnecessary nonrestrictive (usually relative) clauses (e.g., large dogs, not dogs that are large in nature).
- Break long compound and complex sentences into separate sentences. Keep sentences that are both compound and complex to a minimum.
- Avoid stringing together independent clauses with colons, semicolons, or dashes.
- Do not place key content in parenthetical expressions, and eliminate parenthetical asides.
- Break long blocks of narrative text into separate shorter paragraphs.
- Increase the number of subheadings and reword them to guide reading comprehension.
- Add clear transitions between paragraphs and sections of text.
- Define technical terms fully in narrative context where they first appear.
- Operationalize concepts by giving concise, concrete examples.

Principles of Reading Comprehension

Some authors mistake simple straightforward language and sentences of modest length for accessible reading. They oversimplify language in hopes that this will make their thought more comprehensible. However, writing for readability does not involve this kind of dumbing down. Contrary to popular misconception, your college textbook publisher hopes that you are not writing *Anthropology for Dummies* or *Physics Made Easy as Pie*. Enriched vocabulary and suitable complexity actually are desirable in a college textbook. These characteristics usually are not the problem in reading comprehension, especially when a glossary is provided.

What matters in reading comprehension is your progression of thought, connections between one thought and the next, and support of abstractions using concrete examples. Your heuristic devices, unsupported generalizations, intellectual assumptions, undefined jargon, and leaps of logic (or of faith) leave readers in the dust. Consider the reading levels of the following excerpts from (unnamed) introductory college textbooks. Which is easier both to read and to comprehend, and why?

Example A: Readability

The table indicates a difference of 1.8 percentage points between the proportion of the Indian population living in urban places in 1972 and 1980, a span of eight years. Given this fact, it may be surprising to learn that there is great concern over urban growth in India, while there is not much concern in Spain where the urban population shows nearly 7 percentage points difference between 1972 and 1980. To understand the concern over the Indian rate, one has only to look at the actual numbers involved. In the eight years between 1972 and 1978, through migration *and* natural increase, India increased its total number of urbanites by over thirty-one and a half million people (note that in contrast to industrializing Europe, where urban growth was typically solely the product of migration, Third World cities were experiencing additional growth due to an excess of births over deaths within the urban population). The number of *new* urbanites in India in the span of those eight years was just five million less than the *total* population of Spain in 1978. [Paragraph continues for another 7 sentences.]

Example B: Readability

Hypothermia is arbitrarily defined in humans as a condition in which the core temperature of the body falls below 35° C. It is a major cause of death in boating accidents, in mountaineering and polar expeditions, and in aged people living in cold climates

> in homes with no central heating. Table 12.2 lists the symptoms associated with various levels of hypothermia. It illustrates two important points. The first is that manifestations of cerebral dysfunction (i.e., apathy, amnesia, confusion, poor judgment, and hallucinations) are among the earliest overt signs of hypothermia as the temperature of the body core drops. As a result, the idiosyncratic behavior of people under dangerously frigid conditions often increases the hazardousness of the situation. The second point is that humans can recover from core temperatures below 27° C, although they appear to be dead at such temperatures, with no detectable heart beat, respiration, or EEG (e.g., Niazi & Lewis, 1958). The only certain sign of death in hypothermia is failure to recover when warmed (Lloyd, 1986). [Paragraph ends.]

You no doubt chose Example B as the easier text to read and comprehend. It starts with a definition, provides a concrete context for learning about the subject, and systematically and without digression explains the behavioral significance of the data in the table, thus linking the subject to the course. At the same time the passage retains an enriched vocabulary with many multisyllabic descriptive and technical words. The subject is equally complex as the passage on India's urbanization, yet easier to acquire.

Example A, in contrast, contains only one vaguely interesting word (*urbanites*), yet makes a hash of the reader's effort to construct meaning. For example, the author assumes that the reader will understand what is meant by the conventions of the first sentence, despite the incorrect grammar, and that the significance of a span of eight years will be understood implicitly (i.e., the reader will realize that this is a significantly long or short time). For readability, the first sentences could have been better stated as follows.

> The table indicates a 1.8 percentage increase in the proportion of the Indian population living in cities between 1972 and 1980. This percentage increase is remarkable for the comparatively (short) (long) span of eight years.

Example A goes on to say prematurely, "Given this fact," before any fact has been made clear. The author then immediately introduces a comparison between India and Spain, suggesting we might be surprised. But we are baffled. Why Spain? In what way is Spain comparable to India? Why not Italy or Pakistan? Then we are asked to believe that urbanization in Spain is not so great a concern as urbanization in India, despite the fact that Spain's rate of urbanization is so much greater than India's.

At the very next sentence, most readers will stop struggling with text and will study the table instead or will skip to the next paragraph, for in the next sentence the span of "eight" years changes from "1972–1980" to "1972–1978"! Readers who try to read on may start to feel stupid as they come to the long digression in parentheses, which obliquely suggests the point of the comparison between India and Spain, and the italicized words *and*, *new*, and *total*. These words have been singled out for emphasis, and the author assumes emphasis alone will cue readers as to significance. Pondering that significance, an intelligent reader might wonder why the text is making such a big deal of a simple matter of scale. Why should we be surprised if a pond concentrates proportionally more fish through natural increase and migration than does an ocean? But what reader has the time and level of commitment to extract or construct meaning from page after page of abstruse text?

The proof is in the learning, and learning is what it is all about. If you think now about what you read, you will find that you remember more about hypothermia than about urbanization in India.

What Is Clarity?

Part of the reason that Example A was difficult to read and comprehend is that it lacked clarity of expression. Clarity is clearness; there is no doubt as to what is being said and what is meant by it. Writing for clarity in exposition, like writing for readability, also does not involve dumbing down. It involves crafting your writing style. As Strunk and White pointed out so famously so long ago, being clear, coherent, and concise (the three Cs) are the foundations of all good writing. Here are some avoidable writing problems that interfere with clarity.

What Makes Writing "Not Clear?"

- Wordiness
- Convoluted sentence structure in which the subject, verb, and predicate are separated by too many words, phrases, and clauses
- Overuse of passive voice, forms of the verb *be*
- Overuse of the past perfect and conditional tenses (e.g., *had had, would have had*)
- Lack of grammatical agreement in tense and number
- Inappropriate uses of personal and relative pronouns; unclear referents for pronouns
- Lack of transitions
- Lack of concrete examples or illustrations
- Archaic and formal usages unrelated to the purpose of exposition
- Undefined or unnecessary jargon
- Skipped steps in logical development, progression of ideas, or cause and effect

- Statements of the obvious, causing readers to doubt their comprehension
- A focus on accuracy before basic comprehension has been achieved, e.g., premature presentation of alternatives, disclaimers, and exceptions
- Digression
- Repetition or redundancy

If you find you tend to write above or beyond the reading comprehension level of your audience, as an alternative to using readability analyses, enlist the aid of one or more student readers. Give them copies of a chapter of your manuscript and ask them to write "Not Clear" alongside any passages that trip them up. Your analysis of those passages should help you identify and overcome patterns of exposition that reduce comprehension and learning rate in your readers. Also keep in mind, by the way, that when editors mark passages "Not Clear," they are basing their judgments on the perceived needs of your audience.

Write Well

Writing well is discussed further in Chapter 13, where you will find a list of selected references on academic and expository writing and editing. In composition, all good writing for any audience at any educational level has the same basic qualities, including clarity, concision, unity, coherence, and emphasis. Just as poor writing habits and habits of thought compromise clarity, wordiness compromises concision.

What Is Wordiness?

Wordiness is the habitual practice of using more words than are necessary to convey information or an idea or a feeling. Passive constructions and optional adjectives, adverbs, and prepositional phrases cause the greatest offense. In addition, wordiness comes from uncertainty and self-regard. That is, authors tend to use more words when they are unsure of the information they are attempting to convey, or the points they are trying to make, or their efficacy in communicating on the page. Self-regarding authors, who like to hear themselves talk and extemporize on the page, also use more words. Whatever the reason for it, wordiness is to be scrupulously avoided. However careful or fascinating you believe you are in your writing, in reality your wordiness bores readers to death and interferes with their learning.

Consider the following unedited passage for a college textbook on criminal justice.

> **Example of Wordiness:**
> Rehabilitation and restorative justice are more contemporary philosophies defining the purpose of criminal sanctions.

> Rehabilitation and restorative justice philosophies argue that criminal sanctions should provide for a "cure" of the criminality of the offender. The rehabilitation model is often referred to as the medical model in that it views criminality as a "disease" to be "cured." Rehabilitation of the offender is considered to be impossible by some. For those who believe that it is possible to rehabilitate the offender through rehabilitation and restorative justice models the most common approaches involve psychology, the biological/medical approach, self-esteem treatment, and programs aimed at developing ethical values and work skills.

Here is the same passage with 35 fewer words. Note that in tightening the paragraph the editor preserved, even improved, the author's intention and meaning.

> **Improved Version:**
> Rehabilitation and restoration are contemporary philosophies of obtaining justice through criminal sanctions. Rehabilitation calls for sanctions that "cure" the offender of criminality. Because criminality is seen as a disease to be cured, this model often is referred to as a medical model. Some believe that rehabilitating offenders is impossible. Others, however, believe that effective rehabilitation is possible through psychological approaches, medical treatment, self-esteem counseling, and programs promoting ethical values and work skills.

Eliminating unnecessary words and phrases helps control manuscript length as well as improve clarity in exposition. Following are some tips on eliminating wordiness.

> **Wordiness Elimination Guide**
> **Example:** *One of the most important factors that ambiguity is caused by that is often ignored is wordiness.*
>
> **1st Pass:** Change the sentence to active voice. *One of the most important factors that causes ambiguity that is often ignored is wordiness.*
>
> **2nd Pass:** Eliminate unnecessary articles and prepositional phrases. *An important factor that causes ambiguity that is often ignored is wordiness.*
>
> **3rd Pass:** Eliminate unnecessary words and relative phrases and clauses, including parenthetical asides. *An important, often ignored cause of ambiguity is wordiness.*

4th Pass: Delete additional adjectives or adjectival forms that do not directly advance the purpose or point of the sentence. *An oft-ignored cause of ambiguity is wordiness*, or, *An important cause of ambiguity is wordiness*, or, *A cause of ambiguity is wordiness.*

5th Pass: Change the word order so that the subject comes first, directly followed by an active verb. Isn't the following statement the point? *Wordiness causes ambiguity.*

6th Pass: Beyond the sentence level, delete every sentence that does not directly support the paragraph in which it is embedded.

What Are Unity, Coherence, and Emphasis?

In addition to clarity and concision, all good expository writing exhibits unity, coherence, and emphasis. Unity is the quality of centrality and relevance, or belongingness. That is, all the paragraphs in a section relate to the purpose of that section, and all the sentences in a paragraph relate to the point set out in the paragraph's topic sentence or thesis statement. In prose, irrelevancies, tangential remarks, digressions, sudden insights, flashbacks, cosmic syntheses, and brainstorming on the page can all compromise unity.

Coherence is the quality of sequentiality and integrity, or togetherness. Sentences and paragraphs progress in a logical or natural order, flowing smoothly from one to the next while sticking together in meaning. The writing and the meanings it conveys have direction and thrust. Coherence is compromised most by lack of transitions, derailment of logic, stagnation of thought, and non sequiturs—statements that do not follow what has just been said.

Emphasis in writing is the quality of focus, interest, and control. Words, ideas, and images are subtly weighted or ranked such that the most important word, idea, or image in each sentence, paragraph, and chapter stands out. Emphasis guides the reader in constructing meaning from text by distinguishing what is to be regarded as important. Emphasis is compromised when words, ideas, and images are all given equal importance or when the reader's attention is focused inappropriately.

The above section of text, "What Are Unity, Coherence, and Emphasis?", exhibits the qualities described in it. The three paragraphs all address the same implied purpose to define and illustrate these qualities, which is unity. The progression of thought within and between paragraphs facilitates sense-making—through the repetition of a pattern of exposition, which is coherence. And the section ends with the application in this paragraph, which reinforces the emphasis introduced in the first sentence of the section. Good writers and editors evaluate writing in terms of these qualities of unity, coherence, and emphasis.

What Is Style?

The elements of style are word choices, word usages, sentence constructions, paragraph constructions, writing rules and conventions and formats, and your personal distinguishing communication values and expression of self. Read a list of the standard rules of style in English composition in the table of contents of Strunk and White, *The Elements of Style*, originally published in 1935. Read the complete 1938 edition online at **bartleby.com/141**.

Keep in mind, however, that many elements of style are arbitrary conventions and matters of taste. These vary nationally and among publishing houses and change over time. Items in a series may or may not require a comma before the last item, for instance; certain abbreviations may or may not be allowed, and so on. Rules that you learned in school—and disobeyed only at your peril—may no longer apply, so it serves to be flexible on matters of style.

Ask your editor about "house style"—the publisher's style guidelines. You might find it helpful to consult the house style sheet as you draft. The copyeditor assigned to vet your manuscript will work to these guidelines as well. House styles are built from manuals of editorial style based on the publisher's list needs, publishing experience, and idiosyncrasies of powerful editors. Preferences include simple matters, such as capitalization and punctuation, and larger decisions, such as using endnotes rather than footnotes. You can save yourself, any coauthors, your editors, and the people who will produce your book a great deal of anguish by choosing and consistently using one agreed-on style.

As mentioned at the beginning of this chapter, editorial styles most commonly used in college textbooks are the Modern Language Association (MLA) style, the American Psychological Association (APA) style, Council of Biology Editors (CBE) style, and Chicago style (*The Chicago Manual of Style*), and several others. These styles differ mainly in their treatment of headings, source citations, notes, references, bibliographies, and technical notational or symbol systems used in the respective disciplines.

Any college handbook on English composition will contain information on these styles for documenting research, but the best source is the current style manual for your discipline. You also can find most style guides online. For your convenience, this chapter's appendix lists the standard editorial style manuals used in academic and higher education writing and where they reside online.

In both the broad and the narrow sense, then, your style is a key ingredient in reaching your true audience and accomplishing your mission in writing a textbook. The other, closely related, key ingredient is your authorial voice, the subject of the next chapter.

APPENDIX
Academic Style Manuals, by Discipline

Anthropology
The American Anthropological Association uses *The Chicago Manual of Style* and *Merriam Webster's Collegiate Dictionary*. Official website: **aaanet.org/pubs/style_guide.htm**.

Biology
CBE Style Manual Committee, Edward J. Huth. *Scientific Style and Format: The CBE Manual for Authors, Editors, and Publishers*, 6th ed. Cambridge University Press, 1994. Official website, Council of Science Editors: **councilscienceeditors.org**.

Business and Management
American Management Association. *The AMA Style Guide for Business Writing*, AMACOM, 1996. Official website: **amanet.org**. Accounting and business also use Chicago and APA.

Chemistry
Coghill, Anne M., and Lorrin R Garson. *The ACS Style Guide: Effective Communication of Scientific Information*, 3rd ed. Oxford University Press, 2005. Official website, American Chemical Society: **pubs.acs.org**. Explanatory website: **pubs.acs.org/books/references.shtml**

Chicago Style (**used in many disciplines; it is a default style**)
The Chicago Manual of Style. 15th ed. University of Chicago Press, 2006. Official website: **chicagomanualofstyle.org**

Engineering
Institute of Electrical and Electronics Engineers (IEEE) uses the Chicago Manual of Style. Official website, American Society of Civil Engineers: **pubs.asce.org/authors/index.html**. Official website, IEEE Computer Society: **computer.org/portal/site/ieeecs**. Some engineering publications use the APA (American Psychological Association) style.

English (**and some other disciplines in the humanities, e.g., philosophy**)
Gibaldi, Joseph. *MLA Style Manual and Guide to Scholarly Publishing*, 2nd ed. New York: The Modern Language Association of America, 1998. Official website: **mla.org**. Explanatory website: **owl.english.purdue.edu/handouts/research/r_mla.html**. Chicago also is used. See also European Union English style guide: **europa.eu.int/comm/translation/writing/style_guides/English/style_guide_en.pdf**.

Geology
Bates, Robert L., et al., Eds. *Geowriting: A Guide to Writing, Editing, and Printing in Earth Science*, 5th ed. 1995.; online at **nwrc.usgs.gov/lib.** Official website, American Geological Institute: **agiweb.org.** *Suggestions to Authors (STA)* style guide for the U.S. Geological Survey: **usgs.gov/library**; see also *Geoscience Reporting Guidelines* (Canada).

Government
Garner, Diane L., et al., *The Complete Guide to Citing Government Information Resources: A Manual for Writers and Librarians* (Rev. ed.). Congressional Information Service, 1993. "Brief Guide to Citing Government Publications": **exlibris.memphis.edu/resource/unclesam/citeweb.html.** *U.S. Government Printing Office Style Manual*: **gpoaccess.gov/stylemanual.**

History
Gray, Wood. *Historian's Handbook: A Key to the Study and Writing of History*, 2nd ed. Houghton Mifflin, 1991. Explanatory website: **dianahacker.com/resdoc.** Most historians use either Chicago or Turabian style.

Humanities
Modern Humanities Research Association: *MHRA Style Guide* (2002, free download): **mhra.org.uk/Publications/Books/StyleGuide/download.shtml.**

Information Sciences and Computer Science
"New ANSI Style Guidesheet" (2003), downloadable from **publicaa.ansi.org.** Official website, American National Standard for Information Sciences: **ansi.org.** See also *Microsoft Manual of Style for Technical Publications* (2003): **winwriters.com/msmanualofstyle.htm.**

Journalism
The AP Stylebook and Briefing on Media Law (Rev. ed., 2004): **apstylebook.com.** Official website, Associated Press: **ap.org.** *UPI Stylebook and Guide to Newswriting*, 4th ed. Capital Books, 2004. *The Canadian Press Stylebook*, 14th ed. (2007) and *Guide de rédaction* (for French language writers and editors): **cp.org.** See also *The New York Times Manual of Style and Usage*, the *Wall Street Journal Style Guide*, *The BBC News Style Guide*, and others.

Law and Legal Studies
The Bluebook: A Uniform System of Citation, 18th ed. Harvard Law Review Association, 2005. Official website: **legalbluebook.com.** Explanatory website: **law.cornell.edu/citation.**

Linguistics
Linguistic Society of America, "Language Style Sheet." Official website: **lsadc.org/info/pubs-lang-style.cfm**. Computational Linguistics style guide: **clt.mq.edu.au/compling/style.html**. Others, including historical and comparative linguists, commonly use MLA, APA, or Chicago style.

Mathematics
American Mathematical Society. *Manual for Authors of Mathematical Papers*, 8th ed. 1990. Also, *LaTex: A Document Preparation System*, 2nd ed. 1994. Official website, American Mathematical Society: **www.ams.org**. *American Statistical Association Style Guide:* **amstat.org/publications.**

Medicine
American Medical Association. *AMA Manual of Style*, 9th ed. 1998. Official website: **ama-assn.org**. Explanatory website: **healthlinks.washington.edu/hsl/styleguides/ama.html.**

Oxford Style
Oxford University Press, *The Oxford Style Manual.* 2003. Official website: **oup.com/uk.**

Physics
American Institute of Physics. *Style Manual for Guidelines in the Preparation of Papers*, 4th ed. 1990. Official website: **aip.org/pubservs/style/4thed/toc.html** (free download). Astronomy also uses the AIP and Chicago styles.

Psychology (and other social sciences)
American Psychological Association. *Publication Manual of the American Psychological Association*, 5th ed. 2001. Official website: **apastyle.apa.org/index.html**. Explanatory website: **owl.english.purdue.edu/owl/resource/560/01.**

Political Science
American Political Science Association, *The Style Manual for Political Science.* 2002. Official website: **apsanet.org**. Explanatory website: **wisc.edu/writing/Handbook/DocAPSA.html.**

Sociology
American Sociological Association. *ASA Style Guide*. 1997. Official website: **asanet.org**. Explanatory website: **owl.english.purdue.edu/handouts/research/r_docsocio.html.**

Turabian Style
Kate Turabian, et al., *A Manual for Writers of Research Papers, Theses, and Dissertations*, 7th Ed. University of Chicago Press, 2007. Explanatory website: **isr.buckness.edu/img/assets/6535/ turabian.pdf.** See a comparison between Turabian and Chicago at **lib.berkeley.edu/ instruct/guides/chicago-turabianstyle.pdf.**

Sources: Adapted from "Examples of Style Guides" at **en.wikipedia. org,** accessed August 28, 2007, and "The Owl at Purdue" (last updated July 2007, accessed August 25, 2007) at **owl.english.purdue.edu/owl.**

7

Establish an Effective Authorial Voice

AN AUTHORIAL VOICE is achieved through (1) your attitudes toward your subject as revealed in the language you use and your carefully disclosed theoretical, philosophical, or political orientations; (2) your attitudes toward the reader as revealed in the style and tone you use; and (3) elements of your personality that inevitably leak through your prose. Voice is tricky. If voice is missing, your textbook is likely to fail. If readers are put off by the voice, it will fail faster.

Reflect on Your Voice

As you read in Chapter 6, a common complaint is that textbook writing can go overboard in avoiding offending or being too difficult for anyone, with the result that a textbook lacks a true authorial voice. Exposition becomes anonymous, noncommittal, sanitized. However, the best textbooks are not, need not, and should not be "soulless and bland." They do have distinctive authorial voices. A person and a teacher, not just an expert, is talking to us. Who are you as a person and a teacher? Who will you be to your readers? To begin with, how do you feel about what you are saying? And how do you feel about the people who will read what you write?

How would you answer these questions for the voice in following excerpt?

Example: Features of the Authorial Voice

The title of this chapter mentions an "invitation" to corrections. What does this mean? How can anyone feel "invited" to such a complex field riddled with critical issues and deeply disturbing realities and focusing as it does on human tragedy and failure? How can anyone feel "invited" to a field so shaped by its social context that political and economic realities at times seem impossible either to maintain or to change? The answer

> is that corrections also is inspirational and change is always possible, though not always predictable. In corrections there are opportunities to make a positive difference in people's lives and in correctional institutions at different levels of the system, in ways ranging from common decency and kindness to penal reform.

This author conveys his passion for his subject in a way that inspires confidence in his authority to address that subject. Further, he shares with the reader the personal beliefs and values that shape his motivation to write. He cares for the reader, whom he hopes to entice into his field, and has compassion for all the players, it seems, in the system he is about to describe. His will be an unblinkered story of hope.

Your Attitudes Toward Your Subject

A surprising number of authors write as if they were bored by their subject. An effective authorial voice uses language that conveys respect for the subject, focuses attention on it, arouses curiosity about it, and generates excitement for learning it. Education research supports the importance of these ingredients in preparing readers to "listen and learn." Compare the following paragraphs from two world history texts introducing chapters on the scientific revolution, for example. Which one would you prefer to read? Why?

> **Sample Voice A:**
> The foremost cause of the change in worldview was the scientific revolution. Modern science crystallized in the seventeenth century. Whereas science had been secondary and subordinate in medieval intellectual life, it became independent and even primary for many educated people in the eighteenth century.

> **Sample Voice B:**
> The sixteenth and seventeenth centuries witnessed a sweeping change in the scientific view of the universe. An earth-centered picture of the universe gave way to one in which the earth was only another planet orbiting about the sun. The sun itself became one of millions of stars. This transformation of humankind's perception of its place in the larger scheme of things led to a vast rethinking of moral and religious matters as well as of scientific theory.

Both samples are perfectly clear, but Sample B presents a more positive attitude toward the subject, as the following comparison shows:

	SAMPLE A	SAMPLE B
Verb Forms	was	witnessed
	crystallized	gave way
	had been	became
	became	led to
Adjectives	foremost	sweeping
	subordinate	earth-centered
	secondary	larger
	intellectual	vast
	primary	moral
	independent	religious
	educated	scientific
Key Nouns	cause	change
	change	universe
	worldview	picture
	science	earth
	life	planet
	people	sun
		stars
		transformation
		humankind
		perception
		place
		scheme
		rethinking
		matters
		theory

You undoubtedly chose Sample B, the more attractive piece. Sample B contains more interesting verbs in an active rather than a passive voice (*witnessed* vs. *was*). Sample B also provides adjectives that are distinctly more compelling; that is, you would probably prefer to read about something that is *sweeping* and *earth-centered* rather than about something that is *foremost* and *subordinate*. Sample B also contains a number of engaging concrete nouns (*planet*, *sun*, etc.) in contrast to Sample A's more abstract nouns.

Consider also the subtle differences in attitude toward the subject that are revealed in the language. Sample A interprets the subject as *science*, which is reinforced through the use of the pronoun *it*. *Crystallized* conveys the idea that science was in a muddle until the scientific revolution made it right. The relevance of science is confined to "medieval intellectual life" and "educated people." The net effect is stuffiness. The author of Sample A seems to want us to feel inferior to the subject.

In Sample B, on the other hand, relevance is extended to "humankind's perception of its place in the larger scheme of things." Sample B interprets the subject as a "change." *Witnessed* focuses attention on the impact of the change. Sample B further identifies knowledge of planets and stars as the basis of the change. The author of Sample B seems to want us to feel a bit in awe of the subject, the experience of which we are being let in on. We readers can feel connected to the subject, as we are a part of this universe. Our preference for Sample B is an outgrowth of the author's attitudes toward us and toward the subject as reflected in the authorial voice.

Your Philosophical and Political Orientations

Philosophical orientation consists of your beliefs and values concerning your subject, including your professional judgments and personal political, religious, or ideological biases. These beliefs and values come though in subtle ways in your writing, much like the fabled subliminal images and messages in advertising. Like truth in advertising, intellectual honesty is an entitlement of the consumer.

Consider, for example, an introductory cultural anthropology textbook that dishonestly skews its presentation of modern theoretical frameworks without indicating its own orientation. Cultural materialism is linked with Marxism and given twice the space of other perspectives. Interpretivism and structuralism are dismissed in four paragraphs. Conflict perspectives are treated synonymously with both Marxism and gender studies. Students have no way of evaluating the significance of the presence of three unique chapters: "Inequality, "Conflict," and "Colonialism." For all they know, all introductory textbooks on cultural anthropology have these chapters. Their instructors know, of course. They chose this textbook as a reflection of their own undeclared view that power is the root of all evil. All the examples, features, photos, and photo captions point this out, forcing the heartsick reader to bear witness. This reader is in the dark, exploited as surely and completely by the author as the world's aboriginals have been by others.

Intellectual honesty also requires including ideas with which you do not agree. Authors of an introductory psychology textbook who reject Freud must nevertheless discuss Freud and his followers in their book and must manage to do so evenhandedly. Intellectual honesty is expressed not in avoiding a point of view but in clearly identifying a point of view for what it is, perhaps identifying strengths and weaknesses of that view, and providing information about the existence of other points of view, all the time using fair, value-free language.

"Value-free" does not mean that you must not convey a point of view, simply that your point of view and the assumptions on which it is based must be expressed openly and defended, and that readers must be allowed to evaluate it for themselves. The following excerpt is a simple and concise example of such a self-declaration.

> **Example: Self-Declaration**
> This textbook is written to inform you about corrections—the institutions and methods that society uses to punish, control, and change the behavior of convicted offenders. Throughout, four major themes are developed. First, corrections is a system that functions as a subsystem of the criminal justice system. Second, corrections takes place in particular social contexts—environments and situations that influence people's responses to events. A sociological approach sheds light on how corrections functions in various social settings. Third, all the participants in the corrections process are important—victims, reformers, individuals who work within the system, offenders who are sentenced to the system and others. Fourth, and last, the field of corrections offers many opportunities for a challenging, satisfying career.

As mentioned earlier, and it bears repeating, an undergraduate introductory textbook also is not the place for political posturing, grandstanding, or proselytizing. Achieving balance and objectivity in exposition is easier said than done, however. In writing, as in life, honesty and authenticity are a struggle. Let us continue with the scientific revolution example from world history.

> **Sample Voice A:**
> The emergence of modern science was a development of tremendous long-term significance. A noted historian has even said that the scientific revolution of the late sixteenth and seventeenth centuries "outshines everything since the rise of Christianity and reduces the Renaissance and Reformation to the rank of mere episodes, mere internal displacements within the system of medieval Christendom." The scientific revolution was "the real origin both of the modern world and the modern mentality."[1] This statement is an exaggeration, but not much of one. Of all the great civilizations, only that of the West developed modern science. It was with the scientific revolution that Western society began to acquire its most distinctive traits.

Sample Voice B:

The process by which this new view of the universe and of scientific knowledge came to be established is normally termed the "Scientific Revolution." However, care must be taken in the use of this metaphor. The word revolution normally denotes fairly rapid changes in the political world, involving large numbers of people. The Scientific Revolution was not rapid, nor did it involve more than a few hundred human beings. It was a complex movement with many false starts and many brilliant people with wrong as well as useful ideas. However, the ultimate result of this transformation of thought revolutionized the manner in which Europeans thought about physical nature and themselves. This new outlook would later be exported to every other major world civilization.

Sample A is full of value statements. Author A says that the subject is "tremendous" and that we don't have to take Author A's word for it, because others, such as the footnoted historian, claim that the subject is even more important than that, that it "outshines everything since [Christ]." Author A doesn't buy this entirely; it's a slight exaggeration. In the last two sentences, Author A concludes that we should value the subject because it was unique to Western civilization—a conservative, somewhat Eurocentric, view. It is important to Author A that we correctly interpret the degree of importance of the subject. Meanwhile, the material reveals (a) a belief in the absolute ranking of historical events in terms of importance, and (b) the value judgment that the rise of Christianity should receive the highest rank. The quoted historian also has a metaphysical stance (defining a selected origin as the "real" one) and assumes that the notion of a "modern mentality" has validity as a construct.

In the second sample, Author B is not so much concerned with our interpretation of the subject's importance as with our definition of it, our conceptualization. The name for the subject is a metaphor, Author B says, and we should value accuracy in our use of metaphors. The subject's importance is qualified in terms of the rate of change, the number of people involved, the degree of complexity, and the degree of continuity. The qualifiers further encapsulate the views that being brilliant doesn't make you right and that right ideas are ones that are useful. Author B offers a liberal conclusion that the metaphor is appropriate because the subject resulted in a new outlook, and that we should value the subject because it affected not only Europeans, but the world.

Few readers analyze what they read in this critical way, however. They simply acquire your undeclared assumptions and attitudes toward the subject. This fact imparts to you a grave responsibility.

What Is Tone?

The stinginess or stuffiness of Sample A in the history examples, and the generousness or openness of Sample B, are aspects of tone. Tone refers to the quality of voice that reflects how an author feels about the subject and about the reader. Thus, tone is your affective response as revealed through the words and phrases you choose. These choices have a cumulative and subtle psychological net effect on readers. Consider, for example, these examples of positive and negative tones.

Examples of Positive and Negative Tone	
POSITIVE	NEGATIVE
open	stuffy
respectful	disparaging
earnest	insincere
honest	defensive
enthusiastic	neutral
down to earth	imperial
warm	cold
pleasant	cranky
forthright	sneaky
excited	bored
friendly	mean-spirited
intimate	hostile

Viewed this way, few authors would consciously choose a negative tone. However, negativity can creep into the writing of authors who are inwardly angry or resentful or have private agenda. Be aware that regardless of subject matter, any audience at any age and level of educational attainment is more motivated to read and learn text that has a positive tone.

Your Attitudes Toward the Reader

Your tone and the language you use should convey respect for your audience as well as for your subject. Authors sometimes convey negative expectations of readers or imply that readers are deficient, ignorant, immature, inexperienced, inferior, stupid, dumb, lazy, repulsive, pathetic, helpless, or irrelevant. Other messages are that readers need the author to enlighten them; to parent, counsel, patronize, chastise, or reform them; to put them in their place, show them a thing or two, or trick them into learning something.

Authors who convey these negative messages usually do so unintentionally. These messages are not lost on readers, though they may be equally unaware. Like the participants in Zimbardo's prison experiment, your readers will become complicit in your definition of their roles in the learning enterprise, based on your expectations of them as reflected in your writing.

The most common faults in authorial tone involve language that is avuncular and gratuitous, seconded by the frosty, stern, or authoritarian voice of the taskmaster. Third is the neutral or "pure" voice, devoid of affect—the android's synthesized voice. Fourth is the manipulative voice of the propagandist or spinmaster. The fifth most common fault is ambivalence toward the audience, at times championing the readers and at times criticizing them. You may recognize this fifth fault as a tendency of the voice of this book—and of editors in general. This chapter's appendix attempts to offer examples of "bad-voice" problems in the form of archetypes.

Who Are You?

Because of its duration and intensity, writing a textbook is unavoidably a self-defining endeavor. Authors working with development editors sometimes feel a bit exposed. Your persona thins, and, for better or worse, aspects of your personality become visible. In any case, authors often unintentionally reveal interesting self-concepts or character traits in their writing. "I am omniscient" or "I am brilliant" is the commonest message. "I'm plain folks just like you" or "I'm just a good ole boy" are close seconds.

Intellectual arrogance, however subtle, tips us off to authors who regard themselves as geniuses (and who among us does not?). Our narratives might contain self-congratulatory nuggets, arguments or dialectics with the self, highly competitive judgments of others, self-conscious claims of authority, self-promotion, self-justification, and summary condemnations of others' views or works. "Of course," "obviously," "in fact," "clearly," and "perhaps," are identifying markers, along with prodigious use of jargon.

Often, textbooks with ego also are peppered with "I" and "we," sometimes in the form of "the author(s)." In some textbooks, authors' first-person accounts of their experiences or research are an asset. For example, authors of a textbook on archaeology who describe their most challenging digs and amazing finds may well be serving their readers and mission. The problem with *we* is that usually it has too many referents, confusing the reader as to which "we" is meant—the authors, structural engineers or paleontologists as a group, Americans or Canadians or Westerners, or human beings in general.

In addition, the use of *we* can establish a power and control issue that distracts the reader and detracts from the instructional content. In the following (ungrammatical) excerpt, for example, the authors appropriate the information and make themselves the subject of the paragraph instead.

> **Example: Inappropriate Use of First Person**
> If multicultural education efforts are to be successful as the school accepts the growing diversity among its student body, we see a multitude of social, cultural, and educational issues that need to be addressed. We present here what we believe some of those major issues to be. As prospective teachers, we suggest that you examine these issues with us and build them into your concerns about education as you embark on your career. We no longer accept that the problems of cultural differences are so great that the school cannot respond to them. There must be a beginning and we believe it should start here with the major point we have attempted to stress in this chapter: the school we know today will become vastly different as we enter the next century.

As you can see, "we" becomes the subject of the paragraph. While the use of personal pronouns is accepted, even expected, in professional and scientific journals, "the author(s)" is not an appropriate focus for a textbook. In introductory textbooks, especially those that consciously adopt an informal tone, the student reader ("you") and the subject are paramount.

> **Example: Appropriate Use of Second Person**
> When you look at this pattern, what do you see? You probably recognize it as part of a human eyeball, even though all that's physically present in the photos are many different colored dots. In this case perception actually creates an object from sensory stimulation. That is, your perceptual processes determine that certain features go together to form objects. This is challenging because you often see only parts of objects, with some nearer or more distant or obscured by other objects. Nevertheless, in the photo below, you recognize that the orange is one object even through it is partially hidden by the apple.

Achieving a Voice Through Style

Inexperienced authors who have not yet felt the copyeditor's lash often try to establish a distinctive voice through the use of colloquialisms, regionalisms, clichés, dialect, or slang, often in the mistaken belief that a Prairie Home Companion presentation makes their textbook more accessible. In exposition these usages cannot substitute for authorial voice, however, and in most contexts constitute bad style as well.

Distinctive authorial voices come through in subtle choices among words and expressions that cumulatively create an impression of the author as a person and as a teacher in the reader's mind. Following are three passages from different, older textbooks on the same subject, suggesting the diversity, subtlety, range, and effectiveness of authors' voices.

Example: Voice A

As an educational reform movement, multicultural education seeks to change the effects described above. Exactly *how* to do this is the topic of heated debate. Should education emphasize the similarities *or* the differences among people? Some reformers urge schools to focus on improving human relations so that students will learn to respect *all* people. Other educators press for in-depth studies of various racial and ethnic groups as part of the curriculum. But critics believe this is not enough. They want to *infuse* the entire curriculum with material written by and about minority group members. Still another approach to multicultural education is to *transform* the entire educational system so that students learn to be politically effective in reshaping society.

Voice A briefly but persuasively describes alternative approaches to addressing problems that have been presented previously. The writing conveys the feeling that the subject is important. Without going into detail, the voice wants us to advance our appreciation of a complex matter by considering degrees of response to the problems. The tone is sincere and informal, even personal and warm. The use of italics—which actually is not good style—emphasizes comprehension through oral rhythms, as if this author-teacher were speaking to us directly.

Example: Voice B

General disagreements about multicultural education have followed some of the same lines as the specific arguments about Afrocentric and other minority-oriented curricula. For example, critics contend that multicultural education may divide society by emphasizing ethnic separatism rather than developing citizens who will work together to accomplish common goals.[70] Some believe that multicultural education will fragment and overload the school curriculum, reinforcing tendencies for teachers to stress memorization and regurgitation of disconnected facts and concepts.[71] Furthermore, critics argue that multicultural concerns may be misused to justify second-rate education for economically disadvantaged or minority students.[72] If "ethnic studies" programs do not make great efforts to maintain a high quality of instruction, the diplomas or degrees students receive may be viewed as second-rate.

Voice B struggles to present fairly an issue on which he or she has strong views. In this passage those views are largely conservative or negative, but perhaps the writing will go on to present the opposing views. The language is straightforward and precise but mildly shocking, edgy with implied harsh judgments. The tone is authoritative, hard-edged, and aggressive, and statements are supported by source citations through which this author-teacher perhaps seeks to overwhelm us. Nevertheless, although admonitory, Voice B is not claiming that he or she has all the right answers.

Example: Voice C

Why is multicultural education so controversial? The debate about multicultural education is neither new nor faddish. It is part of the larger, continuing dialogue about the meaning of e pluribus unum. As one country composed of many states and many peoples, the nation continues to struggle to define itself. How is America to conceptualize and deliver a public education that is appropriate for all its people? This question arises in many forms and many languages in political forums, churches, social organizations, and schools across the country.

Voice C conveys the feeling that the subject is important but should not be taken too seriously because it is a perennially unresolved issue. The tone is inflated or passionate, depending on your point of view, and the language can be taken as pretentious or imitative of stump speeches. This author does not seem as knowledgeable about the subject as the others. This voice is easy to listen to, the prose stirring but empty.

Consider now the readers of these three passages. What relationship to the text and to the subject might they develop based on their experience of Voice A, Voice B, or Voice C? In each case how does the voice invite learning or motivate the learner to read? Most important, what would readers learn or take away from these passages?

Integrating Coauthors' Voices and Styles

Because introductory undergraduate textbooks are by nature far-ranging, many have two or more coauthors whose overlapping areas of expertise can cover the subject adequately. Too often, however, each coauthor does things his or her way. The author of Chapter 1 decides to underline everything that seems important, the author of Chapter 2 writes verbosely above grade level, and the author of Chapter 3 provides 25 figures and tables thinly connected by text. In addition, Chapter 1 is warm and inviting, Chapter 2 is distinctly contemptuous in tone, and Chapter 3 admits no affective response at all. The reader, meanwhile, is doomed. Random differences and mixed messages from chapter to chapter foil any attempt at coherent learning. As a result, whatever first-year sales the publisher can garner quickly slip away and the book fails, never to see royalty, reprint, or revision.

In professional circles it is common practice for a group of colleagues to put their names to a journal article authored principally by only one of their number. The order of their names in bibliographies and references rotates as each "partner" takes a turn as lead author of an article, thus avoiding the lack of recognition implicit in et al. In textbook publishing, however, silent partners are rare. They include original authors who are too far into retirement to contribute or who are deceased, and new recruits to author teams who have minor or highly specialized roles in a revision. In cases of multiple authorship, therefore, integrating authoring styles is critical. This integration is difficult, because authors usually have strong and unique personalities, attitudes, backgrounds, and professional agendas. The object in integration is not to bury the individual voices but to provide a consistent style and "metavoice" for the book as a whole.

There are three ways to make a metavoice: (1) The publisher hires an editor at your expense to "smooth" the book, rectifying styles and rewriting narrative as necessary, an expensive project and one that many authors find painful; (2) one of the authors on the team is chosen consensually to make a final edit of the whole manuscript for the purpose of smoothing; or (3) the authors collaborate in advance to decide the ground rules for style, format, and voice, based on the publisher's input concerning house style and the book's market. If carried out, the third option usually works best for all concerned.

Whether you are sole author or coauthor, establishing, integrating, and monitoring your authorial voice is a key to your book's instructional and commercial success. As you can see, establishing an effective authorial voice involves far more than merely expressing one's individuality and putting one's best foot forward in print. However experienced you may be as a professional and a human being, take time to reflect on yourself in your role as textbook author.

Engaging Your Reader

Your role as textbook author is similar in many ways to your role as classroom instructor. How do you engage your students in class? What makes them listen and pay attention? What makes them care? Is engaging students something you usually do successfully? What do you do when you walk into your classroom? How can your experiences inform your writing? Classroom instructors engage students through eye contact, voice and tone, verbal emphasis, and expression of affect, as well as through delivery of content. Traditionally, instructors begin classes in some combination of the following ways (except in wired classrooms, which work differently).

Nonverbal Activities

- Use of chalkboard
- Setup of any relevant display or equipment
- Writing of topic, terms, outline, diagram, formula, assignment
- Collection of assignments or papers
- Spot quiz

Verbal Acts

- Greeting
- Announcement of the topic
- Explanation of the topic's place in the course
- Review of the previous topic and its connection
- Questions for students' verbal response
- Example or anecdote relating to the topic
- Learning activity
- Demonstration
- Lecture
- Questions for students' written response

Aside from providing eye contact, is there any reason that a textbook chapter cannot do the same kinds of things to engage the learner? Chapter apparatus and pedagogy help accomplish this, but first, let's look at how to develop the learning objectives that should drive your choices of apparatus and pedagogy along with chapter content.

APPENDIX
Some "Bad-Voice" Archetypes

Uncle

Tipoffs: Low-level (dumbed down) language, over-explanation, overuse of personal or down-home anecdotes or homilies, oversimplified examples, the use of repetitions and refrains as in storytelling, and use of statements that go without saying.
Message to Readers: You are children (and all that being a child implies).

> **Example:** Unlike scientific theories, intuitive theories come from personal experience. For example, you probably have an intuitive theory about crossing the street. Crossing the street is a daily event in most people's lives. I have an intuitive theory about crossing the street in downtown Boston. As Figure 1.1 shows, many cars turn onto Boylston Street from Massachusetts Avenue, the intersection I cross on my way to work. As a result, many cars occupy the space I must use. Through reflection on my experiences at the intersection, I have developed an intuitive theory that explains how I cross the street. At the heart of my theory is a hypothesis: If I make eye contact with the driver, the driver goes and I have to wait, whereas if I avoid making eye contact, the driver waits while I cross. My theory works fairly well. After all, here I am to write about it. Your intuitive theory about crossing the street must work well too, for here you are to read about it.

Possible Reader Response: Give me a break! (Or, Get over yourself!)
Reader Motivation: Don't bother; this is a gut course.

Taskmaster

Tipoffs: Lots of rules, conditions, and injunctions; extensive use of "should" and "must;" moralistic or legalistic overtones.
Message to Readers: You are bad and had better shape up.

> **Example:** As a teacher, you should make it your business to learn how to use the computer to instructional advantage in your classroom. Unfortunately, teachers often resist this kind of change. If you do not overcome resistance to educational technology, however, your students will go into the world without the background they need for success in the world

of the future. Increasingly, as schools must devote more resources to acquiring equipment and training teachers in their use, teachers will be expected to fulfill society's mandate for technologically literate graduates.

Possible Reader Response: Shame on me! (Or, Bug off!)
Reader Motivation: Feel righteous, or seek to avoid further punishment.

Android

Tipoffs: Slavish devotion to logic, precision, and rigor; lack of warmth; impersonal tone.
Message to Readers: You are unworthy as human beings and unlovable.

Example: An organization is a group of people, working toward objectives, which develops and maintains stable and predictable behavior patterns. These behavior patterns persist over time, while the individuals who make up the organization may change. The two factors that determine behavior patterns in organizations are organizational structure and organizational culture. Organizational structure is determined by the tasks the organization performs. Organizational culture is determined by the beliefs, values, attitudes, and norms that are the basis for the behavior patterns in the organization.

Possible Reader Response: What a bore! (Or, Who cares!)
Reader Motivation: Skip the book; get the study guide.

Spinmaster

Tipoffs: Evocation of strong feelings through media formats, including tendency to write in sound bites; use of present tense in descriptions of past events; exaggerated claims, overuse of hypothetical scenarios; dramatic or inaccurate language used purely for effect; no source citations.
Message to Readers: You are stupid or unmotivated and cannot be trusted to learn.

Example: It's 1862 and a curious young biologist is moving mollusks. He moves them from the calm water they are used to to a turbulent shore. What will happen? Will they be dashed to bits? Will they survive to reproduce? If they survive, will their descendants be adapted to the new environment? The biologist, who will become known as the greatest scientist of his day, watches. Mollusks, he muses, like other life forms, must evolve.

Possible Reader Response: What a joke!
Reader Motivation: Read for pleasure; I'm not going to learn anything from this.

8

Why You Need Learning Objectives

IN TEXTBOOK DEVELOPMENT, most decisions are made in advance. The publisher, editor, and author agree in advance about the book's audience, mission, and story. They agree about the scope and sequence of content. They agree about the chapter apparatus and pedagogy. The length, schedule, editorial style, and even the art and photo counts may be decided in advance. Among the first tasks in textbook development, often accomplished before writing a single word of text, is to develop the learning objectives and to build the text headings that will directly address those objectives. Development of the learning objectives and heading system begins with reflecting on your instructional goals for the course.

Reflect on Your Instructional Goals

Your instructional goals, or teaching objectives, are a good starting point. They provide an overall framework for developing your textbook. That is, what are you trying to do? How will you do it? How will your textbook structure and content express your goals?

Suppose you have the following four goals for your Introduction to Geology course.

- Link geology to students' everyday lives.
- Help students acquire and retain geologic information.
- Foster scientific reasoning about geology-related issues.
- Create geologically literate citizens.

You may decide to link geology to life through news items or anecdotes at the beginning of every chapter. To help students learn geological information, you would first identify exactly which information you believe is important for them to acquire and retain. You may decide to help them in this through your chapter apparatus, pedagogy, illustrations, and a glossary.

To foster scientific reasoning about geology-related issues you would first decide what geology-related issues are important to include (mining, oil drilling, soil use, water use, dam building, etc.). Then you might decide to model scientific thinking in text features about geology-related situations in which disasters were avoided (or not) through the application (or not) of scientific reasoning. To figure out how to create geologically literate citizens, you would first define what you mean both by geologic literacy and by citizenship.

Now think about your readers' learning goals. What do they hope to get out of their intro to geology course aside from a grade and distribution credits in science? They might want to identify geologic objects and features of interest to them (e.g., the plagioclase feldspar in this rock, the terminal moraine in the woods out back, the stratigraphy in the roadworks downtown, that mudslide in the news). They very likely want to satisfy their curiosity about dramatic geologic phenomena (earthquakes, tsunamis) and get a sense of whether they might like to major in your subject. What will you provide in your textbook package that will address their goals?

How Learning Objectives Differ From Goals

Instructor and student goals provide an overall framework, but each chapter must then address specific learning objectives (whether stated or implied)—what it is that students will know or be able to do after learning the chapter content. Each learning objective is expressed in a text heading and is taken up in one section of the chapter. That is, each main heading of text, along with its subheadings, addresses only one learning objective.

For example, suppose you have the following learning objectives for your chapter on plate tectonics.

After studying this chapter you will:

- Define plate tectonics using the language of geology.
- Name and show the plates on a map.
- Trace the history of Earth's lithosphere.
- Explain the causes of plate formation, continental drift, and seafloor spreading.
- Compare and contrast three types of plate boundary.
- Describe the geologic changes that occur at plate boundaries.
- Discuss the implications of plate tectonics for life on Earth.

This chapter thus will have seven main headings of text, and all the content under each main heading will address a learning objective in the sequence. You would consider your four instructional goals in the context of providing the content that would enable readers to achieve each objective. For example, in providing content for the first learning objective (define plate tectonics using the language of geology), you would consider how to present the relevance of the topic to students, provide charts and diagrams and glosses to help them acquire and retain geologic information, and develop features to foster scientific reasoning and geologic literacy.

How Learning Objectives Guide Chapter Development

As you develop your learning objectives, consider what combination of information, observations, and experiences will best help students meet each one. For each, ask yourself the following questions.

- What prior knowledge and skills will students need to master the new content?
- What terms and concepts will need to be defined?
- What subtopical content or documents will students read?
- What content can be given via non–text media (image, video, audio, animation)?
- What online resources will students access?
- With whom and how will students communicate or interact?
- How will students know if they are meeting the objective?
- What will be the outcome of their learning?
- How will learning outcomes be measured and evaluated?
- How will the evaluation of outcomes affect your instructional goals?

These are the questions that teachers ask when developing lesson plans for classroom instruction or learning objectives for online courses. How does this play out for the second learning objective in the chapter on plate tectonics (name and identify the plates on a map)?

- Students will need prior knowledge of geography and map reading skills.
- The terms and concepts to be defined will include tectonic plate, plate boundary, mid-ocean ridge, continental shelf, (etc.).
- The subtopics will be the Eurasian Plate, North American Plate, Pacific Plate, Nazca Plate, Caribbean Plate, (etc.), with maps of the plate boundaries and the ring of fire.
- Students will use the following links to online animations of plates: ucmp.berkeley.edu/geology/tectonics.html, (etc.).
- Students will know they are meeting the objective if they can label the plates and draw the general plate boundaries on a blank map.
- The learning outcome will be that students will improve their geologic literacy (one of the four instructional goals).

Note that just as objectives are not the same as goals, outcomes are not the same as objectives. A statement of learning *outcomes* answers the question, "What will happen as a result of achieving the learning objective?" Learning objectives also are different from *skill sets*, which are considered separately either as prerequisite knowledge or as new skills to be acquired. Finally, note how learning objectives tie in with assessment and evaluation as well as with course supplements. As you will see, learning objectives can legitimately serve as a solid basis for systematically developing textbook content from start to finish.

Apply Findings from Educational Psychology

Learning objectives come from the field of educational psychology. This field is multidisciplinary and focuses on all factors that affect learning and teaching. Most authors of college textbooks are not aware of this body of knowledge and its theoretical perspectives, however, or else they reject it as irrelevant to their work. Yet many educational publishers, development editors, and learning design specialists rely on input from educational psychology and other fields—such as cognitive psychology—to help them craft and market textbooks.

Take what is known about motivation, for example, without which learning cannot occur. Are teachers (including textbook authors) responsible for students' motivation? No, students clearly have some kind of motivation when they enroll in a chosen course and open the textbook their instructor has assigned. But do you have a responsibility to engage the student in the particular learning enterprise you set forth in each chapter? Yes, and the better you get at this, the more successful your textbook will be.

Activate Motivation To Learn

Educational psychologists identify several sources of motivational needs; your chapters could create or satisfy selected ones in one way or another. Consider the following possibilities from just one motivational source.

Sources	Motivational Needs	Textbook Applicatons
Cognitive	Maintain attention. Develop understanding. Decrease uncertainty. Figure something out; solve a problem. Eliminate a threat or risk. Increase or decrease cognitive dissonance.	Exciting chapter openers. Provocative opening vignette. Chapter outline. Probing focus questions. List of key terms. Stated learning objectives. Common myths about subject. Open-ended scenario. Puzzle or quest. Application activity. Review questions. Practice test. Counterintuitive example. Pro–con argument. Positive model.

Research findings from educational psychology also show how the rate, efficiency, and long-term effectiveness of learning improve for all learners when study is guided by learning objectives. Learning objectives identify the competencies on which student performance will be measured. They also focus attention, mobilize prior knowledge, and activate motivation to learn. According to most cognitive scientists, these are the key brain-mediated events that initiate the learning process.

Use Learning Objectives Well

Authors of college textbooks often complain that learning objectives are for K–12 students and are not appropriate or desired for adult learners. K–12 textbooks are organized around statements describing the information, tasks, and behaviors students should master. These statements of objectives are written according to venerable rules developed for elementary and secondary education to ensure functional interrelatedness between the planning and delivery of instruction and the assessment of learning based on measurable performance (Mager, 1975).

Classically, the desired behaviors, the conditions of performance, and the criteria for mastery are included in learning objective statements, as in the statement, "Given 10 complete sentences containing 20 nouns, students will correctly circle 18 or more nouns." Naming measurable indicators of learning is important in this scheme. To identify, list, trace, compare, solve, write, or argue are directly measurable. To learn, reflect, understand, or appreciate, however, are not directly measurable.

Example: Learning Objectives

After reading this chapter [in a U.S. government text], you should be able to:

- Define public opinion and identify the forces that shape it.
- Trace the process of political socialization in American life.
- Analyze the role of technology and the media in shaping public opinion.
- Explain and illustrate how demography shapes political participation.
- List and describe six basic forms of political participation.
- Evaluate protests, political action groups, and lobbies as expressions of American political participation.

Notice that these statements specify in behavioral terms what students will do. College-level texts tend to emphasize learning objectives in the cognitive domain. Cognitive objectives address internal or conceptual changes in the learner, for example, by asking students to recognize, create, interrelate, apply, demonstrate comprehension, hypothesize, predict, or transfer learning to real-life situations. For example, students will:

- Demonstrate an understanding of the relationship between mass communication and public opinion.
- Create advertising copy for and against a particular political action committee.
- Apply their knowledge of political socialization to plan increased participation in student government.
- Present hypotheses explaining the institutionalization of dissent in a democracy.

Authors also often have unexpressed affective objectives; that is, they want students to care enough to vote, to become entrepreneurs, to love chemistry, to change their health habits, or to appreciate art, for example. Affective outcomes such as these involve the reader learning to value something or feel differently about something. Affective outcomes often are embedded or implied in behavioral and cognitive objectives.

In college-level texts above the introductory level, specific measurable behaviors, conditions of performance, and levels of mastery often are omitted. Instead, authors express objectives more generally as goals of learning or learning outcomes that students should keep before them as they read and should anticipate on tests. Anticipation is key. All learners of any age have a right to know up front what will be expected of them minimally, and the use of learning objectives accomplishes this.

Some authors nevertheless reject the use of learning objectives as too elementary, utilitarian, or restrictive. They claim that stated objectives guide the student to acquire only the specified knowledge and skills, without extension or choice. However, it bears repeating that educational research clearly supports the explicit use of learning objectives with students at any age or level of educational attainment and in any field of study. Research also suggests the importance of engaging the full range of cognitive abilities in both directing and assessing all students' learning (Slavin, 2005).

Write Good Learning Objectives

Learning objectives can be behavioral, cognitive, or affective. That is, students will be able to do, think, and feel differently after studying your chapter content. As noted above, all objectives are stated in behavioral terms using descriptors of observable behavior. Because learning is a mind–body phenomenon of marvelous complexity, direct observation of behavior is the only way to determine if it is taking place. Stating cognitive objectives correctly thus involves choosing action words that describe the observable behavior from which learning can be inferred. Examples of such action words include to *define, trace, analyze, explain, illustrate, list, describe, evaluate, demonstrate, discuss, present, solve, prove, apply, draw, create, infer, compare, contrast, predict, write, design, outline, exemplify*, and so on.

Bloom's Taxonomy

Everyone knows about Bloom's Taxonomy of cognitive learning objectives (Bloom et al., 1956), but you may not know that most commercial publishers of college textbooks ask authors to use this taxonomy or one of its many variants to ensure that accountability is built into the instructional materials they publish. The various rubrics for cognitive objectives all move from simple to complex learning, from factual to conceptual learning, and from lower to higher levels of cognitive functioning. Bloom's six-step rubric reflects these progressions.

Bloom's Taxonomy of Cognitive Objectives

1. **Knowledge**
   Remember; recall factual information (e.g., *define, describe, list, itemize, name, state*)
2. **Comprehension**
   Understand concepts (e.g., *explain, predict, translate, infer, exemplify, interpret, extrapolate, hypothesize*)
3. **Application**
   Use information and abstractions to solve novel or real-life problems (e.g., *compute, apply, solve, prove, calculate, illustrate, show, manipulate, manage, decide*)
4. **Analysis**
   Recognize main points; reduce complex information to explain how parts relate to a whole; understand relationships (e.g., *compare, contrast, identify, analyze, trace, relate, organize, outline, discriminate, distinguish*)
5. **Synthesis**
   Innovate, create something that did not exist before (e.g., *write an essay, design an experiment, draw, create, express, discuss, formulate a thought, represent an idea visually, present a theory, propose a course of action, invent*)
6. **Evaluation**
   Understand values, judge something against given or stated standards (e.g., *assess, evaluate, rate, judge, determine, accept, reject, argue a point of view, qualify, recommend*).

Bloom's scheme is admittedly subjective. For example, the classification of behaviors in terms of the types and levels of cognitive functioning can vary significantly depending on the classifier. Stating a hypothesis, for example, could also be classified as an application or a synthesis. Subjectivity does not invalidate the basic idea, however, which is a useful starting point for writing learning objectives in observable behavioral terms. The different types of learning performance in the taxonomy are all appropriate at the college level for different purposes.

Consider how the taxonomy applies to the learning objectives for the plate tectonics chapter in the intro to geology textbook.

- Define plate tectonics using the language of geology. (1. KNOWLEDGE)
- Name and show the plates on a map. (1. KNOWLEDGE AND 3. APPLICATION)
- Trace the history of Earth's lithosphere. (4. ANALYSIS)
- Explain the causes of plate formation, continental drift, and seafloor spreading. (2. COMPREHENSION)
- Compare and contrast three types of plate boundary. (4. ANALYSIS)
- Describe the geologic changes that occur at plate boundaries. (1. KNOWLEDGE)
- Discuss the implications of plate tectonics for life on Earth. (5. SYNTHESIS)

The plate tectonics chapter engages readers at most of the levels of cognitive functioning, providing good variety. Linking statements of learning objectives to cognitive levels is a good practice, because it helps you keep tabs on difficulty level. If all the objectives in a chapter tapped only factual recall, for example, the chapter (and possibly the text) would be regarded as too low-level. As you read in Chapter 6, "level" (reading level, grade level, cognitive level, difficulty level) is a significant factor in textbook adoption and sales. Consulting a scheme such as Bloom's Taxonomy helps you maintain balance in your intellectual demands on the reader as expressed through your stated learning objectives.

How might you classify the objectives for the chapter on political participation in the U.S. government text in terms of Bloom's taxonomy? Note how they call for a balance of different levels of cognitive functioning.

- Define public opinion and identify the forces that shape it. (1. KNOWLEDGE)
- Trace the process of political socialization in American life. (2. COMPREHENSION)
- Analyze the role of technology and the media in shaping public opinion. (4. ANALYSIS)
- Explain and illustrate how demography shapes political participation. (2. COMPREHENSION)
- List and describe six basic forms of political participation. (1. KNOWLEDGE)

- Evaluate protests, political action groups, and lobbies as expressions of American political participation. (6. EVALUATION)
- Demonstrate an understanding of the relationship between mass communication and public opinion. (4. ANALYSIS)
- Create advertising copy for and against supporting a particular political action committee. (5. SYNTHESIS)
- Apply knowledge of political socialization to increase participation in student government on campus. (3. APPLICATION)
- Present hypotheses explaining the institutionalization of dissent in a democracy. (5. SYNTHESIS)

Construct Chapters from Learning Objectives

Consider the following learning objectives for a chapter on portfolio management in a textbook on securities finance.

- Describe the asset classes in an asset mix and the role of the asset mix in a portfolio. (1. KNOWLEDGE)
- Evaluate strategies for determining asset mix. (6. EVALUATION)
- Compare and contrast portfolio management styles. (4. ANALYSIS)
- Explain the benefits of three asset allocation techniques. (2. COMPREHENSION)
- Trace the steps in monitoring and evaluating portfolio performance. (4. ANALYSIS)
- Calculate total return and risk-adjusted rate of return of a portfolio. (5. APPLICATION)

The portfolio management chapter—the whole text, in fact—can be planned out in advance, objective by objective, using a planning chart like the one on the next page.

Try this kind of development for one of the learning objectives presented in this chapter (for the intro to geology textbook or the one on government). A blank chart for planning your learning objectives is provided in the chapter appendix. Try completing this or a similar form for each learning objective in a chapter you are planning to write. Then adapt the form and process to your uses when planning learning objectives for every chapter in your textbook. You'll be glad you did.

Chapter 11, Portfolio Management	
Statement of Behavior for a Learning Objective (How will we be able to see if there has been a change in what students know/think/feel/do?)	Describe the asset classes in an asset mix and the role of the asset mix in a portfolio.
Cognitive Level (according to Bloom or other rubric)	1. Knowledge
Prerequisite Skill Set (What will students need to meet the objective?)	Understanding of investment policy and what a portfolio is. Definition of asset mix.
Main Heading and Subheadings (for the section of text that provides the content for the learning objective)	What Is In the Asset Mix? Cash Equities Fixed-Income Products Income Trusts and Hedge Funds
Section Support (What verbal and visual section content will give students what they need to meet the objective?)	Chart showing types of assets in asset classes. Annotated examples of asset mixes in actual portfolios.
Model Test Items (How will we know if students are meeting or have met the objective?)	What is the main purpose of each asset class in an asset mix? What role does the asset mix play in portfolio management?
Possible Supplement Tie-ins (What other resources will students have to get what they need to meet the objective?)	N/A
Potential Learning Outcome (What might happen as a result of students achieving this learning objective?)	Student will select appropriate asset classes for setting the asset mix for a customer.

APPENDIX
Plan Your Learning Objectives

Chapter (Number and title)	
Statement of Behavior for Learning Objective (How will we be able to see if there has been a change in what students know/think/feel/do?)	
Cognitive Level (according to Bloom or other rubric)	
Prerequisite Skill Set (What will students need to be able to do to meet the objective?)	
Main Heading and Subheadings (for the section of text that provides the content for the learning objective)	
Section Support (What verbal and visual section content will give students what they need to meet the objective?)	
Model Test Items (How will we know if students are meeting or have met the objective?)	
Possible Supplement Tie-ins (What other resources will students have to get what they need to meet the objective?)	
Potential Learning Outcome (What might happen as a result of students achieving this learning objective?)	

9

Why Heading Structure Matters

THE STEPS OUTLINED in Chapters 5–8 form the foundations of textbook development. These foundations include getting information from competition analysis, market research, instructors who are potential users of the book, and professional peer reviews; reflecting on your mission; identifying your audience; choosing and developing your style and voice; and establishing your teaching goals and learning objectives. The next steps involve organizing your course content into a sequence of parts and chapters and then developing a system of text headings for each chapter. Your final writing outline is the basis for text headings, which you use to develop your table of contents.

Because headings have high visibility, and because your book will be sold largely on the basis of its table of contents (TOC), it is worth whatever time it takes you to get the organization and headings right. This task should be done at the very beginning, not after you have written your manuscript. Authors who try to insert headings after drafting and while rushing to revise often discover that they need to rearrange their chapters. Textbooks are written to outlines rather than outlined after the fact. Thus, you should know what is going to be in every chapter of your book before you even start. This point cannot be stressed enough. Your publisher probably will require that you provide a whole-book working TOC with your prospectus. That TOC goes out for review along with your prospectus before your book is even signed, and your revised TOC may be printed in your publisher's sales catalogue before you have even finished drafting. Take care to develop your TOC on the basis of your mission, market research, and competition analysis. (See Chapter 4.)

The Organization of Your Book

Scope and sequence is a phrase from el-hi publishing referring to the range of topics you will cover and in what order. This is a more challenging task than you may think, even for a well-organized college course, because alternative scopes and sequences may be equally commendable on some grounds. Decide what topics you definitely will, will not, and might cover. Then identify the broadest topical areas and experiment with sequencing them, making sure that prerequisite knowledge is presented first. For example, in a textbook on genetics a chapter on Mendelian inheritance probably should precede a chapter on chromosome theory, and in a textbook on finance a chapter on equities probably should precede a chapter on derivatives.

In the planning stage, begin with a *brief TOC*, which sets out the proposed organization of your book in terms of parts and chapters, with headings and subheadings to follow later in the process. Textbooks commonly have a Part I that serves as an introductory or foundational unit. Chapters in Part I typically cover core concepts and background information necessary for studying the subject. For example, a Part I in an introduction to archaeology textbook might define and describe the basic subdivisions within the field, identify the underlying assumptions or basic theoretical orientations, or briefly survey the field's history and philosophy. Subsequent parts might then cover the rest of the course content in one of several possible ways, depending on the book's story and mission. Parts and chapters may be organized according to timelines of prehistory, for example, or by geographic region, or by steps in the process of doing archaeology.

Develop Parts and Chapters

Parts in a textbook represent units of study. Parts and chapters may progress in a chronological, hierarchical, or horizontal topical fashion, depending on your subject and what you are intending to accomplish. Chronological development is progressive, like a story. The narrative describes steps in a process, a sequence of change, or changes over time. Hierarchical development is classificatory and analytical. The exposition arranges information either inductively (specific to general) or deductively (general to specific). Horizontal development treats all topics equally or in parallel rather than subsuming some in relation to others. Other organizational principles may also apply.

Suppose your mission is to empower readers to find and evaluate information on the Internet efficiently and effectively. Because the mission is processual, chronological development might be best. Chapters in Part I might provide background information on the Internet and might explain why it is useful or important to be able to find and evaluate information there. Chapters in Part II might then go on to describe how to find and evaluate information on the Internet. Part III chapters might follow by laying out the knowledge and skills readers need to find and evaluate online information efficiently and effectively. Chapters in Part IV might demonstrate reader empowerment through specific applications to selected careers or subject areas. Thus, the TOC (completely hypothetical) might look something like this.

Part I The Internet
Chapter 1 Internet Technology and the Information Age
Chapter 2 Living and Working Online

Part II Navigating Cyberspace
Chapter 3 How to Locate Information on the Internet
Chapter 4 How to Read Screens and Websites
Chapter 5 How to Evaluate Online Information

Part III Becoming an Information Expert
Chapter 6 Improving Your Efficiency and Effectiveness on the Internet
Chapter 7 Knowing Where to Go
Chapter 8 Using Databases
Chapter 9 Using Subscription Services
Chapter 10 Taking Advantage of Information Software

Part IV Applying Internet Skills
Chapter 11 Doing Online Academic Research
Chapter 12 Doing Online Market Research
Chapter 13 Being a Smart Online Consumer
Chapter 14 Using Online Resources at Work

Try to have three to six parts, and organize the content so that each part has two or more chapters. For an undergraduate course in which chapters likely will be assigned at a rate of one a week, try to have 14 to 18 chapters to approximate the number of weeks in a semester or other teaching period. By convention each such chapter should be under 40 book pages in length. An alternative is to have more chapters at less length, which may be especially appropriate for complex topics with many technical terms requiring a lot of exposition. Having brief modular chapters is the trend, also adaptive for online applications.

The Art of Chunking

As you determine the boundaries of your chapters, keep in mind the principle of chunking from cognitive psychology. People remember information most efficiently not as bits but as meaningfully networked groups of bits, or chunks (Miller 1956). You remember chunks because of their strong internal associations and their usefulness to you. Learning involves acquiring, relating, and using those chunks.

In textbook development chunking involves choosing the right type and amount of content to present at the right time and place for optimizing learning. For example, In a textbook on financial securities, if being able to trade bonds effectively is a desired learning outcome, you would chunk information about bond trading in a chapter on that subject rather than burying the information in a chapter on fixed-income securities.

Write Good Titles

Giving titles to parts and chapters requires some thought and flexibility. It is not unusual for titles to change from draft to draft as editorial advice comes in and messages and market concerns become clearer. Following are some tips on giving titles to parts and chapters.

Tips on Writing Titles

- Give clear, brief, simple names to parts and chapters.
- Pack as much specific information as possible into titles without making them too long.
- Avoid making part and chapter titles too long through formal usages or subtitles.
- As a rule of thumb, make titles one to eight words in length, including articles and conjunctions. No chapter or part title needs to exceed ten words.
- Identify the core concept, subject, or theme of the part or chapter.
- As much as possible, use concrete nouns.
- Within reason, use parallel structure in wording the names of parts and chapters.
- Most important: Write straightforward titles without attempting to be comic, coy, clever, or cryptic.

With your well-worded brief TOC in hand, you can go on to develop your writing or drafting outline and, better, your system of text headings.

Develop Chapter outlines for Your TOC

Your chapter outlines consist of the system of headings that lay out the contents of each chapter listed in your brief TOC. You can develop a working table of contents from your writing outline (the topical outline or list that authors use as reminders for drafting). Note, however, that a writing outline is not the same as a table of contents. A writing outline formally lists the sequence of topics in a way that is hierarchical and logically exhaustive. It is telling you what to write. A system of text headings and subheadings, on the other hand, is functional and natural for learning a subject rather than for expressing a form. Headings in a TOC chunk information in a way that tells readers what to learn. The chapter outline thus helps the reader to construct meaning from text.

The concept of meaning construction comes from linguistic studies and has been applied to learning theory in education. The idea is that learning is not passive information retrieval but is an active organization of new information in relation to the learner and the learner's past experience. The learner interprets information according to his or her intentions for using it and in relation to his or her existing mental frameworks. Thus, meaning is not exclusively in your text, nor exclusively in your reader; rather, it must be negotiated. The headings that make up your table of contents are a form of this negotiation. Each heading represents a conceptual organizer or framework for acquiring or integrating content.

Distinguish Your Writing Outline from Your TOC

The difference between writing outlines and tables of contents often confuses even experienced authors and editors. That this whole chapter is devoted to the subject of headings testifies to their importance in exposition, however, as well as in textbook publishing. As you will see, headings play a significant role not only in learning, but also in topical balance, textbook packages, and marketing and sales.

A writing outline expresses the book's logical development and the author's progression of thought, using a conventional outline format with Roman numerals, the Roman alphabet, Arabic numbers, etc. The product is layers of logically differentiated subtopics that are exhaustively subsumed under larger topics. Some items serve only as abstract or analytical categories—umbrella concepts that are inclusive of the topics that actually will be addressed in the writing. The outline, then, is a system of classifying information, a taxonomy.

In contrast, the headings in a final chapter outline in a table of contents group information in a functional, informational way. All the headings are real and all have actual content under them; that is, they are not empty pegs or logical abstractions. Every heading is followed preferably by three or more paragraphs of text. Your TOC, therefore, is more like a roadmap or a concept web than a taxonomy.

The following examples illustrate the difference between a writing outline and a corresponding chapter outline. The example assumes that the topic of motivation is intended as one main section of text within a chapter that contains other topics as well.

Example: Writing Outline for a Section of Text

I. Motivation
    A. Definition
    B. Types
        1. Extrinsic
        2. Intrinsic
    C. Sources
        1. External
        2. Internal

D. Theoretical Perspectives
  1. Behavioral
  2. Humanistic
  3. Cognitive
  4. Social Learning

Headings for the Above Section of Text (and the TOC)

<A> What Is Motivation?
<B> Extrinsic and Intrinsic Motivation
<B> External and Internal Sources of Motivation
<B> Theoretical Perspectives on Motivation
<C> Behavioral Views
<C> Humanistic Views
<C> Cognitive Learning Theory
<C> Social Learning Theory

As you can see, the writing outline guides the author, while the text headings serve the reader. The headings convey relationships among core concepts, and these headings are organized in levels different from—but no less logical than—the formal writing outline.

Use Levels of Heading Appropriately

Textbooks can have up to five levels of heading, but three is optimal in most subjects and standard practice in introductory texts. The levels of heading are differentiated through book design using different sizes, styles, and colors of type. A-heads (<A>) are the most general and inclusive and also the most prominent visually; B-heads (<B>) are subsumed under A-heads, are next-most prominent visually, and appear on their own lines. C-heads (<C>) are subsumed under B-heads and, like D-heads, often start on the same line as their text. D-heads (<D>) are also distinguished typologically but are the least prominent heading on the page. Glance at pages in textbooks sitting on your bookshelves to see the way levels of heading are differentiated. Notice how different levels of heading use space on the page. You might also see topical subheadings used as marginalia.

Proper headings, like elements in a formal outline, follow the "rule of two;" that is, if an A-head has B-heads, there must be two or more B-heads, and if a B-head has C-heads, there must be two or more C-heads, and so on. A singleton A-head, B-head, or C-head is not good practice and reveals poor organization of content. Also, at every level, headings must have sufficient copy under them to warrant their separate existence and the space they take on the page. Having a one-paragraph A-head section, for instance, is not good practice and usually indicates either topical underdevelopment or inappropriate use of headings as logic pegs or conceptual placeholders.

Not all editors today are aware of these standards or the underlying reasons for them. Also, the style of headings in textbooks differs from styles dictated by professional organizations for journal writing. For example, American Sociological Association guidelines might require that you make A-heads all caps or that you underline and indent A-heads and have B-heads flush left on their own line, etc. However, textbook headings normally are never all capitals, underlined, or indented, and if your book is being designed rather than going to print as camera-ready copy, then all your efforts in formatting will be wasted. A copyeditor must pencil changes or reformat your disk—an unnecessary expense that is charged to your book. For this and other reasons, instead of clinging to formatting guidelines for journal articles, you would be wise to follow consistently your publisher's Author Guidelines for differentiating among levels of heading and keyboarding them.

Unless instructed not to do so, use the <A>, <B>, and <C> notational system to identify levels of heading (the carets indicate you do not intend the actual letters to be set into type). That way, publishing personnel always will be able to tell consistently which level of heading you intend. Alternatively, supply a chapter outline that clearly shows intended levels of heading that your copyeditor can use as an authoritative guide. Inconsistency in heading structure that finds its way into print can destroy the organizational integrity of your book.

How to Craft Headings

The best way to start developing your writing outline into a system of headings—and by extension into your table of contents—is to convert your Roman-numeral items into questions. These questions are your A-heads. They focus the reader's attention on a particular quest for enlightenment and identify your broad theme or unifying concept. The paragraphs you write under an A-head should introduce the theme, define the concept, or provide background or context for the discussion to follow. The last sentence or two of an A-head section can briefly forecast your answer to the question by identifying the topics in your B-heads. This gives the student readers what they need to begin learning what you want them to know.

The question–answer approach to heading development is challenging and works better for some subjects than for others. Initially, however, this approach is worth trying. The question–answer structure is pedagogically sound for exposition, helpful to students, and especially appropriate for instruction based on learning objectives or outcomes. Furthermore, in study skills training, students are coached to convert text headings into questions to answer for reading comprehension and review.

The next level of items in your formal outline—those that are real versus purely logical—become your B-heads. B-heads should be worded to answer directly the question posed in the A-head under which they are subsumed. The paragraphs under B-heads elaborate their function of answering the A-head question. All the B-heads should consistently have wording parallel in structure and grammatical agreement; that is, the wordings should not switch from one form or part of speech to another. Headings also should be worded to provide straightforwardly the most solid and specific information possible in the least possible space. A heading that simply says, "Introduction" or "Research" or "Criticisms" conveys insufficient information.

Based on the discussion so far, what is wrong in the following example of headings?

Example: Poor Subheadings

<A> What Are the Stages of Cognitive Development?
<B> Theories of Cognitive Development
<B> Sensorimotor
<B> Observing the Preoperational Child
<B> Poured Concrete Operations
<B> What Are the Hallmarks of Formal Operational Thought and How Can You Encourage Formal Operational Thinking in Children?

In the example, the first B-head does not directly serve its A-head question; that is, "theories of cognitive development" are not "stages of cognitive development." The reader is confused at the outset. In addition, the B-heads lack parallel grammatical agreement and style; that is, the B-heads switch between noun phrases, verbal phrases, and additional questions. The wording of the fourth B-head contains a distracting, not-so-clever, pun. The last B-head is too nonconforming compared with the other B-heads and would unnecessarily take up a lot of space on the page. The net effect of the headings is that students' efforts to make sense of information are compromised rather than aided.

Example: Corrected Headings

<A> What Are Theories of Cognitive Development?
<A> What Are Piaget's Stages of Cognitive Development?
<B> Sensorimotor Stage
<B> Preoperational Stage
<B> Concrete Operational Stage
<B> Formal Operational Stage

In the first A-head of the corrected version, the concept of stage theories could be defined and contrasted with non-stage theories. Then, key theorists and background information on their work could be identified in added B-heads. In the B-heads under the second A-head of the corrected version, "observations" and "hallmarks" and other conceptual organizers for each stage could be taken up in added C-heads.

Avoid repeating the exact same headings in similar contexts within a chapter or in different chapters. Each heading in a textbook should be unique. In headings, repetition is not "system" but monotony. Imagine reading a chapter describing six alternatives in which six of the B-heads read "Benefits of. . ." and the other six read "Drawbacks of. . ." Your eyes are glazing over at the thought.

Readers intuitively count on your headings to get a clue about the topical differentiations you are making, so keep in mind that headings are supposed to serve the learner. In exposition, obscurantist headings are mean-spirited. It bears repeating that headings should be straightforward, economical, informative, unique, and strong. They articulate the bones to which the sinews and flesh of your prose attach.

The C-heads in your chapter outline are derived from items in your writing outline denoted by Arabic numbers. C-heads give the details, examples, or other elaborations that directly support their B-head. The "rule of two or more" applies throughout, and, again, for every heading, you must have something substantive to say.

What Headings Really Mean

There is no one right way to construct a system of headings. Depending on your goals and emphasis, for example, you might recast your lesson on cognitive development in other ways.

Example: Alternative Heading Structure A

<A> What Is Cognitive Development?
<A> What Are Some Theories of Cognitive Development?
    <B> Piaget's Theory of Cognitive Development
    <B> Neo-Piagetian Theories
    <B> Vygotsky's Theory of Cognitive Development
    <B> The Constructivist View
<A> What Are Piaget's Stages of Cognitive Development?
    <B> The Sensorimotor Stage
    <B> The Preoperational Stage
    <B> The Concrete Operational Stage
    <B> The Formal Operational Stage

Example: Alternative Heading Structure B

<A> What Is Piaget's Theory of Cognitive Development?
<B> Developmental Processes
<C> Schemes
<C> Accommodation
<C> Assimilation
<C> Equilibration
<B> Developmental Stages
<C> Sensorimotor Stage
<C> Preoperational Stage
<C> Concrete Operational Stage
<C> Formal Operational Stage
<A> How Is Piaget's Work Viewed Today?
<B> Criticisms of Piaget's Stages
<C> Limitations of Theories Based on Stages
<C> Impact of Culture on Development
<C> Relationship of Gender to Development
<B> Influences on Neo-Piagetian Theories
<C> Information Processing
<C> Constructivism
<C> Ecological Models of Development
<B> Piaget's Influence on Education
<C> Developmentally Appropriate Education
<C> Focus on the Learning Process
<A> What Is Vygotsky's Theory of Cognitive Development? Etc.

Notice that the differences between these two examples reflect differences in both organization and emphasis. Your heading structure, in other words, reflects the amount of information you are providing, the amount of differentiation you are making within and between topics, and each topic's relative importance in your scheme of things. How much do you have to say? About what? At what level of specificity? And how important is it?

The levels of heading thus signify their function as conceptual organizers. In Example A, for instance, the author regards "The Constructivist View" as a standalone B-level topic equal in importance to the other B-head topics in that section. Author A wants us to remember constructivism as a major theoretical orientation in the study of cognitive development. In Example B, in contrast, "Constructivism" is a C-head subsumed under "Influences on Neo-Piagetian Theories," which the author has chosen as the more important conceptual organizer. Author B wants us to remember constructivism as only one of several Neo-Piagetian theories of cognitive development.

The relative importance you give to your topics in this way becomes a roadmap to your beliefs and values as an author in your subject area, a blueprint to your philosophical stances on the topics you consider. Intentionally or otherwise, your headings reveal what learning you feel is most important for your readers to acquire and retain.

What Is Topical Development?

Topical development refers to the amount of elaboration or depth of coverage, number of subtopics, and number of words (or amount of space) you devote to a topic. For each topic there is an optimal level of development for your course, mission, and audience, and it is up to you to find it.

Example: Thinking about Topical Development

How will you develop the topics in Part III Blood Collection for your introduction to phlebotomy text? Chapters in previous units have already discussed the health, safety, and legal issues involved; the quality, care, and treatment of blood specimens; and some basic background biology. Your readers will be aspiring EMTs, nurses, or phlebotomy technicians, and you hope they will go on to the second-tier course that leads to phlebotomist certification.

For the unit on blood collection, say you decide to have an introductory chapter and a chapter for each of the three main blood collection techniques: venipuncture, skin puncture, and arterial blood collection. The introductory chapter will define the three types of blood collection, when and with whom they are used, and why. The chapters on the three techniques will have A-heads explaining at similar depth the equipment, routine procedures, and possible complications. As needed, subheadings will differentiate techniques for different patients (e.g., adults, children, infants).

To maintain focus, level, and consistency in topical development, you decide to leave out special collections and non-blood collection procedures as well as procedures in special contexts, such as point-of-care testing, and in special settings, such as donor care centers. You also keep the underlying science and medical terminology to a minimum so as not to encroach too much on the second-tier course.

Your plan makes sense. As you draft, however, you discover that venipuncture is requiring much more space and really needs to be two chapters, while dermal puncture and arterial blood collection need only one chapter each. This not a case of topical overdevelopment or underdevelopment, because the facts call for more explanation and therefore greater coverage of one topic over the other two topics with which it is grouped. Thus, this decision probably is appropriate for content that is hierarchically organized.

In the example, topical overdevelopment might occur if you considered additional content and examples only for venipuncture and not for the other methods. Topical underdevelopment might occur if you referred to special collection techniques without elaborating on them, especially if that topic were expected or required in the introductory course. If your chapters expressed chronologically organized content (e.g., steps to becoming a phlebotomist), rather than hierarchically organized content, then you would call out the parts and chapters differently. Venipuncture, skin puncture, and arterial blood collection might be three A-heads in the chapter, "How to Get a Blood Sample," for example, and that chapter might follow "How to Use Blood Collection Equipment" or precede "How to Avoid Complications in Blood Collection."

Overdevelopment and Underdevelopment

Underdevelopment of topics is a serious flaw in exposition, because it does not cover the topic adequately or provide enough information to aid comprehension. With overdevelopment, in contrast, readers always are tempted to skip over unneeded passages once they have achieved comprehension. Overdevelopment also may make your book too dense or too long.

Too many headings can be a sign of overdevelopment in the form of topical over-differentiation. When developing sections in terms of your chapter outline, take care not to chop up text too finely. A surfeit of headings followed by brief copy particulates information, becomes visually confusing to readers, and also eats up valuable space on the page.

Some authors go the other way, however, and spin out page after page of narrative without providing enough subheadings for the reader to organize the material conceptually or to gain some visual relief. As a rule of thumb, chapters in most content areas ideally have a minimum of three and a maximum of eight A-head sections of text. Undergraduate textbooks typically have at least one heading of some type per each spread (two facing book pages). To analyze the organization and heading structure of this book, examine its TOC in the frontmatter.

Characteristics of Good Topical Development

Following is a list of guidelines for providing good topical structure and organization.

Guidelines for Good Topical Structure and Organization

- Begin each A-head, B-head, and C-head section of text with a thesis statement or question in the introductory paragraph.

- Promptly explain the purpose of taking up a topic. Avoid making it a surprise or a mystery for the reader to solve.
- Group or cluster ideas or points into meaningful chunks of closely related information.
- Avoid logically exhaustive or taxonomic development.
- Avoid imbalance or inconsistency in topical development. Each section of narrative should embrace a reasonable amount of meaningful information.
- With topics of equal importance, avoid underdeveloping some (i.e., making them too narrow or brief) and overdeveloping others (making them too broad or long).
- Take care to see that sections of text lead naturally and coherently from one to the next. Avoid abrupt endings, and make clear transitions.
- Avoid encyclopedic exposition in which each topic is treated without reference to any others. This unhelpful kind of organization is known in the trade as the "recipe card," "scattershot," or "encyclopedic" approach to instruction.
- Avoid leaps of faith in which you assume the reader is filling in logical steps (or gaps) in your progression of thought.
- Support each main idea or point using specific examples, data, evidence, or arguments.
- Avoid underdevelopment of abstract ideas and also unsupported claims.
- Treat topics fully in the context of their greatest relevance. Avoid reiterating topics repeatedly in all relevant contexts.
- Define key terms and concepts fully in the context where they are first used meaningfully.
- Avoid introducing a topic that is not taken up substantively until later in the book.
- Cross-refer to previous chapters as needed, but avoid forecasting, as this does not remedy poor topical development. Authors who frequently cross-reference to future chapters undermine the reader's trust.

How Headings Guide Topical Development

A-head and B-head sections are the most important conceptually and thus should contain the longest copy, or the most paragraphs. C-head and D-head sections, while they contain important details, are briefer. Avoid consigning the meat of your chapters to long C-head or D-head sections, especially as these levels of heading typically are omitted from the frontmatter TOC.

At the other extreme, three sentences are regarded as the minimum for copy under a C-head. The following hypothetical example shows an inappropriate treatment of sections in terms of level of heading and length of copy as indications of relative importance.

Example: Inappropriate Topical Development

<A> What Are the Stage Theories of Cognitive Development?

Stage theories postulate that individuals progress in their cognitive development through a specific number of defined stages.

<B> Piaget's Theory

Jean Piaget, a Swiss psychologist, studied children's learning behavior at different ages and concluded that there are specific stages of cognitive development, shown in Table 2.1.

<Insert Table 2.1>

<B> Vygotsky's Theory

Lev S. Vygotsky, a Russian psychologist influenced by the work of Piaget, conducted experiments to clarify Piagetian stages and study how children move from one stage to another.

<B> Neo-Piagetian Theorists

In the decades following Piaget's contributions to cognitive psychology and the study of child development, new research led to criticisms of Piaget's stage theory. It was found that children do not all move through all the stages by certain ages and may not even move through the stages in the same sequence. Piaget's conclusions were also criticized because they did not seem to take into account the impact of culture and enculturation on child development. Neo-Piagetian theorists revised the definitions of the stages to attempt to account for these factors.

<A> What Are Piaget's Stages of Cognitive Development?

<B> The Sensorimotor Stage

The first stage, from birth to two years of age, is called the sensorimotor stage. Etc.

In the foregoing example, the narratives under the first A-head and the first two B-heads are too brief, consisting of single sentences. The length of copy under the third B-head suggests that its topic is more important than the others. The second A-head, meanwhile, is used purely structurally with no copy at all. The example also reveals a serious lack of explanation below the level of highest abstraction—that is, sections lack the specific examples and concrete applications that readers need to make meaningful sense of the information. Without concrete examples, your subject, however worthy, cannot come alive for readers.

Concrete Examples Support Topical Development

Editors of college textbooks often are amazed to find manuscripts with page after page of unrelentingly abstract prose, paragraph after paragraph on constructs with no hint that empirical analogs exist in the real world. What are these authors thinking? Why should readers care to learn anything about stratigraphy, for instance, even when defined, if they cannot imagine what it might look like or where in the world they might see it? How much better it would be to read about archaeological excavations at Ceren, El Salvador, or Harappa, Pakistan, and how the stratigraphy at those sites revealed interesting facts from successive cultural depositions. Or to read about geological surveys in which stratigraphy revealed the history of vulcanism in the Pacific Rim or iridium in Italy or pollen in Greenland ice cores or drought in Yucatán or, frankly, anything empirical. Readers then might be motivated to wade through a closely reasoned, technical, and conceptual argument about stratigraphy as a research tool.

Concrete examples help readers to operationalize concepts—make them into something they can use. They can imagine, visualize, or identify with representations or exemplars of the concept. Vicariously experiencing an exemplar, in turn, engenders self-confidence in the reader, who then becomes more motivated to tackle the difficult or complex idea in aid of which you advanced a concrete example. Offering concrete examples is more than a courtesy to the reader; it is essential to learning.

When asked to provide an example, lazy authors often write abstract examples rather than concrete ones. The following "example," for instance, actually is little help. Why should we, the readers, care about A, B, or C?

> **Example: Concrete Example Gone Abstract**
> For example, imagine stratigraphy in which layer A is overlain by layer B, which was laid down on top of layer A at a later time. Then, layer C was deposited on top of layer B, and, assuming the depositions were not disturbed, layer C is the most recent or represents the present-day surface.

> **Example: Improved Version of Concrete Example Gone Abstract**
> At Harappa, the living floors and material culture of the earliest Stone Age inhabitants were overlain by the cultural remains of early farmers of the Indus Valley. On top of those deposits, later farmers built a small walled city with a sophisticated sanitation system. Still later Harappans expanded the amount of land under cultivation and built extensive irrigation networks, which remain visible at the present-day surface. As you can imagine,

excavating down through Harappa's stratigraphy is a way of going back through time.

"Inhabitants," "farmers," and "Harappans" are inherently more interesting to readers than "A," "B," and "C." Notice that concrete examples typically take up more space on the page, however. Choose them carefully to support topical development and the most important constructs you are trying to teach.

Another refuge of the lazy or unmindful author is hypothetical examples, which in most contexts are not as good as real ones. Readers are keen judges of credibility and tend to put less confidence in invented examples. Readers also often have unpleasant memories of hypothetical examples from earlier schooling. (Mary has two oranges and Jim has three apples. How can they share the fruit equally with Larry and Sandra?)

When they directly involve the reader, fictions also can backfire and convey wrong messages that thwart learning, as in the following example.

Example: Hypothetical Example Gone Wrong

As an example of crime profiling, imagine you are a serial killer. You choose your victim, say a grocery clerk, and assemble your weapons of choice—a cord for strangling, perhaps, and a switchblade for carving your initials in the corpse. You plan the time and place of your attack (behind the grocery store after closing) and also the details of your escape (on foot). You don't bother to disguise your appearance because you will be killing your victim and making sure there are no witnesses.

Whatever is happening here, the reader certainly is not thinking about the concept of crime profiling.

Some authors find developing text sections easier if they go about it in a systematic way. One such way is shown on the next page in a planning grid for topical development for one main section of a chapter. A blank planning grid is provided in the appendix.

Role of Headings in Marketing and Sales

Frontmatter TOCs may not contain all levels of heading, so you would be wise to ensure that the hot topics and buzz words your customers will regard as most important all appear in A-heads and B-heads. For the publisher, the TOC is an important sales tool. It will be published in the sales manual and used to instruct the sales force on how to sell your book. It will be published in the company's catalogue and will appear on the company's website. It may be compared to the TOCs of competing texts to highlight

Example: Planning for Topical Development

Chapter 2: Understanding Chronologies of the Past		
Learning Objective: Students will explain stratigraphy and seriation as forms of relative dating.		
A-Head: Relative Dating: Stratigraphy and Seriation		
Writing Outline	*B-heads and C-heads*	*Concepts and Examples*
I. Relative dating II. Stratigraphy A. Superposition B. Deposition III. Seriation A. Cross-dating B. Sequence Dating	<B> Why Relative Dating? <B> What Is Stratigraphy? <C> The Law of Superposition <C> Cultural Depositions <B> What Is Seriation? <C> Cross-dating <C> Sequence Dating <B> What Can We Infer from Relative Dating?	Vs. Absolute dating; Dendrochronology Strata; sedimentary rock Superposition; index fossils Hohokam, Harappa, Banpo Series; lithic tools New England gravestones Greek ceramics; coins Zimbabwe, Cahokia, Ceren

your book's superior organization and content. It may be printed in full on direct mail advertising brochures sent to faculty members nationwide. Your TOC may be printed in both long and short forms on the endpapers and in the frontmatter of your book. Portions of the TOC might be reproduced on acetate transparencies or electronic slides as lecture aids for adopters.

The TOC also is the key to correlating any supplements planned to accompany your text, such as an instructor's manual, test bank, and study guide. Your supplements authors must use your heading system to organize their content. The test bank author, for example, constructs a certain number of test items for each level of heading, assessing students' mastery at each level of conceptual organization and detail that you have laid out. In an Annotated Instructor's Edition, margin annotations next to each heading might indicate by number which test items cover the information in that section of text. Your study guide author likewise relies on your system of headings to guide the students through your material and to structure their opportunities for self-assessment. In your instructor's manual, lecture notes or instructional strategies may be keyed to specific sections of text. Your headings, in other words, are the scaffolding for your whole textbook package.

As mentioned at the beginning of this chapter, inexperienced authors sometimes wait until they have finished a chapter and then go back to outline the contents according to whatever headings they can stick in or seem to fit. This strategy often leads to extra time and effort, however, for this is when they discover that they have only one A-head for the whole chapter or that they have singleton B-heads and C-heads, or that they have over-differentiated or under-differentiated in topical development. It bears repeating, therefore, that the time you spend retrofitting your chapter to make the headings work is better spent in figuring out your headings in the first place.

Experienced authors and those who grasp the functionality and importance of the TOC often skip the writing outline and go straight to developing a system of headings. As mentioned in Chapter 3, submitting a real working table of contents with your curriculum vitae, prospectus, and sample chapters will win the respect and confidence of your editors. In drafting, exposition flows naturally from your heading structure. Heading structure also provides a convenient mechanism for staying in control of length and schedule, as you assign value, space, and time to each portion of your TOC. With your working heading structure in place and drafting underway, you can the turn your attention to the apparatus and pedagogy of your chapters, the subjects of the next three chapters of this book.

APPENDIX
Developing Your Text Sections

Chapter:		
Learning Objective:		
A-Head:		
Writing Outline	B-heads and C-heads	Concepts and Examples
Learning Objective:		
A-Head:		
Writing Outline	B-heads and C-heads	Concepts and Examples

10

What Pedagogy Does for Your Text

PEDAGOGY IS THE NAME GIVEN to all the written elements of your book that are neither narrative text nor the figures and tables that directly support narrative text. These pedagogical elements include the apparatus—chapter openers and chapter closers; systematic study aids, such as mid-chapter reviews, marginal annotations, or boldfaced key terms—and in-text features, such as thematic boxes, which are distinguished from the narrative through design.

The Functions of Pedagogy

The idea behind pedagogy is that a textbook acts as an instructor—a teacher—and that learning theories and research-based principles of effective instruction therefore apply. An example is the necessity for learning objectives, discussed in detail in Chapter 8. In addition, research supports the theory that people learn more, better, faster, if information is given in ways compatible with what is known about cognitive processing—the way people think, or more accurately, the way the human brain operates in the learning process. Without resorting to jargon, this means that information should be delivered or presented for discovery in proven ways. These ways include teaching sequences in both direct and nondirect instruction.

Principles of Direct Instruction

Textbooks contain expository writing most often in the form of direct instruction—the direct transmission of information that all students are expected to master. During past decades, different researchers have identified similar elements and events in this process (Gagne, 1977; Good et al., 1983; Evertson et al., 1984; Rosenshine and Stevens, 1986; Gagne and Driscoll, 1988). Most research giving rise to models of direct instruction has been done on behalf of elementary and secondary education. Because the studies draw upon general learning theories, however, the findings are equally valid for learners at the college, graduate, and postgraduate levels. All the models can be summarized in terms of the following general sequence (Slavin, 2005). Will your chapters perform the following tasks, reflecting students' learning needs?

Events in a Direct Instruction Lesson

1. State objectives and expectations.
2. Review prerequisite knowledge and skills.
3. Present new material.
4. Question to check for comprehension.
5. Provide opportunities for independent practice.
6. Assess performance and provide feedback.
7. Provide opportunities for outside application.

In many ways, the events in direct instruction relate to what is known about cognitive and psychological processes involved in learning. Event or Step 1, for example, activates motivation by telling learners what to expect and what will be expected of them. This first step also suggests how the information is relevant to learners personally or professionally and how it relates to their prior knowledge and experiences.

In Event or Step 2 students' attention and perception are directed selectively to (1) the topic and (2) to concepts students need to acquire to understand the new information. In Steps 3 and 4 the learner acquires the new information, makes sense of it, and retains it in memory through cognitive processes that encode stimuli and connect responses to those stimuli in neural networks. Steps 5, 6, and 7 reinforce learning, the application of learning, the motivation to learn, and the transfer of learning to new contexts or to the real world. An effective textbook does exactly the same things.

This is not to say that a textbook literally is a series of direct instruction lectures. Many an author has attempted to produce a textbook by having his or her lecture notes or tapes transcribed. These efforts fail, because spoken words do not transfer well to print and the nonverbal communication that takes place in the classroom is lost. The colloquial language, body language, shock tactics, personal fables, Socratic monologues, ironic observations, nostalgic anecdotes, rhetoric, panegyrics, polemics, and folksy or mordant humor that you use to attract students' attention—and that might make you a spellbinding lecturer—will make you look gratuitous, silly, egotistical, dated, eccentric, politically incorrect, and intellectually unsound on the printed page. In print, the events of direct and nondirect instruction occur through skillfully structured narrative and sound pedagogy.

Principles of Nondirect Instruction

In education, *nondirect instruction* includes all the planned learning experiences by which it is intended that students will acquire information on their own or through interaction with their peers and others. Students at all ages and at all levels of educational attainment learn actively and indirectly through observation, inquiry, discussion, modeling, progressive skill approximation, critical thinking, problem solving, decision-making, and hands-on experience. Pedagogical features give you an opportunity to build some of these learning experiences into your textbook. Consider, for example, what pedagogical features you could develop that would encourage students to use some of the following critical thinking skills (Kneedler, 1985). Will your textbook encourage readers to exercise the following skills?

Examples of Critical Thinking Skills

1. Define and clarify the problem.
   a. Identify the central issue.
   b. Compare similarities and differences.
   c. Distinguish relevant from irrelevant information.
   d. Generate appropriate questions.
2. Judge information pertaining to the situation.
   a. Distinguish among fact, opinion, and reasoned judgment.
   b. Evaluate consistency.
   c. Identify unstated assumptions.
   d. Recognize stereotypes and clichés.
   e. Identify factual inaccuracies, misleading information, and false claims.
   f. Identify fallacies in arguments.
   g. Recognize bias, manipulation, propaganda, and semantic loading.
   h. Distinguish between verifiable facts and value claims.
   i. Recognize different value systems and ideologies.
3. Solve problems and draw conclusions.
   a. Evaluate the credibility of a source.
   b. Recognize the adequacy of data.
   c. Weigh competing evidence.
   d. Make inferences from evidence.
   e. Hypothesize and predict probabilities.

For more ideas, see the Foundation for Critical Thinking at **criticalthinking.org**.

Students as Active Learners

Higher education faculties and critics frequently decry the lack of independent thinking and critical thinking skills among college undergraduates. Yet, a glimpse in undergraduate classrooms and textbooks suggests that students generally are expected to be the passive recipients of bodies of knowledge. Both live and in print, higher education faculties often unintentionally discourage learners from interacting with information sources, constructing meaningful knowledge actively, or thinking critically. Thus, the student's right to make reasoned judgments about what to believe and do—the whole point of learning—is preempted.

Part of the reason for this situation is the persistence of the historical role of college instructors as didacts and their lack of education as teachers. One could predict that few college professors would readily identify themselves as "teachers" at all. A "teacher" is the person who terrorized or nurtured them in second grade. Another part of the reason is that college instruction generally centers on the subject and on the instructor as the subject expert. Today, however, the trend in education at all levels is toward active learning, placing the student at the center of learning and actively involving the student in acquiring the subject. As a result, the "I" or "we" implicit in author-centered, subject-centered textbooks now becomes "you"—the student, the person whose learning is at stake.

Effective instruction no longer rests on the lecture model in which the instructor is the "sage on the stage" "telling it like it is" to passive, note-taking students who occasionally are invited to ask questions (but had better be careful not to betray any real curiosity or ignorance). The best textbooks are made to guide the reader through a self-directed learning process. Online courses and wikis are expressions of this process, and active learning is the purpose of having pedagogical features in your textbook. Pedagogical features give readers opportunities to construct, monitor, apply, and extend their own learning through interaction with text.

It is beyond the scope of this book to discuss all the learning theories and theories of instruction. The following links will take you to brief summaries of a sampling of some theories that might inform your textbook development.

Some Resources for Developing Your Pedagogy

Theories of direct instruction: **chiron.valdosta.edu/whuitt/col/instruct/dirprn.html**

Cognitive learning theories: **hsc.csu.edu.au/pro_dev/teaching_online/how_we_learn/cognitive.html**

Advance organizers: **netc.org/focus/strategies/cues.php**

Information processing theory: **tip.psychology.org/miller.html**

hsc.csu.edu.au/pro_dev/teaching_online/how_we_learn/information.html

Dual coding theory: **tip.psychology.org/paivio.html**

Criterion-referenced theory: **tip.psychology.org/mager.html**

Component display theory: **tip.psychology.org/merrill.html**

Problem-based learning: **edweb.sdsu.edu/clrit/home.html**
Andragogy (adult learning): **tecfa.unige.ch/themes/sa2/act-app-dos2-fic-andragog.htm**
Cognitive apprenticeship (case-based learning): **corpus-delicti.com/case_based.html#cognitivea**

Many more theories and applications are listed with links in the University of Colorado at Denver's encyclopedia of instructional models at **carbon.cudenver.edu/~mryder/itc_data/idmodels.html.**

Forms of Apparatus and Pedagogy

Chapter apparatus consists of your opening and closing pedagogy. The chapter opener expresses the subject, theme, aims, topics, and organization of a chapter. Inexperienced authors often resist chapter openers as "taking up space" or "giving away the show." They want to delight and surprise or intentionally, temporarily confuse the reader. Readers, however, have a right to know at the outset what they are reading and why or to what end. Also, readers learn the material better if they are mentally prepared for it. Chapter openers perform the functions of the first steps in models of direct instruction. They arouse curiosity, motivate, direct attention, and activate prior knowledge.

Openers and Closers

Chapter openers may include one or more of the following kinds of pedagogical elements, discussed in more detail in Chapter 11.

- Chapter overview or introduction
- Chapter outline
- Focus questions or anticipation guide
- Learning objectives or outcomes
- Graphic (advance) organizer
- Scenario or vignette
- Quotation or epigram
- Photo or illustration

Chapter closers—all the elements following the chapter narrative—provide psychological closure and give students opportunities to review, reinforce, or extend their learning. Chapter closing pedagogy always includes some kind of a conclusion and summary, and commonly in introductory textbooks, a list of terms and concepts with page cross-references. Closers might also contain one or more of the following elements, essential to learning.

- Review questions

- Self-assessment quizzes with answers
- Content applications
- Reflections or case analyses
- Field, lab, or Internet activities
- Research or writing assignments
- Brief annotated bibliographies for student use

Integrated Internal Pedagogical Devices

Other pedagogical devices to consider as regular internal elements in each chapter include the following possibilities.

- Boldfaced key terms
- Cross-references to relevant material in other sections or chapters
- Highlighted statements of main points
- Callouts of embedded subtopics
- Margin notes, such as glossary annotations, background notes, examples, or applications
- Sidebars with key facts
- Interim study or review questions
- Reflection, discussion, or critical thinking questions
- Reminders of appropriate operations or formulae

When well planned and well written, integrated pedagogical devices such as these aid student learning.

Interior Feature Strands

In-text features, whether boxes or portions of text set off through design, function pedagogically to attract attention; arouse curiosity; increase motivation to read; stimulate critical thinking; and provide opportunities for reflection, application, or problem solving. You might consider including one of more of the following kinds of feature strands in your textbook.

- Case studies
- Profiles
- Debates
- Primary source excerpts
- Models
- Reflections
- Thematic boxes

The development of feature strands is discussed in more detail in Chapter 12.

Pedagogy Pitfalls

Pedagogy has pitfalls. Some authors, readers, and textbook critics complain that features replace content, dumb down a text, are gimmicky, interrupt the narrative flow, create a boxy appearance, or cause confusion about what is important to know. Others claim that features serve only as window dressing, filler, fluff, or the publisher's hype, and that students don't bother to read them unless they are on the test. These complaints can be valid and usually stem from one or more of the following problems:

- Poor design of features
- Poorly written features
- Features that are too long
- Too many features (or too few)
- Inconsistent types or uses of features
- Lack of fit between features and chapter content
- Lack of clear purpose or relevance in using features
- Strained or insincere features based on the latest buzz in the field.

Some textbook features obviously pander to marketing directives rather than educative value and look and sound like television infomercials.

Other pitfalls stem from authors' lack of enthusiasm in supplying pedagogy or publishers' lack of investment in commissioning contributions to it. Plugging in two pages of boring or irrelevant prose per chapter to fulfill a marketing plan calling for an emphasis on diversity, technology, or globalism, for example, does not help to put your book on the road to success. You can avoid the pitfalls of pedagogy by observing the general rules of thumb outlined below.

Tips for Avoiding Pedagogy Pitfalls

- Choose a small number of specific chapter-opening and chapter-closing elements and use them consistently in every chapter.
- Develop at least one, but not more than four, types of feature strands.
- For each type of feature, have a clear purpose that reflects both key market concerns and real concerns in the course.
- Link features intimately to content; embed features in content-appropriate contexts.
- Try to have one of each type of feature in every chapter or every other chapter as a regular way of maintaining feature strands throughout the text.
- Ask to have some features designed as boxes and others as portions of text embedded in the narrative flow but set off through design.

- Establish a consistent standard for the desired length and content of each feature type.
- In most cases, keep features to less than one book page in length. In most subjects a two-page spread (a comprehensive, often illustrated, feature on facing pages) might be regarded as a maximum.
- Build in opportunities for readers to respond to feature content, for example, by adding comprehension, critical thinking, reflection, or discussion questions.
- Take personal responsibility for writing the pedagogical elements and features or for checking the quality of material written by contributors or freelancers.

If done right, features can greatly enhance both the salability of your text and its instructional value and effectiveness for readers. Doing pedagogy right involves planning, selecting, creating, integrating, and designing a chapter apparatus and feature strands.

If a development editor is assigned to your book, the development plan will contain a pedagogy plan similar to the one in this chapter's Appendix B. This pedagogy plan will be based on what you already have provided in your draft manuscript, what competing texts have to show, what reviewers say, and what marketing research suggests is desirable. You will receive guidelines and models for drafting or subcontracting the agreed-upon features. The development editor might provide models for some pedagogical elements for you, or your publisher might have features written by contributors or freelance writers on a work-for-hire basis.

Lacking editorial assistance, you will need to make all the decisions about apparatus and pedagogy yourself and supply all the elements and features. The next two chapters are intended to help you in this task. In addition, these chapters direct you to actual examples of pedagogy in sample chapters of textbooks posted on publishers' websites. You can see how effective pedagogical features look and work. Start, for example, by reading about the "New Features" for a child development textbook at **ablongman.com/html/fabestour**. Or select your discipline at **vig.prenhall.com/catalog/academic** to explore features in current titles relevant to you and your textbook. Google "sample chapter textbook" to locate publishers' sites with downloadable chapters, such as Jones and Bartlett's *Fundamentals of Nursing*, 3rd edition, at **nursing.jbpub.com/brockopp/sample_textbook_chapter.cfm**. Even upper level technical textbooks, such as *Medical Microbiology*, 17th edition, from Elsevier Health has some pedagogy (**intl.elsevierhealth.com/e-books/viewbook.cfm?ID=1490**).

Note that these URLs may have been discontinued or renamed by the time you are using this book. Just go to your keyword search. As you survey publishers' descriptions of their products and sample textbook chapters, continue thinking about your apparatus and pedagogy. You may wish to record your ideas using the form in this chapter's Appendix A, "Developing Your Pedagogy Plan." In the chart, list your ideas for your textbook's apparatus and pedagogy. Then, for each item in your list, identify the pedagogical function it will serve in relation to learning theories, principles of instruction, students' learning needs or thinking skills, the learning objectives for the chapter, and your teaching goals.

APPENDIX A
Developing Your Pedagogy Plan

Apparatus and Pedagogy	**Pedagogical Function**
Chapter Opening Elements	
Chapter Closing Elements	
Internal Pedagogical Devices	
Feature Strands	

APPENDIX B
Outline of a Sample Pedagogy Plan

This sample pedagogy plan is for an undergraduate textbook in archaeology.

Chapter Openers

- Chapter number and title
- Chapter opening photo
- Field notes or excavation account relating to chapter topic or theme
- Focus question linking field note or account to first A-head content
- Chapter outline with embedded statements of learning objectives

Apparatus

- Boldfaced key terms with margin glosses
- Marginal correlation icons linked to lab manual and website
- Interim review questions at end of each A-head section

Feature Strands

1. GREAT DISCOVERIES illustrated spread, one per chapter, historical information including early and contemporary archaeologists and sites, focusing on developments in scientific thinking and problem solving in archaeology, with one to three critical thinking questions.
2. VISUALIZING THE PAST illustrated box feature, two or three per chapter, up to one page in length, with captioned photos, diagrams, or computer arrays showing how archaeological problems can be modeled or represented.
3. SITES map feature, one per chapter as relevant, showing labeled locations of sites mentioned in the chapter.
4. TIMES timeline feature, one per chapter as relevant, showing labeled times of events or periods mentioned in the chapter.

Chapter Closers

- Commentary on or conclusion to the chapter opening field notes or excavation account
- Bulleted summary organized by A-head
- Annotated links list
- Quiz with ten objective items and answer feedback

11

Create Truly Useful Chapter Apparatus

THE FOLLOWING SECTIONS describe some options and suggestions for the structural aspects of your chapter pedagogy, such as your chapter openers and chapter closers. Suggestions are based on educational research and principles of effective direct and nondirect instruction, discussed briefly in Chapter 10. Suggestions also reflect standard practice in college textbook publishing. As preparation for reading this chapter, you might examine several textbooks on your office shelves and observe how chapters begin and end. Notice page layout and design elements that both distinguish and tie together these parts of the chapter apparatus.

The Chapter Opener

The chapter opening elements or devices that you and your editor choose will be applied consistently at the beginning of every chapter. Your publisher will incorporate the elements into a design for the page or spread that begins each chapter. Through their consistency in type and design and their appropriateness to your mission, these elements will become a distinguishing feature of your text. In addition, they will connect both to chapter content and to the chapter closers in a way that will unify your instruction.

The Overview and Introduction

An overview and introduction collectively explain what the chapter is about, why readers should learn about the material (or how they should begin thinking about it), and what kinds of information are involved (or what topics will be taken up).

Chapters may be grouped into parts, or units, and presented in part-opening overviews, or there may be a separate overview for each chapter. In other instances, part divisions are indicated in the table of contents (TOC) as a window on the textbook's organization, but the parts do not have actual text pages devoted to them for part openers. Part openers take up space in a book, so their use should have clear justification.

Overviews and introductions introduce the chapter theme and central concepts and also relate each chapter or part to the previous one, showing how the readers are advancing their knowledge by connecting intelligently to what they already have studied or already know. Well-considered and well-wrought overviews and introductions give your book integrity.

How, then, do overviews and introductions differ? Notice in the following examples from an international business text that the overview and the introduction, while interrelated, are not the same thing. The overview gives the big picture, while the introduction prepares readers for acquiring details from the chapter at hand. The last sentence of the introduction briefly foreshadows the six A-head sections that organize the chapter content.

Example: Chapter Overview
Chapter 9 outlined the main financial institutions that affect companies doing business internationally, including institutions for raising capital, managing debt, making investments, and facilitating the flow of funds. Now, Chapter 10 explores in greater depth the flow of direct foreign investment, in particular the efforts of both home and host countries to influence that flow to regulate multinational enterprises. You have seen how the actions of MNEs affect nations and individuals as citizens, as consumers, and as producers. Now, what efforts are made to control the actions of MNEs, and what impact do those efforts have on international business?

Example: Chapter Introduction
The reasons that MNEs engage in direct investment ownership are to expand markets by selling abroad; to acquire foreign resources, such as raw materials, inexpensive labor, and expertise; and, at a government level, to attain some political advantage. MNEs pursue these goals and seek to extend their control mainly through trade and direct investment. Home and host countries, in turn, control MNEs principally through trade restrictions, investment incentives, government ownership, regional economic cooperation, commodity and trade agreements, and foreign exchange rates.

Authors often slight overviews and introductions as nuisance writing or mere obligatory, pro forma gestures. Inexperienced authors often save them for last or leave them out entirely. Yet these elements are more than a matter of good exposition or sound instructional practice. They serve as self-monitoring devices, an author's best weapons against incoherence and a host of other follies. If you cannot write a two- or three-paragraph description of your chapter, encapsulating an explanation of why anybody should read it, then you are not ready to draft it.

However, overviews should not be first-person catalogues of authors' intentions. Consider, for instance, "In this chapter, first we talk about this; next we take up this other thing; then we cover that, that, and that; and finally we close with a consideration of this." In such an introduction, the focus is on the authors, secondarily on the subject, and not at all on the learners and the state of their knowledge. You are talking only to yourself. Rather, good introductions invite the student to read and learn the material.

The Outline and Focus Questions

Other than providing an overview or introduction, or both, the simplest way to prepare the reader for what is to come is to provide a chapter outline or a list of focus questions, or both. An outline at the beginning of each chapter presents the chapter headings and subheadings in the order they appear—a TOC without page references. Outlines can present all the levels of headings or just the main ones (see Chapter 9 on heading structure) and can include titled pedagogical features.

As a chapter-opening element, a list of questions at the beginning of a chapter or with a chapter outline alerts readers to the most important material to learn and thus guides their reading. If you conceptualize and frame your main headings as questions, then they automatically will suggest or serve as focus questions. In the following example of a chapter-opening outline, the focus questions are embedded in the chapter's A-heads.

Example: Embedded Focus Questions

Chapter 6 History of the Bantu to 1497
- What are the origins of the Bantu?
  - The Bantu Homeland in Western Africa
  - The Bantu Migrations
  - Bantu-Speaking Peoples Today
- What were the economic impacts of the Bantu migrations?
  - Farming and Herding
  - Cattle and Taro
  - Copper and Iron
- What Bantu kingdoms arose by the 15th century A.D.?
  - The Luba States
  - The Kongo Empire
  - Great Zimbabwe
- How did trade link the Bantu states with other peoples?
  - The East-West Central African Trade

African Trade in the Roman Era
The Arab and Asian Trade
The Portuguese

Alternatively, list focus questions after the outline, or key them to sections of the outline, letting readers know in more detail what they should expect to learn.

Example: Chapter Outline Followed by Focus Questions

Chapter 6 History of the Bantu to 1497
- Origins of the Bantu
  - The Bantu Homeland in Western Africa
  - The Bantu Migrations
  - Bantu-Speaking Peoples Today
- Economic Impacts of the Bantu Migrations
  - Farming and Herding
  - Cattle and Taro
  - Copper and Iron
- Bantu Kingdoms by the 15th Century A.D.
  - The Luba States
  - The Kongo Empire
  - Great Zimbabwe
- Trade Links Between the Bantu States and Other Peoples
  - The East-West Central African Trade
  - African Trade in the Roman Era
  - The Arabs and Asian Trade
  - The Portuguese

Focus Questions:

1. What are the geographic and ethnic origins of Bantu-speaking peoples in relation to their present-day distributions?
2. What were the patterns and trends of Bantu migration?
3. How did the Bantu migrations affect demographic, economic, and technological developments in Sub-Saharan Africa?
4. What factors contributed to the rise and spread of Bantu states?
5. How were the Luba, Lunda, Kongo, and Mwenenmutapa states alike and different?
6. How did trade link the Bantu states with peoples of Africa, the Middle East, Asia, and Europe?

As you can see, focus questions provide a basis for Steps 4, 5, and 6 in the model of direct instruction presented in Chapter 10. That is, students can assess their own levels of knowledge and comprehension by answering the questions independently, and instructors can assess students' learning by asking the questions in class or adapting them for use as test items. Thus, focus questions aid the instructor who assigns your chapters as well as the students who read them.

Learning Objectives or Outcomes

An alternative to focus questions, also useful to both students and instructors, is a list of learning objectives—another chapter opening device, like focus questions, with multiple functions. As you read in Chapter 8, learning objectives specify precisely what students are expected to know or be able to do after reading the chapter and studying the information. Learning outcomes state the intended result of meeting the objectives. These pedagogical devices are especially appropriate for introductory and second-tier college textbooks. Stating objectives or outcomes in your chapter openers is optional, an alternative to using focus questions.

Together with your system of text headings, learning objectives can integrate your pedagogy and drive your supplements. Objectives also provide you with clear goals for creating text features to support what you want your readers to gain from reading your textbook. Whether you state them or not, as you draft each chapter you should know what objectives or outcomes are guiding your efforts as an author–educator.

Scenarios and Vignettes

Another chapter-opening device is the scenario, also sometimes called a vignette. Scenarios and vignettes are brief descriptions of simulated or real-life situations, usually involving named characters or the reader. The situation is expressed in the form of a description, account, news clipping, dialogue, or story problem. Technically a *scenario* (Italian) is an outline of a plot or hypothesized chain of events, and a *vignette* (French) is a borderless image that blends decoratively into the page—a metaphor for writing that produces the same effect; that is, the situation merges seamlessly with text.

> **Example: Scenario**
> Imagine that you are being interviewed by a government census taker, who is asking you questions—how many people live in your household, what are their relationships to one another, and so on. Then the census taker asks you about your race and gives you five choices: White, Black, Asian/Pacific Islander, American Indian/Alaskan Native, and Other. You hesitate to answer. Although you are listed officially as White on your birth certificate and your mother's parents were from Western Europe, your father's grandparents included a Chinese, a Filipino, and an African American. What does that make you? You decide not to answer the question, but on the basis of your appearance

and your name the census taker records you as "White" and "of Spanish/Hispanic origin." You've been counted.

Example: Vignette

The facts of U.S. racial diversity were acknowledged in the 2000 census, which permitted multiracial classifications for the first time in American history. Previously, census takers gave respondents only five choices: White, Black, Asian/Pacific Islander, American Indian/Alaskan Native, and Other. (Persons of Spanish/Hispanic origin can be any race.) But what if your unofficial racial identity were a combination of these categories. Say you were listed officially as White on your birth certificate—your mother's parents were from Western Europe. But your father's grandparents included a Chinese, a Filipino, and an African American. How would you be classified according to the old census? How might you feel to be "Other?" The Census Bureau's addition of the category "Multiracial" in the 2000 census signaled an important change in American cultural perceptions of race.

Both scenarios and vignettes present situations, and situations stimulate interest. The situations let readers activate any prior knowledge or experience they have with the subject and enable them possibly to identify with the subjects. The situations also call attention to key issues the chapter will address and suggest the relevance of those issues for readers.

In some subject areas, chapter opening biographies, profiles, case studies, or product samples can serve the same purpose as scenarios. The value of scenarios and vignettes depends almost entirely on their reality or authenticity and their interest to readers. Following are some tips for writing effective scenarios.

Tips for Writing Effective Scenarios

- Be as authentic, true to life, and credible as possible.
- Avoid logically abstract scenarios (unless logic is the subject).
- Prefer real to hypothetical examples.
- Make hypothetical scenarios relate closely to the actual subject of the chapter.
- Use language to engender some excitement, but avoid tabloid style.
- Use present tense for immediacy, as appropriate.
- Use natural-sounding dialogue, as appropriate.
- Avoid stereotyping or bias in characterization.
- Include characters of both sexes who accurately reflect cultural diversity.

- Consider first-person accounts of your own or others' experiences.
- Edit verbatim accounts for audience appropriateness in print form.
- Refrain from prurient subjects and manipulations of readers' emotions.
- Avoid voyeurism, gratuitousness, excessive morbidity, and righteousness in tone.
- Include the outcome or result of the action or situation.
- Tie in the situation or example to the chapter's opening exposition.

To be effective, vignettes and scenarios must link directly to the content in the chapter introduction or the first A-head section of text. Vignettes by definition are embedded in relevant text, but for scenarios you need to call attention to how they link to chapter content rather than assume that students will make the connection automatically. For example, the following report of a school homicide could open a chapter about issues and trends in criminal justice, or about causes of violent crime, or about juvenile justice.

Example: Scenario

On April 20, 1999, in Littleton, Colorado, Columbine High School students Erik Harris and Dylan Klebold walked into their school with a semiautomatic pistol, a carbine, and two sawed-off shotguns. They laughed as they shot at people, ultimately killing twelve students and a coach. They also planted at least thirty pipe bombs and other explosives, discovered later, around the school. The pair often wrote and talked about killing people. They even made a video for class that showed them walking down the halls of their school, pretending to shoot friends dressed as hated classmates who had taunted or insulted them in the past. Then it all took a terrible turn into reality. Several copycat school homicides occurred—and some were prevented—in the weeks following the Columbine massacre.

This scenario could be tied to text quite simply by beginning the narrative exposition with a sentence of transition, as in the following examples.

Examples: Alternative transitions for linking the scenario to the chapter narrative

1. Public reaction to school homicides like this one in Colorado includes heightened fear of victimization, which often is heightened further by media coverage. The role of the media in public

perceptions of crime is a major issue in criminal justice today. What is that role?
2. The Colorado massacre described at the beginning of this chapter raises serious issues for contemporary society and the criminal justice system. What causes this type of crime? How can mass murders in schools be prevented? Who, or what, is accountable for the shocking rise in youth violence?
3. Today, school homicides—unheard of a century ago—and other violent crimes perpetrated by juveniles challenge the U.S. criminal justice system. School shootings topped the list of trends in crime in the 1990s. What are some of those trends?

Without a direct tie-in to the chapter content, the opening scenario is just a gimmick floating in the space allotted for chapter openers. Ending a scenario or vignette or its transition with a question to the reader enhances its pedagogical value, especially if you refer to the vignette again within your narrative as chapter concepts come to apply. A chapter-closing application can then ask students to answer the scenario question (or to solve the problem or correct the sample), using what they have learned in the chapter. Used in a functional, integrated way, then, scenarios can add pedagogical value to your book by reinforcing learning and permitting self-assessment. Examples of effective integrated scenarios follow.

Example: Effective Scenario A
Chapter 3 Language and Politics
In the opener: Bruce, a journalism student, researched and wrote a story on Christopher Columbus. His piece has been rejected without comment, however, by every paper he has sent it to. One editor drew a red X through the following paragraph:

> Columbus discovered the Caribbean islands, but he was slow on the uptake when it came to understanding where he was. Seeing near-naked redskins cowering behind the tree line, he realized he could not be in China. That he nevertheless named the natives Indians shows just how badly he wanted to believe that he was somewhere in the Orient.

After reading Chapter 2, you no doubt can spot Bruce's stylistic errors—his colloquialisms, euphemisms, and clichés, such as "slow on the uptake," "when it came to understanding," and "shows just how badly." However, even if Bruce edited the paragraph to eliminate these expressions, no really responsible editor would publish it. Why? What else does Bruce have to learn about appropriate usage in professional journalism?

In the body of the chapter narrative: <Elements of Bruce's paragraph are reiterated in connection with the concepts of attributions, racial and ethnic representations, and political correctness.>

In the chapter closer:
1. As the editor who crossed out Bruce's paragraph, write Bruce a letter explaining why you are not publishing his piece.
2. Using what you have learned in this chapter, rewrite Bruce's paragraph.

Example: Effective Scenario B

Chapter 11 Teachers' Rights and Responsibilities in School Law

In the opener: Mr. Wilson is a tenured physical education teacher at a suburban high school. He has been a teacher in good standing there for the last ten years. Lately, however, school administrators have received three complaints from parents of the girls' varsity basketball team that he has used offensive language and has invaded the privacy of team members in the girls' locker room. On the basis of these complaints, he has been given notice of dismissal. Can Mr. Wilson be dismissed legally for these reasons? What are his rights in the matter? What procedures must the school board follow in seeking to dismiss him?

In the narrative: <The case of Mr. Wilson is reiterated in connection with the concepts and provisions of tenure, dismissal, and due process, and the outcome of the case is explained.>

In the closer: <A related or parallel case is presented, and readers are asked to address the same questions, applying what they have learned.>

Example: Effective Scenario C

Chapter 18 Alcohols

In the opener: Lara and Hector are following all the steps that lead to the synthesis of complex alcohols. They have a firm grasp of the chemical properties and preparations involved, but their sequence of reactions keeps leading them deeper and deeper into a labyrinth of possibilities, and they are running out of time. Here is what they have so far.

<Figure 18.1, diagram of faulty chemical formula>

What is the source of their problem? How would you approach this challenge?

In the first section of narrative text: In the example at the beginning of this chapter, Hector and Lara forgot that organic synthesis of complex compounds involves working backwards. They knew the chemistry of the individual steps, but did not plan the most efficient route from their goal. In almost every organic synthesis it is best to begin with the molecule you want—the target molecule—and work backwards from it. In reality, there are only a few ways to make a complicated alcohol. For example, there are comparatively few ways to make a Grignard reagent or an aldehyde or ketone, and so on—back to your primary starting materials. Working the other way around, your starting materials can undergo so many different reactions that you discover a bewildering number of paths, few of which take you to where you want to go.

In the closer: Lara and Hector were attempting to make tricyclopropylmethanol, although you wouldn't know it from their partial formula. Using the basic principle of organic synthesis, draw your own formula for achieving this product.

As you can see, scenarios or vignettes take a little thought. They are, however, among the most effective chapter openers in any subject, which is why they are so common in textbooks.

Epigrams and Quotes

Epigrams—brief quotations—prepare the reader in a more reflective way and can be very effective when combined with chapter opening photographs. The use of chapter opening photos is an industry standard in introductory textbooks. With or without photos, however, epigrams can set the tone of a chapter and reinforce its principal theme.

Epigrams should be more than merely inspirational or decorative. Authors too often leave epigrams floating without narrative or pedagogical context, as if the clever, witty, coy, cute, ironic, telling, acerbic, harrowing, or nostalgic little nuggets of thought were themselves entirely sufficient. For follow-through, the chapter closer might reiterate the quotation and ask students to reinterpret it in terms of what they have learned.

Example: Epigram A

For a chapter on "getting started" in a textbook on writing:

> "The great enemy of clear language is insincerity. When there is a gap between one's real and one's declared aims, one turns, as it were instinctively, to long words and exhausted idioms, like a cuttlefish squirting out ink."
>
> —George Orwell

In the closer: Review the epigram at the beginning of this chapter and clarify its meaning in light of what you have read. Then write three paragraphs using specific examples to answer each of the following questions.

1. How does clarity of expression depend on clear intentions?
2. How does Orwell's statement reflect his claim?
3. What problems of style other than "long words and exhausted idioms" can develop when writers are "insincere?"

Example B: Epigram
For a chapter on "pragmatism" in a philosophy textbook:

> "The philosophy which is so important in each of us is not a technical matter; it is our more or less dumb sense of what life honestly and deeply means. It is only partly got from books; it is our individual way of just seeing and feeling the total push and pressure of the cosmos."
>
> —William James

In the closer: To what philosophy does William James refer in the quotation at the beginning of this chapter? According to James, what is the basis of this philosophy and what is its source? How does the quotation suggest the influence James had on the educational philosophy of John Dewey and his followers?

The epigram is an old-fashioned but timeless device. It is suitable not only for the arts and humanities, but for any textbook in which the intended primary learning objective is to reflect on ideas.

Internal Apparatus

Introductory college textbooks often have internal pedagogy as part of chapter apparatus. Each A-head section may begin with a thesis statement or main point, for example, and each A-head section may end with a summative statement or review question. These regular elements of internal apparatus may be distinguished from the regular text through book design.

As noted in Chapter 10, another common treatment is to boldface key terms in the narrative and define them in margin glosses. Regular marginalia, such as definitions, topical headings, cross-references, URLs, or other kinds of information, may contribute to the internal structure of chapters, especially if your textbook will be an annotated instructor's edition or an interactive edition.

When choosing elements of your internal apparatus, consider how much structure, direction, assistance, and convenience your readers need to learn what you want them to know most quickly and most efficiently. Too many elements will clutter the page and confuse the reader. Too few will raise the difficulty level and reduce the learning rate.

Some college instructors, unsympathetic toward learners, believe that internal apparatus spoon-feeds readers, who should be struggling for enlightenment. The assumption seems to be that only hard-won knowledge will be retained. However, removing obstacles to learning, rather than creating them, should be your goal as an author–educator.

Chapter Closers

Much has already been said about the pedagogical value of chapter closers (see Chapter 10). Among the most useful closers—and often the most underrated by authors—are the conclusion and summary. In structure and function, a chapter's conclusion and summary mirror its overview and introduction. Other kinds of chapter closers serve to satisfy the requirements of knowledge transfer or application.

The Conclusion

Just as the introduction is not a list of intentions, the conclusion is not a rehash of what you covered or tried to accomplish in the chapter. Such a rehash focuses on you as an author and subject expert rather than on knowledge. Some conclusion is needed, however. Consider the following paragraph, which ends a chapter on millenarian movements in a comparative religion textbook and is immediately followed by a new chapter.

Example: Lack of Conclusion

Finally, an example from nineteenth-century North America is the ghost dance cult, a millenarian movement among Native Americans of the Great Plains. This religious movement had two spreads in the 1870s and the 1880s at times of increasing population pressure and dislocation through contact with westward-migrating Anglo-Europeans. The second movement began among the Paiutes in Nevada, initiated by the prophet Wovoka, and quickly spread to the Arapaho, Cheyenne, Dakota, and others. Wovoka received from the Great Spirit a vision of the resurrection of the dead and the restoration of traditional ways of life. He returned to his people with a message of hope and a dance ritual to be performed for five consecutive days at frequent intervals. His message was reinterpreted and added to wherever it was carried. In some groups, it included the return of buffalo—slaughtered by plainsmen for sport or to supply railroad builders—and the destruction of the white man. The cult was expressed through religious symbolisms as well as through the trance-inducing collective dancing. The ghost dance cult did not die out until after the massacre of more than 300 Sioux at Wounded Knee Creek, South Dakota, in 1890.

What will readers make of the information in this chapter? Not much. There is no conclusion, no interpretation of significance, no unifying thought. The readers are intended merely to acquire information as discrete bits for their own sake and for no other apparent reason than that the author regards these bits as important for them to know. This is the "flash card" or "encyclopedia" approach to education, evident in many college textbooks. While flash cards and encyclopedias have their place, educational research shows that students taught this way never learn to connect up information or even ask, "So what?" The chapter needs a conclusion. Consider the value of even a brief conclusion such as the following for the chapter on millenarian movements.

Example: Conclusion

Thus, the spread of religious ideas in response to conquest, missionary activity, and other intercultural contact has occurred throughout the ages and throughout the world. As you have seen, whatever form they take, millenarian movements constitute an adaptive response to changes that have led to real or perceived cultural inadequacy or that have resulted in profound physical, cultural, or psychological loss.

Conclusions and the ability to draw conclusions are indispensable to learning. At the same time, conclusions and summaries are not appropriate places for introducing new information or adding new details.

The Summary

Experienced authors look forward to writing their chapter summaries. These are moments of truth. While drafting a summary you find out if your chapter contains everything that it should, progresses logically, and makes sense as a whole. If the summary proves a difficult task or takes more than 20 minutes to draft, then something is wrong with the way the chapter has been conceived and executed. In a textbook, a chapter summary is a test of teaching effectiveness.

Ideally, your main headings for each section are in the form of questions, or at least are convertible to questions or imply them. Your summary, whether in the form of paragraphs or a numbered or bulleted list of main points, should answer those questions in a clear, concise way. Some authors even restate the questions as subheadings that structure the summary. Answers then emerge naturally during a review of the content in each section.

In the following example, a five-page A-head section from an introduction to teaching textbook is summarized using one sentence (more or less) per heading, for an average of less than two lines of type per page of text.

Example: Summary for a Section of Text

Outline of Section:

<A> What Is Taught in the Schools?
- <B> Kinds of Curriculum
  - <C> Explicit Curriculum
  - <C> Hidden Curriculum
  - <C> Null Curriculum
  - <C> Extracurriculum
- <B> Curriculum Content

Summary of Section:

What is taught (and not taught) is called the curriculum—the subject areas, course content, learning outcomes, and planned and unplanned experiences that affect student learning. Four curricula that all students experience are the explicit curriculum, the hidden (implicit) curriculum, the null curriculum, and extracurricular programs. In all four forms, curriculum content reflects what communities and the wider society believe is important for students to learn.

A summary should be a content review, but not a catalogue of what has been covered, which is sure to be boring and unhelpful to learners. Compare the following poor summary to the one above for the section on curriculum in the education textbook.

Example: Summary in an Inappropriate Style

In this chapter we first discussed the problem of defining what is meant by curriculum, pointing out the lack of universal agreement on what the concept of curriculum should entail. We then offered a broad definition that takes into account all the experiences that affect students and their education. We

> discussed the explicit curriculum, the hidden curriculum, the null curriculum, and the extracurriculum. Last, we turned our attention to curriculum content.

A summary such as the above might be reassuring to you in your role as author, but it does not bespeak your role as teacher, and it imparts little or nothing of value to the reader.

Other Chapter Endmatter

Chapter closers also can include activities for application or extension, such as problem sets or Internet activities, chapter quizzes, annotated recommended readings for students, topical cross-references, chapter notes or references, key terms and glosses, or other pedagogical devices. For example, a chapter in a textbook on applied finite mathematics might have end-of-chapter application activities in which students use linear programming to solve real-life problems in production scheduling, shipping costs, asset allocation, crop planning, mining production, and diet planning in fields as diverse as transportation and advertising.

One of the most difficult ideas for authors and editors to grasp is that elements in the chapter apparatus are intended to have functional interrelationships. As you have seen, for example, openers and closers have related or matched content, like bookends. An effective closing application relates to the opening scenario. Functional interrelationships usually extend even to design. Design motifs may represent classes or sources of information and be mirrored in text features. Design elements also may link text content to supplements and other external resources.

The number of elements in chapter closers and their length depends on your audience, subject, teaching goals, learning objectives, market, and competition. Decisions about closing elements also depend on the relative need for independent practice or concept transfer on the part of learners. In mathematics and English composition textbooks for required undergraduate courses, for example, chapter closers can run several pages. Chapter closers in textbooks with built-in readings, annotated book lists, study guides, or practice tests also run long. Regardless, all pedagogical elements add to the length, bulk, weight, and cost of a book—more reason for choosing wisely.

In keeping with the message of this chapter, here is a brief conclusion. In this case, however, it is you who must draw the conclusions, based on your answers to the following questions: What will be the right mix of functionally interrelated chapter openers and chapter closers for your book? What are you providing to students in your chapter apparatus to aid their active learning and to make your textbook indispensable to them? You may find the planning sheet in the chapter appendix useful to start choosing and defining specific apparatus for your textbook.

APPENDIX
Planning Your Apparatus

PART OPENING ELEMENTS	POSSIBLE TEXT APPLICATIONS
Part Overview	
Part Outline	
Other	
CHAPTER OPENING ELEMENTS	POSSIBLE TEXT APPLICATIONS
Chapter Overview	
Introduction	
Chapter Outline	
Focus Questions	
Learning Objectives/Outcomes	
Scenario/Vignette	
Epigram/Other	
INTERNAL APPARATUS	POSSIBLE TEXT APPLICATIONS
Section Openers	
Section Closers	
Terms and Definitions	
Marginalia/Other	
CHAPTER CLOSING ELEMENTS	POSSIBLE TEXT APPLICATIONS
Conclusion	
Summary	
Key Terms/Vocab. Review	
Discussion/Review Questions	
Chapter Quiz/Study Guide	
Applications/Problems	
Activities	
Annotated Readings	
Chapter End Notes	
PART CLOSING ELEMENTS	POSSIBLE TEXT APPLICATIONS
Part Summary	
Other	

12

Develop Successful Feature Strands

PEDAGOGY ONLY BEGINS with the chapter apparatus, the subject of Chapter 11. Regularly occurring pedagogical features within the body of each chapter, often called feature strands, also contribute to the educative value and visual appeal of your textbook. The features described in the following sections—case studies, debates, primary source excerpts, models or how-tos, reflection and critical thinking questions, thematic boxes, and supplement tie-ins—need not be restricted to internal use, however. In some textbooks they are successfully located at the beginning or end of a chapter. Features such as case studies, reflections, primary source documents, and biographical profiles are especially adaptable as chapter openers or as material on which chapter-closing activities are based. As a rule of thumb, place each feature where it will do students the most good—that is, in its most relevant context in relation to chapter content and to what you are trying to put across.

Types of Internal Text Features

The types of features you choose should be guided by what your market requires or prefers, what your competition has, what your publisher suggests, and your own ideas. Whatever features you choose, you must use them systematically in every chapter, or at least regularly and not just here and there. Authors sometimes resist this kind of consistency, especially when they think certain features are more suitable for some chapters than for others. Yet consistency is necessary. In the following promotion for a biology textbook revision, imagine the impression the new feature strands might make.

> **Example: Poor Impression Caused by Inconsistent Feature Strands**
> The following text features, new to this edition, were designed to capture the interest of your students and help them integrate the knowledge they gain in this course.

BIOLOGY IN SPACE: A news feature that links chapter content to NASA research, including findings from the Space Shuttle program and SpaceLab experiments. This feature appears in Chapters 2, 3, and 7.

PIONEERS IN BIOLOGICAL SCIENCE: An illustrated biographical feature that briefly tells the stories of the people and events behind historically significant developments in biology. This feature appears in Chapters 1, 14, and 15.

Randomly scattered features like these do not inspire confidence. Feature strands by definition are carried out regularly throughout a textbook, ideally in every chapter. You can overcome the problem of consistency and fit by conceptualizing a feature strand in broad enough terms to make it applicable in every chapter. For instance, in the above example, if relevant information were insufficient to have a BIOLOGY IN SPACE box in every chapter (not likely), you could call the feature strand BIOLOGY IN LIFE instead (pun intended) and include your NASA examples among others.

Each type of feature has a name or title—sometimes called a tag line—and is distinguished from the running text through design. A real title and a design help unify a feature strand throughout your book and generate readership. Titles such as Box 1.1, Box 1.2, and Box 1.3 do not invite readership, but feature strands called SOCIOLOGY IN ACTION or ASTRONOMY'S GREATEST DISCOVERIES do. Subtitles then identify the specific subject of each box. Titled feature strands also help your publisher promote your book, and the sales force sell it.

As mentioned in Chapter 10, some authors and instructors scorn all "boxes" and do not provide or assign them. Critics claim that features make the text too boxy or jumpy, distract the reader from the "real" reading, or compromise intellectual rigor for interest or popularity. These are the authors and instructors who believe strongly that textbooks should not pander to students and that students rightly should struggle to decipher text. When properly done, however, boxes are integral parts of the chapter, not dispensable frills or add-ons. Good feature strands help fulfill your mission in writing a textbook, can add rigor as well as interest, and often provide the in-depth concrete examples that students need to grasp or apply core concepts. Therefore, consider the following feature strands with an open mind. What kinds could you use in your textbook?

Case Studies

Case-based instruction is a mainstay in fields such as business, advertising, management, law, education, social work, and others in which the particulars of an actual circumstance are used to test or demonstrate chapter concepts or principles in action. The best cases are real and situational, consist of accurate reportage, and end with questions for the reader. The questions invite readers to reflect on, analyze, compare or contrast, apply, or evaluate the information in the case. Case studies engage readers in cognitive processes that are desirable in active learners, such as critical thinking and problem solving. They also give instructors the option of using case analysis as a basis for class discussion or course assessment. In some courses, such as law, cases are regarded as mandatory.

Following are two examples of case studies, one for a chapter on the impact of cultural environments on multinational business and one for a chapter on assimilation and pluralism in a textbook on multicultural education.

Example: Case Study A
CASE TO CONSIDER: Cultural Assumptions

In the 1970s, a publishing house set up an operation in Bahrain to edit the first telephone and business directories for thirteen Arab states. Problems began when the company could not find sufficient qualified personnel on or near the Arabian Peninsula to work on the project. The publisher filled four key positions through ads in newspapers. Its staff then included a young single woman as editor and three salesmen.

None of the new hires had visited the Middle East before, and all expected to conduct business as usual. The salesmen, on commission, expected to make the usual number of calls in a 9-to-5 day. They also expected to have appointments at scheduled times, the undivided attention of potential clients, and efficient business transactions. These expectations were not met, however. After many complaints from Arab businessmen, the salesmen were replaced, but the damage to sales could not be recovered.

The editor found that she was not free to travel unaccompanied in Arab countries and could not easily hire freelance assistants during her travels. She had assumed that collecting the data for the telephone directories would be a simple, cost-effective task. The publisher had quoted prices on the assumption that all streets would have names and that all residences and businesses would have street numbers, which proved not to be the case.

After two years, the company had to sell its floundering Bahraini operations. What, exactly, went wrong? What factors contributed to failure there, and how might the problems have been prevented or addressed? What guidelines would you propose for multinational firms planning to conduct foreign operations?

Example: Case Study B
THE CASE OF MARIA GONZALEZ

Maria sits proudly in the student lounge of a prestigious U.S. university. She thinks how if had not been for her mother and grandmother her life would be completely different now. She recalls her mother's immigrant stories about her childhood: the move from Mexico City; the humiliation of not speaking English; the move to the suburbs and becoming American at all costs. Then her mother was introduced to Carlos Gonzales, rediscovered her roots and the joys of Latin dancing, music, and poetry. There were feasts with grandmother's cooking and trips back to the old village for the Day of the Dead. Maria and her brothers were taught to be proud of their Mexican heritage, and all are fluent in Spanish and English. Maria wonders about the other students in the student lounge and if they will expect her to be like them. She vows that she will succeed at the university while still maintaining her roots.

As with chapter openers, the pedagogical value of case studies increases when they are reiterated in some way within the chapter narrative and in the closing elements. The case of Maria, for example, might employ any of the following strategies.

Examples: Linking cases to instruction in the chapter introduction
The case of Maria Gonzalez suggests the pressures and conflicts that students from microcultures often confront as they try to adjust to the macroculture of a school. Maria determines to retain her Chicana identity as a U.S. citizen. Her decision reflects the process of cultural pluralism or accommodation, as distinct from assimilation or absorption into the host culture.

In the body of the narrative in a discussion of degrees of assimilation:

Recall Maria Gonzalez's story at the beginning of this chapter. If cultural assimilation is at one end of the continuum and cultural suppression is at the other, where would Maria's position fall on the continuum?

In the body of the narrative in a discussion of Mexican–American race relations:

The story of Maria Gonzalez illustrates the tension between cultural pluralism and assimilation felt by many Mexican-Americans who are bicultural. She is pulled in two different directions and must adjust to two different needs: the need to keep her identity as a Chicana with a rich culture and history and the need to be accepted by her classmates.

In the chapter conclusion:

Students like Maria Gonzalez experience cultural conflict. Most American schools have students who, like Maria, feel the pressures of a dual identity as a result of living within two cultures simultaneously. Multicultural education has developed in recognition of this reality.

As a closing activity or an item in the test bank or study guide supplement:

Contrast the case of Maria Gonzalez to that of Isaac Washington. What are the essential differences in their experiences as members of microcultures? What are the essential differences in their responses to biculturalism?

Case studies are not suitable for all subject areas. Consider them for your textbook, however. Like scenarios and vignettes, cases often are easily and appropriately adaptable for both "soft" and "hard" academic courses.

Profiles

Profiles offer detailed descriptive accounts of particular examples (or exemplars) of chapter content. Like case studies, profiles explore a selected topic in greater depth. Business, management, and marketing texts, for example, often highlight the success stories of particular individuals, firms, or advertising campaigns. An archaeology text might profile excavations of particularly important sites. A professional book might have career profiles. Literature surveys might have biographical or historical profiles to provide context for selections of literature; and texts on government, international politics, urban sociology, or cultural geography might offer chapter-by-chapter cartographic and statistical profiles.

In addition to providing data, profiles most often feature positive exemplars, such as famous or successful people, places, products, or events. Positive real-life profiles in each chapter can provide strong motivation to read. A marketing textbook might profile the founders of Ben and Jerry's Ice Cream and other entrepreneurs. A teacher education textbook might profile winners of the national Teacher of the Year award. An American architectural history textbook might profile the F. W. Woolworth Building and other famous edifices, and so on.

As with other kinds of feature strands, the pedagogical value of profiles increases with opportunities for students to interact with the information beyond simple comprehension. Applications at the end of the marketing profiles might ask students to find other current examples of the kinds of success shown or to visit the profiled companies' websites. Applications at the end of the teacher profiles might ask students to identify positive attributes or to find out more about the subjects.

Debates

Some textbooks lend themselves to features that present opposing views on chapter-relevant issues. Pro–con or point–counterpoint features are especially appropriate for textbooks in the social sciences and related fields and for introductions to the professions. The keys to successful debate formats are balance, fairness, and credibility, so some care must be taken in selecting spokespersons for opposing views. Identify those persons by name and source, and give their views equal space. Again, end the features with questions for the reader. The following example suggests possible topics for a debate feature for a half-page, two-column feature in a behavioral psychology text.

Example: Topics for a Debate Feature

Chapter 3 Biology and Behavior—DEBATE FORUM: Are there sex differences in the way people think?

Chapter 5 Environment and Behavior—DEBATE FORUM: Can environmental controls on behavior solve social problems?

Chapter 8 Motivation and Behavior—DEBATE FORUM: Do people fear success as much as they do failure?

The design formats for a debate feature may be based on polarization, with a "PRO" or "YES" column juxtaposed beside a "CON" or "NO" column. Another option is to present the feature in three parts: Part one states the issue, part two describes the debate, and part three asks readers about a solution. Debate features might end with specific versions of some of the following generic questions.

Example: Questions for a Debate Feature

- With which view or combination of views do you agree most?
- Which evidence or argument did you find most persuasive, and why?

- How do your past experiences relate to these opposing views?
- What further evidence or argument might you add to the debate?
- How does the information in this chapter relate to this debate?
- What are the implications of each view for practice or policy?
- What questions would you ask and what answers would you need to strengthen or change your view?

To make effective debate features, choose current and authentic issues and avoid insulting the reader's intelligence. The best debates represent true dilemmas in which both or all positions on an issue can be believably defended. Above all, avoid the language of high-minded sentiment or propaganda and offer documented evidence and arguments based on facts. Note that values clarification typically is not a goal of debate features in college textbooks today, but ethical or professional dilemmas may be entirely appropriate along with policy debates.

Primary Source Excerpts

Excerpts from documents, first-person accounts, artifacts or exhibits of evidence, and passages from literature are examples of the use of primary sources in textbooks. Primary source material is all but indispensable in some arts and humanities—including history, philosophy, and literature—and also in the social sciences. If your field is document-based, why not build the need for primary source material into a regular chapter feature?

> **Examples: Primary Source Feature Strands**
>
> SNAPSHOTS OF THE PAST (in an undergraduate U.S. history textbook, 1865 to the present): a half-page-per-chapter feature on the interpretation of photographs as historical evidence. Each photograph relates to the period or theme of the chapter and supports a main point. An extended caption identifies the link between the photo and the chapter, provides background information on the event captured, guides the reader through the image, models the historiographical process involved in treating the image as evidence, and asks questions pertaining to all of the above.
>
> THE PHILOSOPHER'S STONE (in a textbook on philosophy for a survey course): two, one-page features per chapter with excerpts from classic works by noted philosophers representative of the chapter's period, theme, or main point. Excerpts end with questions to readers to stimulate reflection, aid comprehension, or guide analysis. This model is also commonly used in literature surveys.

FIELD NOTES (in a textbook on cultural anthropology): a one-page feature in each chapter with a transcription of a noted ethnographer's first-person account of his or her field experiences. Students are asked to interpret the field notes or to explain their significance in relation to chapter content.

TEACHER TALK (in a textbook on becoming a teacher): one-page, first-person accounts by practicing master teachers on how they deal with situations pertaining to main chapter topics.

Substantive excerpts are best for primary source features because they enable readers to examine critical material in some depth or detail. An in-depth feature also can serve as an antidote to a common complaint about survey texts—that in attempting to cover too much they merely "mention" everything superficially. If your textbook is for a survey course, therefore, consider that primary sources, cases, debates, or profiles might systematically permit more depth.

Arguments against using primary source material are the time it takes to find them and the permissions costs, which in some cases can be prohibitively high. Whatever the course, in addition to primary source documents, consider the role that brief first-person accounts or documentary excerpts might play in your exposition. Anecdotes, famous quotations, unusual newspaper headlines, or provocative government statistics might contribute to your pedagogical aims as well as your publisher's marketing campaign.

Models or How-Tos

Models in any field are applications or demonstrations of practices, principles, theories, or laws expressed in form or function. Models are examples of perfection, or at least of excellence or ideal cases (all other things being equal). The implicit message of any model is that it should be followed.

English composition textbooks, for example, model good writing. An emphasis on decision-making processes in marketing could be translated into a feature strand in which a model marketing decision is presented in each chapter. A textbook on research might model steps in the scientific method. A textbook on law enforcement or on accounting might model professional routines or procedures. A primatology or climatology textbook might present predictive models that readers run to answer questions. A chemistry textbook might contain diagrams of reactions and compounds, an example of models in the most literal sense as illustrations. Textbooks on chemistry, mathematics, photography, and architectural design typically rely on physical models in the form of graphical representations.

Related to models are "how-to" features, usually presented as numbered lists set off from the narrative. The lists briefly call out the sequence of steps needed to accomplish something or to apply a method. In some textbooks, the lists give reminders or tips for successful practice. Eye-catching how-to boxes offer the reader a resource for quick reference or immediate access to what you are attempting to teach in each chapter. How-tos are especially appropriate if your textbook and its market have a practical or applied orientation. This book contains many such lists, for instance.

In any field, educational research strongly supports the use of modeling as a method of instruction. Activities calling for applications to new contexts are an ideal way to maximize the pedagogical value of models. Consider, for example, an educational psychology textbook that zeroes in on teaching standards and teaching practice as the central purposes of study in the course. All the chapter pedagogy directly supports these purposes, such as an opening case, self-checks relating to the INTASC and PRAXIS II standards, "Theory into Practice" features, a teaching practice checklist, and a self-assessment in the chapter closer.

Reflection and Critical Thinking Questions

Reflective features present situations and invite readers to perceive, think about, and respond to those situations in relation to themselves as individuals. The goal is to engage the reader's personal identification with the subject, prior knowledge, thought processes, and affective responses. Reflections often are built around questions and include an activity such as recording thoughts and feelings in a journal or filling out a rating form. Questionnaires, opinion polls, and self-assessments also are forms of this type of feature. Reflection questions are geared to the individual learner and often are not well suited for class discussion.

In an introductory American government text, for example, chapters might contain reflection features built on the following questions.

Example: Reflection-Based Feature Strand

Chapter 1 Understanding American Government
REFLECTION: What are three questions you have about American government to which you wish you had answers?

Chapter 2 The Constitutional Foundations
REFLECTION: As a participant in the Constitutional Convention, what part of the Constitution might you have tried to change from its present form, and why?

Chapter 3 Civil Liberties
REFLECTION: On any given day, how, specifically, does the way you live your life reflect the Constitutional Amendments?

Chapter 4 Public Opinion
REFLECTION: What is your opinion on the following issues? Which issues would you feel strongly enough about to try to influence lawmakers if you had the opportunity?

Chapter 5 Political Parties
REFLECTION: Where do you stand on the liberal–conservative continuum?

Questions for reflection features might also take specific forms of the following general patterns:

- If you were presented with the following situation what would you do?
- In the following situation what could you say [e.g., to reduce tension and redirect the conversation]?
- Rate the following statements on a five-point scale from "strongly agree" (1) to "strongly disagree" (5). Your ratings will help you clarify your philosophical stance on this issue.
- Record in your journal three reasons you think you would like to become a gerontologist.

Some textbooks have reflection-based rating forms that invite readers to interact with text literally by writing in the book. Write-on lines are provided in the margins or in spaces designed to resemble note cards. At one time, if students wrote in your book, its sales would increase, because many college bookstores would not buy back "defaced" books for resale as used books. However, that standard, too, has fallen. Resale operators buy back books at the full used book price regardless of students' underlinings, marginal notes, or completed exercises.

In addition, blank spaces for student write-ins can take up a lot of expensive space in a textbook, leaving you with less room to accomplish your instructional goals. If your course requires many opportunities for on-page student practice, it might be best to plan a lower-cost student supplement to accompany your textbook, such as a manual, workbook, or study guide.

Reflection questions often require critical thinking, and many college textbooks offer sets of critical thinking questions as part of the chapter pedagogy rather than as a feature strand. Critical thinking questions also can be appended to other feature strands to make them interactive, to link them to chapter content, and to guarantee reader response. This book contains many such examples.

Unlike discussion and review questions, critical thinking questions are not answerable directly from the chapter narrative and do not have one right answer or established parameters for an expected range of answers. Critical thinking questions are not merely rhetorical, however, nor are they simply statements of opinion. The questions involve the reader's experiences and expectations outside the course, and students support their opinions with reasoned judgments or argue from premises or data.

The best way to get students to keep your title on their shelves is to provide a work that is so full of valuable, relevant information that users see it as indispensable. Students tend to hold on to reference books, handbooks, bibliographies, directories, and professional resource guides. Many authors add appendices or reference sections to their books that serve student interests and encourage retention. The reality is, however, that by the end of your textbook's first semester of availability, students will sell back as much as 60 percent of your print run, which will be sold as used books to the next semester's students.

Thematic Boxes

A selling point for a textbook is its currency, not only in source citations, but in the presence of themes that reflect the latest hot topics or professional concerns and trends in the field. For example, genome research may be a central concern in the life sciences, new medications and new assistive technologies may be issues in special education, crime scene investigation and crime mapping may be hot in criminal justice, and non-ethnocentric reinterpretation may be a trend in U.S. history. Each of these examples could serve as a unifying theme for a feature strand in the form of thematic boxes.

Each chapter in a life sciences textbook, for example, could have an informational box on how genetics research relates to the chapter or on the implications of genetics research for the chapter's main subject. There could be boxes on food staple genomes in relation to world hunger, mutagenic environments, the preservation of natural pharmacopoeia, endangered species, gene therapies, square watermelons, pharaonic DNA, and so on, throughout. In the special education textbook, each chapter could have an informational box on medications or assistive technologies for students with disabilities or for inclusive classrooms. Each chapter of the criminal justice textbook could feature a relevant technology, such as 911 emergency systems, crime mapping, electronic surveillance, DNA testing, sex crimes databasing, interrogation videotaping, cruiser-mounted cameras or computers, and the like. Finally, each chapter of the history text could have a cultural awareness box that calls attention to interesting or relevant ethnocentric views or interpretations of historical figures and events.

The content of thematic boxes reinforces points made in the narrative but does not attempt to substitute for narrative text, where all important exposition should appear. Reinforcement of information in a history textbook, for instance, might be provided through thematic chronologies or timelines, or through descriptions of critical decisions, benchmarks, or turning points.

A theme adaptable to many disciplines is the investigative report, media application, or research brief. For example, you might have a box in each chapter describing recent important research in your field in the form of an abstract or a summary of the findings. Imaginative, well-written, and well-designed thematic boxes add contemporaneity, interest, pertinence, and visual appeal for your readers. In addition, thematic feature strands support one of the chief metacognitive aims of education: the integration of knowledge.

Supplement Tie-Ins

In integrated textbook packages, having pedagogical features that link supplements to the text can be an important selling point. If your textbook will come with a reader, magazine, videotape, software, CD-ROM, or companion website, for example, you and your editor should think about embedding feature strands in the text that relate to them. Likewise, your instructor's manual should suggest ways that instructors can use the textbook's features in conjunction with supplements to aid learning.

Your ability to tie in supplements will depend on what your publisher plans to include with your textbook. If your package will include a videotape, for example, you might have a feature that addresses the subject of a related video segment. If your textbook will appear as an interactive edition with web links and other media assets, you may want to plan an in-text feature strand that relates to these capabilities. Decisions about supplements, a subject that is beyond the scope of this book, are made by managers and editors in consultation with authors. See *Writing and Developing College Textbook Supplement*s (Atlantic Path Publishing).

Firming Up Your Pedagogy Plan

Consider surveying the textbooks you have at hand to examine and analyze the use of pedagogical features. As a framework for this study, use your notes from the Chapter 10 Appendix, "Developing Your Pedagogy Plan," and the Chapter 11 Appendix, "Planning Your Apparatus." Then use the planning grid in this chapter's appendix, "Planning Your Feature Strands," to think of possibilities for features for your textbook. Choose feature strands with the following characteristics.

- Address proven needs in your course.
- Address new concerns in your field.

- Fit your subject.
- Match or top what your competitors offer.
- Make visible a special strength or unique aspect of your textbook.
- Express your mission or key themes.
- Are relevant to the audience.
- Engage student interest, curiosity, and desire.
- Can be fulfilled realistically and efficiently.
- Can be provided systematically throughout the textbook.

After choosing the feature types that have the most promising applications for your book, consult your working TOC to start brainstorming suitable topics for each feature type in each chapter. Also note sources of information for each feature or the names of possible contributors. Add these ideas to the ideas you developed for chapter apparatus, and then communicate these ideas to your sponsoring editor or development editor, who might also have some useful suggestions, samples, or models for you to consider. Then, reflecting on this input, revise and submit the pedagogy plan you developed after reading Chapter 10.

In some cases your editors may submit a proposed pedagogy plan to you for your review. Either way, everyone eventually must buy in to the planned apparatus and pedagogy for your textbook, and once this happens you may not change it. You will be expected to carry out the approved plan or to arrange for it to be carried out, or the publisher might hire someone to carry out the pedagogy plan in your place. The reason that changes may not be made after a certain point is that changes cost time and money. Substantive changes to a book's approved design, for example, which includes complex coding for each element of your apparatus and pedagogy, often are too costly.

Now you have a plan for your chapter apparatus and pedagogy that will make your book competitive in the marketplace and that everyone likes. Include your feature strands (titles and subtitles) in your working TOC, putting them in their respective contexts. Now you are ready to draft or revise your manuscript in earnest, and this is the subject of the next chapter.

APPENDIX
Planning Your Feature Strands

Feature Type	Possible Applications to Your Textbook
Case Studies	
Profiles	
Debates	
Primary Sources	
Models/How-Tos	
Reflections	
Critical Thinking	
Thematic Boxes	
Supplement Tie-Ins	
Other	

YOUR DECISIONS ABOUT FEATURE STRANDS	
Feature Name	**Possible Topical Applications by Chapter**
STRAND 1:	1
	2
	3
	4
	5
	6
	7
	8
	9
	10
	11
	12
	13
	14
	15

YOUR DECISIONS ABOUT FEATURE STRANDS	
Feature Name	**Possible Topical Applications by Chapter**
STRAND 2:	1
	2
	3
	4
	5
	6
	7
	8
	9
	10
	11
	12
	13
	14
	15

STRAND 3:	1
	2
	3
	4
	5
	6
	7
	8
	9
	10
	11
	12
	13
	14
	15

13

Make Drafting and Revising Easier

YOU CAN MAKE AUTHORING EASIER on yourself and your editors in basic ways, beginning with the following.

- Observe requirements for manuscript preparation.
- Submit complete manuscript.
- Make a commitment to consistency in style.
- Develop checklists to manage the drafting process.
- Systematically manage chapter resources.
- Monitor balance in topical development.
- Complete references as you draft.
- Respond productively to the copyeditor's work.
- Develop a revision plan.

How can you accomplish these tasks efficiently?

Preparing Manuscript

Authors who follow manuscript preparation guidelines decrease the cost of producing their books in countless small ways. These costs affect your earnings as well as your publishers'. Thus, as mentioned previously, you should follow or question even seemingly trivial requests in author guidelines and from editors, because there are practical or technical reasons for those requests. More than in the past, many houses are unwilling to incur extra production costs, even when these costs are charged against your book and passed back to you. Your improperly prepared manuscript is simply rejected as "unacceptable" and is returned to you for correction. Depending on how long it takes you to fix it, your book can lose its place in the publishing queue.

Manuscript Preparation Guiidelines

The University of Florida's manuscript preparation guidelines for authors are among the best generally applicable ones I've seen. (**upf.com/**

MSGuidelines.pdf). See other all-purpose guidelines at Harvard University Press (**hup.harvard.edu/authors**) and the University of Chicago Press guidelines for electronic manuscripts (**press.uchicago.edu/Misc/Chicago/emsguide.html**). Each house has its own unique rules for how manuscript should be prepared, but all will request that the hard copy and disc copy that you submit as final manuscript match exactly. You also must be vigilant to ensure that the correct, most current version of each chapter is the one that goes into production.

Following are some examples of generic manuscript preparation guidelines that help control a book's production costs.

If your manuscript will be copyedited by hand on hard copy:

- Double-space all copy, without exception, regardless of its context or intended use (i.e., including even figure captions).
- Do not underline anything for any purpose unless the editor agrees. Use italics only for words as words, and use boldface sparingly and consistently (e.g., for key terms).
- Do not use hard returns in text except after headings and to start new paragraphs.
- Put each figure and table on a separate sheet (unless instructed otherwise), keyed to text for location.
- Identify each photo, figure, and table and its caption by double-number and title.
- Be consistent in heading styles, text formats, and fonts; use a single simple basic font, such as Times New Roman or Arial, and do not change type sizes for effect or use design features.
- Unless otherwise instructed, number all pages consecutively with each chapter starting on page 1.
- Completely fill manuscript pages, leaving standard or wider margins.
- Complete all parenthetical source citations and notes or references.
- Submit complete chapter manuscript all at once or in batches as the publisher allows.

If your manuscript will be copyedited electronically:

- Single-space all copy.
- Do not underline for emphasis. Use italics only for words as words, and use boldface sparingly and consistently (e.g., for key terms).
- Do not use hard returns except after headings and to start new paragraphs.
- Insert finished double-numbered tables and figures or placeholders for them. Supply unfinished art and captions in separate manuscripts.

- Use a single font and type size throughout. Be consistent in heading styles.
- Establish a small set of document styles (A-head, B-head, C-head, running text, numbered list, bulleted list, list headings, caption headings for figures, tables, and photos) and apply it systematically. (To set styles in Word go to the message screen at Format, Style.)
- Do not insert extra spaces at the ends of lines, and do not use spaces for indentation (i.e., use tabs).
- Insert page breaks appropriately throughout rather than paragraphing down.

Manuscript preparation can be a real pain. The level of detail involved definitely is not for everyone. If attention to these mechanics proves a burden to you, take the initiative in advance and enlist the aid of a paid or volunteer helper who can provide it. Authors are wise who optimize the time and attention they can give to content over form.

Camera-Ready Copy

In some houses, especially subsidy presses and publishers of upper-level texts and supplements, whatever you send is published as-is, as camera-ready copy, whether it is "acceptable" or not. In camera-ready copy, your physical manuscript pages are mounted in a vacuum frame, photographed one by one, and printed from the film. The advantage of camera-ready copy is that the publisher does not have to invest in book design or page make-up. What you see is what you get, and for this reason the rules for manuscript preparation and page formatting are especially stringent for manuscripts being produced in this way. This technology may represent a cost savings over other printing methods, but the results depend on the author and thus are highly variable in quality.

Submit Complete Manuscript

A chapter that lacks a summary, the figures, or the boxes is not complete. Furthermore, your manuscript technically is not complete even when you submit all your chapters, as a textbook also may contain some or all of the following elements.

- Preface and acknowledgments
- Table of contents
- Parts and chapters
- Figures and tables
- Apparatus and pedagogy
- Appendices

- Photos or photo specifications and captions
- Source citations, notes, references, and credit lines
- Annotations or glossary entries
- Author index and subject index
- Permissions log and grants to date

As noted previously, some or all of these elements will be your responsibility to provide, depending on your agreement with the publisher. Many houses treat frontmatter and endmatter separately, in which case these elements are permitted to trail the rest of the manuscript into production. An index, especially, cannot be completed until the manuscript has been put into type and paged. Nevertheless, a "complete" manuscript technically includes all the listed elements. Some houses put manuscripts into production in batches, while others will do absolutely nothing for your book until the manuscript is 100% complete, including all grants of permission. An incomplete manuscript can mean significant delay and unanticipated, extra costs.

Commit to Consistency

In publishing, consistency is rarely foolish (and therefore is not a hobgoblin of little minds). Inconsistency, large or small, leads to structural weakness, imbalance in exposition, and loss of reader confidence. Consistency can be difficult to achieve, however—another authoring task that requires mindfulness and self-monitoring. Issues of consistency in the fulfillment of chapter apparatus and pedagogical feature strands have already been addressed in Chapters 10–12. When editors or reviewers identify a pattern of inconsistency, they might also be referring to discrepancies in voice, tone, reading level, writing style, editorial style, heading structure, or amounts of topical detail, discussed in Chapters 6–9.

As noted in Chapter 6, if the editor does not send you Author Guidelines with information on house style, you should request them. Consistently follow house style first, then consistently follow the preferred style of your discipline (for textbooks, not for journal articles) on everything the house style does not cover.

In drafting, some authors get into a muddle over style and format. For instance, they arbitrarily switch verb tenses, subject pronouns, reference styles, or formats for headings and key terms. Because of the sheer number of details, it is hard to remember in later chapters all the conventions you adopted in earlier ones. Drafting checklists can help with this.

During the production phase, professional copyeditors catch these inconsistencies and rightfully insist on congruence, but this comes just at a time when you thought you were done with your book and perhaps have exhausted yourself. You can save yourself eleventh-hour hassles by attending to these matters as much as possible beforehand. You can also save yourself money (directly or indirectly, depending on your contract) and embarrassment. Professional copyeditors make $25 to $40 an hour or as much as $4 per page. Whatever inconsistencies they miss end up in print.

Develop Drafting Checklists

The trick to achieving consistency is to decide at the outset how you will treat various mechanics and to draft a checklist of those decisions. Such a checklist saves you from having to re-decide repeatedly, risking inconsistency, or to lose time by flipping through manuscript to see how you did things previously or by constantly consulting manuals of style. As you go along using a personalized checklist, you will establish time- and hassle-saving drafting habits. Eventually you will not need to refer to your checklists at all.

The following list identifies the decisions you should include on your checklist for manuscript mechanics and style. For your own use, create a checklist like this by recording a sample of how you plan to treat each of the following elements. A blank checklist is provided in Chapter Appendix A, "Mechanics and Style Checklist."

- A-heads
- B-heads
- C-heads
- D-heads
- Bulleted lists
- Numbered lists
- Quotations
- Examples
- Source citations
- Endnotes
- Credit lines
- References
- Figure captions
- Table captions
- Photo captions
- Key terms
- Glossary definitions
- Annotations
- Other

Inconsistency in even small things, such as embedded lists, can lead to error and confusion. If some of your lists are numbered, some bulleted, and some plain, there must be a rationale. If some of your key terms are boldfaced, some italicized, and some undistinguished, what should the reader conclude?

Your mechanics and style checklist also can include miscellaneous reminders based on your particular needs, such as remembering to reference your figures and tables by number in the narrative, remembering to key the placement of figures and tables in your manuscript, or remembering to monitor length.

Keep your mechanics and style checklist on hand along with an apparatus and pedagogy checklist, which should contain reminders for what to include in every chapter and self-directions for how you will treat your pedagogy. Chapter Appendix B provides this checklist for your use. At the least, for your own reference, record the following decisions about apparatus and pedagogy to remember and apply in every chapter.

- The title and subtitle style of each feature
- The number of each type of feature per chapter
- What has to be in each chapter opener and in what order
- What has to be in each chapter closer and in what order

In addition, some authors keep a separate style sheet listing reminders about the publisher's house style and the editorial style they have chosen. Some authors personalize their style sheets by noting errors of English composition, spelling, and grammar to which they are prone, and specific usages they need to include or avoid, such as technical or politically sensitive terms.

Common usage errors in college texts include, for example, *may* and *might, can* and *could, if* and *whether, which* and *that, reason why* (redundant), etc. Finding these kinds of errors is the copyeditor's job, however. As author, once you have recorded your decisions in drafting checklists and have achieved consistency, your time and effort are better spent attending to the content of your book rather than to English composition, even if you are writing in English as a second language.

There is one important exception, however. If your first draft chapters are being sent out for peer review, you should make every effort to provide error-free copy. Reviewers tend to be indignant, even harsh, over errors of spelling and grammar, which negatively skew their perceptions of your content. Your editor must then defend your book to the publisher against negative reviews. Following are some resources on writing and revising for academic authors.

Selected Sources on Writing

Boice, Robert, *Professors as Writers*. New Forums Press, 1990.
Germano, William. *Getting It Published: A Guide for Scholars...* University of Chicago Press, 2001.

Luey, B. *Handbook for Academic Authors*. Cambridge University Press, 2002.
Munger, David, and Shireen Campbell. *Researching Online*, 5th ed. Pearson Longman, 2001.
Rankin, Elizabeth. *The Work of Writing: Insights and Strategies for Academics and Professionals*. Jossey–Bass, 2001.
Strunk, William, Jr., and E. B. White. *The Elements of Style*, 4th ed. Allyn & Bacon, 2000.

Selected Sources on Revising

Cheney, Theodore A. Rees. *Getting the Words Right: How to Revise, Edit and Rewrite*. F&W Publications, 2005.
Cook, Claire Kehrwald. *Line by Line: How to Edit Your Own Writing*. Houghton Mifflin, 1985.
Einsohn, Amy. *The Copyeditor's Handbook: A Guide for Book Publishing and Corporate Communication*. University of California Press, 2000.
Judd, Karen. *Copyediting: A Practical Guide*, 3rd ed. Crisp Learning, 2001.

Some Useful Links

Bibliofind (rare and out-of-print books): **bibliofind.com**
Columbia Guide to Online Style, 2nd ed.: columbia.edu/cu/cup/cgos2006/basic.html
David Brower's Why Textbook Writing Matters in Academia (October 28, 2005): **dateline.ucdavis.edu/dl_detail.lasso?id=8495**
Greg Mankiw's blog on textbook writing: gregmankiw.blogspot.com/2007/03/on-textbook-writing.html
Library Spot (library of libraries, with links): **libraryspot.com**
Purdue Online Writing Lab: **owl.english.purdue.edu**
Text and Academic Authors Association (TAA): **TAAonline.net**

Manage Resources

As you research, network, develop checklists, and gather materials for your textbook, arrange these resources in a way that will help you manage your project. Resource management can include setting up chapter-by-chapter folders (actual or virtual). Each chapter file could include items such as clippings or bookmarks to current articles and events, references, notes, bibliographies, instructional strategies, student activities, applications, illustrations, or examples, as relevant. Include complete information as to sources and copyright holders, because these are a nightmare to search for after the fact.

Chapter folders will make life easier for you as you draft or revise. They have multiple uses, serving as reminders of what to beef up or add; models for pedagogical features; ideas for figures or special content; concrete examples to use in exposition; or items for your instructor's manual, margin notes, or test bank.

Systematically managing resources by chapter is a way of chunking a complexity of materials. Even if you are an experienced writer, cumulative resource folders can be a comfort as you begin each chapter on a blank screen. The ability to drag and drop information files into chapter folders on your desktop can work wonders for you.

Monitor Topical Balance

Chapter 9 explained how your system of headings can aid you in topical development, but you will need to monitor topical balance as you draft or revise. As a textbook author, you naturally will have more to say about your favorite topics and those you know best. At the same time, you might be tempted to skimp or over-generalize on topics at the fringes of your interest or expertise. You might even be tempted to omit some topics even though they are within the scope of your book and are expected by your customers. Overcoming these temptations is another authoring task requiring self-discipline. The overall balance of your book is at stake, not to mention perceived intellectual soundness.

Fortunately, you can check for topical development in each chapter and between chapters as you draft by considering the amount of space and degree of differentiation you are using for each topic or section of text. For instance, does your Chapter 6 list three times as many key terms as Chapters 4 and 5? Perhaps you have gone into too much technical detail in Chapter 6 and not enough detail in the other chapters. If so, maybe you need to redistribute your material.

In each chapter, do the most important topics use the most space and the least important the least space? The number of lines or paragraphs devoted to a topic indicates its comparative importance, and the reader naturally uses comparative length and detail to make judgments about degree of importance. You may need to drop paragraphs from some topics and add paragraphs to others.

In each chapter do your topics of clearly equal importance have roughly equal space? For example, does your chapter on child development devote a similar number of pages to early, middle, and later childhood? Assuming you are not attempting to propagandize the readers of your economics textbook, does your section on the pros and cons of regulating interest rates devote a similar number of paragraphs to both the pros and the cons? Research shows that the amount of exposure a reader has to a topic will affect what the reader both values and retains in memory.

A good way to prevent problems of balance in exposition is to map out topics in advance, noting the numbers of paragraphs, pages, or chapters you plan to devote to each one. Enter these counts on a copy of your drafting outline or TOC and keep this information with your drafting checklists. Classroom instructors perform a similar content analysis when they decide how much class time to spend on each part of a lesson, unit, or course. This practice also will help you meet the length requirements for each chapter and for the book as a whole, while still saying everything that really needs to be said in the limited space you have.

Manage Source Citations

Cite sources. It is expected in all academic disciplines. And it is expected at all levels. Some authors claim that first-year, "low-level," vocational, or community college students don't need source citations. Other authors actually claim that they are the source of all the ideas in their book or that all the facts cited are common knowledge. These authors are an embarrassment to themselves and their publishers. Sometimes (in lawsuits) they are liabilities as well. Another excuse for malfeasance is that source citations clutter up the text, interrupt reading, and anyway are lost on undergraduate readers, who don't know enough to use them. However, all students in postsecondary education are entitled to know the origins of ideas and information they read, whether or not they appreciate or use them.

Generally, undergraduate textbooks should contain either parenthetical source citations or superscript note numbers with chapter endnotes. The latter often are preferred, especially if citing is extensive, because parentheticals consume valuable space within the running text. Sometimes the chapter endnotes are collected by chapter in the endmatter of the book rather than at the ends of chapters.

Echew Footnotes

Many authors pride themselves on their footnotes and regard them as a sign of true scholarship. In textbook writing, however, you would be wise not to insist on footnotes. If the information is not important enough to include in the narrative and cannot be treated as a source note, then it probably is a conceit—a costly conceit, because it involves printing outside the normal text block. Footnotes are more expensive to copyedit, set into type, and correct. In addition, in the trade, footnotes immediately identify a text as graduate or postgraduate level. You also would be wise to complete source citations as you draft. Do not leave strings of parentheses enclosing only question marks, to be completed later, for you no doubt will regret it. Complete source citations also should accompany all figures and tables.

Complete Notes and References

Publishing a textbook is contingent on the completion of key authoring tasks other than writing the book manuscript. Chief among these are citing sources, completing notes and references, and acquiring permissions.

Consider Author X, who has not made time to update the sources for her revision. She feels that stopping to check references interferes with her creative flow. Getting to the library is inconvenient, and she's sure she remembers where she saw something or can scrounge what she needs from her bookcase. She plans to rectify everything in her final draft. As a result, her manuscript contains many passages like the following.

> At the turn of the twentieth century architects and architectural engineers shifted their focus from facades to infrastructures (DeVries ???). According to Eldridge, this shift was "a direct consequence of further technological developments in the manufacture of steel" (1993, ??).

Her draft references look like this.

Davis, Arnold. 1952. *Twentieth Century Architecture*. Boston: Little, Brown.
DeVries
Eggan, Charles. 1987. *Facades Through the Ages*. New York: Macmillan.
Eldridge. 1993. ***Steel.***

Author X would have acted differently if she knew what agonies were in store for her. The copyeditor repeatedly flags or queries every incomplete source and reminds her that authors cited within the narrative rather than in parenthetical citations must be identified by both their first and last names. Just when she is working day and night to make deadline for page proof, Author X discovers she needs to hire someone to track down her sources and fill in the missing information in both the narrative and the references. She also discovers that no authoring task is more spirit-killing than trying to find page numbers after the fact. (Ask anyone who has suffered this lapse.)

In addition, Author X worries that the graduate student she has shanghaied into helping isn't really up to the task. Bad things have been known to happen. She's thinking, perhaps, of historian Doris Kearns Goodwin's ordeal with alleged plagiarism in 2002 (**pbs.org/newshour/bb/law/jan-june02/history_1-28.html**). Unknown to Author X, her hired hand, frustrated, is not above fudging things when necessary. And the publisher won't help, insisting that sources and references are strictly the author's responsibility. So Author X is out of pocket as well.

Don't think like Author X. Source citations, notes, references, and credit lines can be a torture for everyone involved in the publishing process. Together with permissions, they are among the most common reasons for a book being pulled from production, missing its publication date, missing its copyright year, or failing to see print. The best time to complete citations and references is in your first draft, even if some material is later dropped.

You can also make drafting easier on yourself by drafting to length, meeting authoring schedules, and by doing permissions right. These are the subjects of Chapters 14 and 15.

Working with a Copyeditor

Developmental editing is concerned with your content and organization, copyediting is concerned with your writing and language, and production editing is concerned with formatting and design. Your publisher or acquisitions editor will choose a level of edit—minor (light), medium, or heavy. In a light edit the copyeditor corrects errors in spelling, punctuation, grammar (such as verb disagreement), and usage (incorrect word choices, such as *effect* for *affect*). If a light edit is ordered, it means that your manuscript has been judged to be fairly "clean" (reliably complete and executed consistently) and is in pretty good shape.

A heavy edit, on the other hand, may involve restructuring your sentences, converting passive verbs to active voice, making word substitutions, moving paragraphs around, adding transitional sentences, and the like. A heavy edit also may tell you if your facts are accurate and if your writing makes sense and communicates clearly. Be aware that a publisher requesting a heavy edit essentially is authorizing the editor to fix it, i.e., to rewrite.

You might want to find out what level of edit your publisher plans for your manuscript, so you can know what to expect. Rest assured, however, that a professional copyeditor will never knowingly make any change to your manuscript that alters your meaning or intention. That is their cardinal rule. The mission of a copyeditor is to improve your communication to your audience and to make sure your manuscript hits its market and adheres to house style.

Editors vary in the extent to which they comment on your manuscript. Some can be maddening in their demand for explanation and exacting in their insistence on detail. You probably will come to appreciate this, however. A copyeditor might return a manuscript to you that is full of self-stick notes with written queries or claims such as "Not Clear" (or the equivalent if the edit is done on computer). Your job then is to address each query so the changes can be inputted. Other editors might simply correct a sentence (in a shorter time than it takes to write a note about it). In any case, any professional editor can and will explain the logic, rationale, precedent, or dictionary reference for every change that he or she makes. It is very important, therefore, not to ignore a comment just because you don't understand it.

The manuscript that comes back to you from the copyeditor is the master manuscript. After you respond to the edit, the editor (or you) inputs the final changes and your manuscript is released to the typesetter or compositor to have galleys or page proof made. If you are inputting edits using Word's "Track Changes" feature, you can easily see every proposed deletion, addition, or substitution the editor makes and you can accept or reject each change. It saves time to do it this way. If you work from double-spaced hardcopy manuscript, all the edits have to be keyboarded from handwritten notes, possibly introducing new errors.

The copyeditor's job is to help ensure that your book fulfills its mission and is appropriate, accessible, and appealing to its market and readers. There should be no other agenda, even for editors who also are experts in your subject (should you be so lucky). Most important, understand that the editor is your ally. Don't be the kind of author who immediately assumes a defensive position, sparring needlessly with editors in a perceived war for control of content.

Revising

Today authors revise on screen using the printer's text files or scans from the previous edition. In the old days, publishers would cut the spines off copies of your previous edition and send you the cut copies as tearsheet to cut and paste. Manuscript preparation typically included writing minor changes by hand on the tearsheet and typing any change or addition consisting of more than three words. These elements were then cut and pasted to cobble together new manuscript pages. The advantage of using tearsheet for a revision was the savings in copyediting costs; only new material had to be copyedited. Tearsheet may still be used for minor revisions, but now the same economy can be obtained through electronic editing.

Authors still must adhere to manuscript preparation guidelines. A manuscript with the wrong margins and headings and other formatting or style errors may be returned as unacceptable. Following are some rules of thumb for preparing a revision manuscript.

Guidelines for Revising on Hard Copy

- Neatly write minor corrections legibly using a medium that photocopies easily (for example, not hard pencil or non-reproducible blue). Take care to form numbers correctly.
- Write corrections above or beside text to be edited, using insertion carets to show where the changes go. Do not write at

the top or bottom of the page and then indicate changes with long arrows. Also, do not write sideways up the margins.
- Type any change involving more than a few words. Key the correction or addition for location, and insert the new copy on a separate sheet as the next page. Number additional pages the same as the insertion page plus (a), (b), etc. Double-space all keyboarded corrections and additions.
- Avoid using numbered and circled paragraphs to indicate a change in the sequence of text, especially if the change affects more than one page. Rather, cut and paste these sections (physically or electronically) into the new order.
- Cut and paste (or print out) each tearsheet figure and table and place it on a separate page.
- Check changes in the wording of headings and feature strands and in the numbering of figures and tables.
- Pay special attention to updating statistics, parenthetical source citations, credit lines, and references.
- Use standard-size paper and fill each page with roughly the same number of lines. Both incomplete and overfilled pages make it difficult to estimate manuscript length accurately.
- Exclude the previous edition's photos or any other elements that are being dropped.
- Create separate annotation, reference, caption, and glossary manuscripts, as relevant, re-alphabetizing as needed.

Additional Guidelines for Revising Electronically

- Read Microsoft's online help documents on using Track Changes efficiently and effectively.
- Address each comment and accept or reject each change.
- Accept all formatting changes (unless they introduce an error).
- Remain faithful to the styles in use.
- Do not make any changes or additions that will remain hidden from the copyeditor (i.e., make sure that Track Changes is on).
- Check that the correct levels of heading are shown.
- Do not use the space bar for anything except spaces between words.
- Do not use the return key for anything except a new paragraph.
- Save your revised document to your hard drive before sending it as an e-mail attachment.

Will Your Textbook Have Legs?

There is an expression in publishing that predicts the longevity or shelf life of a textbook. "It's got legs" means that editors have reason to expect many successful revisions over a span of many years. In all fields, books with legs have characteristics in common. They have strong ongoing markets. They are well written and written by recognized authorities in the field. The authors address their real readers in a distinctive and appealing voice. The content is technically accurate, complete, up to date, topically balanced, intellectually honest, interesting, and pedagogically sound.

Many textbooks are not revised, however, and publishers may have legitimate business reasons for this. Sales of your previous edition may have proven disappointing, for example, with high rates of return and declining sales. After its 7th or 11th edition, a textbook starts to get old. Perhaps your book can no longer hold its own against strong, new, outside competition, or perhaps it is losing out to new inside competition.

Revision Roulette

Other changes could put you at a disadvantage. Perhaps, as part of its branding efforts, your publisher has shifted its focus to other parts of its list and no longer wishes to invest heavily in your subject area. Why revise your book, however good it is, if the sales reps will no longer visit the departments where your course is taught? Or perhaps your editor has left the company, which essentially orphans your book. Staff turnovers are high in publishing houses, because moving out often is the only way to move up. New editors won't know you or your history with the company, and they will be under a lot of pressure to acquire new product. Thus, leadership changes, list changes, industry changes, and market changes can result in an unfavorable environment for you and your book, and there really is nothing you can do about it.

The publisher also might drop your book if you are a senior author who no longer teaches and is no longer active in your field, especially if your text reflects older paradigms or issues that your editor feels you would not or could not change. A history of ignoring editorial advice, reviewers' concerns, and market intelligence could be the nail in the coffin. Needless to say, the best defense in this case is always to revise thoroughly with enthusiasm and vigor and with a view to commercial success.

Savvy authors understand the publishing world enough to know that they must be proactive in promoting themselves as well as their textbooks. You might write a letter of welcome to the new editor, for example, introducing yourself and explaining the long, happy, profitable history you've had with the company. Send the editor publicity releases or news articles about your doings, publications, or awards. Ask for postproduction reviews so you can see how your book was received and where it might be revised. Find new ways to help with marketing and promotion. And develop a revision plan—much like a prospectus—to explain to the editor chapter-by-chapter the changes and updates you intend to make in addition to addressing customers' concerns. Develop new, exciting, contemporary ideas for chapter apparatus and pedagogy or for instructor and student supplements.

Another strategy is to suggest that you would consider adding a coauthor, someone "up-and-coming" or at the forefront of a new or "hot" area in your field. For senior authors especially, accepting the contributions of one or more coauthors is a valid survival strategy and one that typically enhances textbook currency and quality. It can also be a way to help promote the career of a younger colleague or protégé. Some authors recoil at the idea, but publishers who suggest that you add a coauthor are offering to help you keep your book alive.

If, despite your attentions, the decision has been made not to revise your textbook, then you would be wise to walk away. Negotiate a release from your contract or a reversion of rights, and seek out another publisher, or consider self-publishing. In any case, you win by breathing new life into your book and finding new ways to bring it to readers. With a good revision plan, you could give your textbook new "legs" on your own—even a whole new life.

APPENDIX A
Mechanics and Style Checklist

Record a sample of how you plan to treat each element.

ELEMENTS	RULE OR EXAMPLE OR STYLE
A-heads	
B-heads	
C-heads	
D-heads	
Bulleted lists	
Numbered lists	
Quotations	
Examples	
Parenthetical source citations	
Endnotes	
Credit lines	
References	
Figure captions	
Table captions	
Photo captions	
Key terms	
Glossary definitions	
Other	

APPENDIX B
Apparatus and Pedagogy Checklist

ELEMENTS	DECISIONS
Parts Number of Parts:	Title/Subtitle Style: Part Opener Contents: Part Closer Contents:
Chapters Number of Chapters:	Number/Title Style:
Chapter Openers	Contents: 1. 2. 3. 4. 5. 1st A-head
Chapter Closers	Contents: 1. Summary 2. 3. 4. 5.
Other Apparatus	Contents: 1. 2. 3. 4. 5.
Feature Strands Number per Chapter:	Title/Subtitle Style: Contents: 1. 2. 3. 4. 5.

14

Control Length and Manage Schedule

As you now know, publishers have length requirements for books, based on what they know of their markets, what directly competing books do, and what they think they can sell. There are practical considerations as well. College courses typically run on a semester basis for 15 or 16 weeks, including a week or more for testing, but at some schools semesters run for only 10 to 12 weeks. Your book realistically might have 12 to 16 chapters to be read and studied at a rate of one chapter per week, or 20 or more brief ones that can be absorbed at a rate of two chapters a week.

An average of 50 pages of reading and study per week per course is the recommended maximum on a majority of campuses nationwide. In bookmaking for undergraduate markets, 40 pages or fewer per chapter is the general preferred standard, depending on the nature, scope, and level of the course. Using the preferred maximums, and depending on the trim size (the actual physical dimensions), your introductory textbook might be around 544 book pages, for example, with frontmatter and endmatter adding another 64 pages for a total of 608 pages—a mid-range size.

Why Length Is Important

Book length is determined in advance. That is, in commercial textbook publishing you do not have the luxury of waiting to see what you come up with. The publisher will want to know how many pages you estimate your book will be or will tell you how many pages of manuscript or how many words to supply. This number probably will be in your contract, and you will be expected to meet it. If your manuscript is significantly shorter, you will be asked to supply more copy, and if it is significantly longer, you will be asked to cut. As you read in Chapter 4, contracts often give publishers the power to hire someone else to meet length requirements if you cannot or will not do so.

Why is length so important? As you may recall from Chapter 2, the publisher has book buyers who contract for the materials, such as paper, and the vendors who will manufacture your book. All decisions about your book as a physical object, such as the number of pages and grade of paper and type of cover and binding, and about the budget for your book, are made well before the book is ready for production, sometimes even before it exists in reality as a manuscript. (The term *vaporware* from software publishing applies here.) No money can be dispensed on behalf of your book until the budget is approved, and, once approved, the budget tends to be regarded as bottom line.

The budget includes the cost of the paper, which usually is bought in bolts by weight and allocated to each title according to the number of *signatures* and *half signatures* in a book. A signature is 32 pages, and in traditional manufacturing the imposition (sequence) of pages at the printer typically is based on eighth-of-a-signature flats. A flat (a sheet of paper with four pages printed on it) might juxtapose pages 3, 35, 67, and 99, which, when merged with other flats, folded, cut, and bound, all come out in their right places for the correct numerical sequence of pages. Books are bound in signatures whether or not there is type on all the pages, which is why you sometimes see books with blank pages at the end.

Even with POD technology and sheet fed press runs, the cost of paper is why you must take length seriously. If the company had to buy (or reallocate) an extra signature of paper for your book, possibly at a higher price because of the small quantity and the rush, and if your print run were 20,000 copies (although initial print runs usually are much lower), that comes to 8 flats and 640,000 pages that are not in the budget. Your book also would have more bulk, taking up more space, and more weight, which would raise the cost of storing, packaging, and shipping each copy. As you can imagine, the cost of those extra pages ultimately would add significantly to the overall cost of manufacturing your book and bringing it to customers. This example is moot, however. Publishers who often incur these kinds of costs do not stay in business for long.

Publishers attempt to cut costs by exporting manufacturing to developing countries and by taking advantage of new computer-based technologies, which are more efficient but by no means cheap. Extra length always translates into extra cost. And what costs your publisher costs you. It is worth your while, therefore, to estimate the length of your book accurately in advance in collaboration with your publisher. The market for your book dictates its optimal length for it to be competitive. Depending on the market, your introductory textbook might max out at 624 pages and your brief or concise edition might need to come in at 432 pages.

Calculating Length

Managing length is an author's responsibility, and along with managing schedule it is one of the most important responsibilities a textbook author has. The best way to prevent a length problem is to draft to length in the first place and then to monitor for length creep from draft to draft.

1. Start by deciding how much space (number of pages, paragraphs, lines, or words) you would like to allot to each topic, and note these decisions on a copy of your chapter outline. These decisions relate to your previous decisions about topical coverage and topical balance, as reflected in your table of contents and heading structure (recall Chapters 7 and 11). Allot space on the basis of a maximum total of 40 book pages per chapter or on whatever maximum your publisher gives you.
2. Set a standard format for your margins, number of lines per page, and page numbering system, and draft continuously, filling each page. Avoid unnecessary blank space or page breaks, which make length estimation less accurate.
3. Calculate the average number of words per line you are getting as you draft, and multiply this number by the average number of lines per page. This gives you your average number of words per manuscript page (msp).
4. Find out the planned trim size of your book. If it will be an 8- by 10-inch book, for instance, you can expect to fit at least 500 words on a book page (bp). To convert msp to bp in this case, you would multiply the average number of words per msp by the number of pages in the chapter manuscript to find the total number of words in the chapter. You would then divide this figure by 500—the number of words you can expect to fit on an 8 by 10 page. Even easier, your word processing program will tell you the total number of words you have keyboarded, which you can then divide by the trim size figure.
5. The result is the number of book pages your chapter will occupy, not counting photos, figures, and tables. To add in these elements, tally the number of photos, figures, and tables and multiply by .33. If you have 3 photos, 2 figures, and 4 tables in Chapter 5, for instance, you would multiply 9 X .33 = 2.97 = 3 book pages. This calculation assumes that each of these elements will occupy an average of about one-third of a book page. If you have a very long figure or table, therefore, count it as two to get a more accurate page count.
6. As a final step in getting an accurate page count, multiply your subtotal for the number of book pages by .05 and add the result to the overall bp count. This result accounts for the white or blank spaces on each page before and after headings, around photos, and between figure captions and text. The following

formula for estimating length summarizes these steps. Note that the trim sizes are rounded up, as the exact measures are fractions accounting for the amount of paper lost when a book block is folded, trimmed, and grinded on one side to receive the cover. For example, an 8 x 11 book actually measures 7.69 x 10.63. A 7 x 10 book may actually measure 6.5 x 9.75 inches (16.51 cm x 24.76 cm). On press, an 8 x 10.5 book runs 20.5 x 26.7 cm.

Formula for Estimating Length

Trim size (inches)	Estimated words per book page
Under 7 × 9	350–400 words
7 × 9	450 words
8 × 10	500 words
Above 8 × 10	550–600 words

To convert manuscript pages to book pages:
(Words per line) × (number of lines per page)
= (number of words per page) × (number of pages)
= (total number of words in the manuscript) / (number of words per book page, obtained from table above)
= (number of book pages) + (total number of photos, tables, and figures) × (0.33 for space used by images) + (subtotal) × (0.05 for white space)
= (number of book pages).
Suggested maximum number of book pages per chapter = 40.

Your publisher may have different trim size counts and a different system for calculating length than the one shown above. If this information is not provided in the company's Author Guidelines, ask your sponsoring editor, especially if you are working without other editorial assistance.

If the total bp in any chapter exceeds 40, be prepared to make cuts before final draft or to move material to other locations in the book or its ancillaries. A topic might go just as well in another chapter, for instance. Your very long table might make a good handout master, your extra chapter closing activity might be a good addition to your instructor's manual, and your extra mini-case might make a good basis for items in your test bank, interactive edition, or companion website.

Depending on your purposes and the needs of your subject, it is a good idea to plan chapters of roughly equal length, as a practical strategy and for consistency. Once you find out how many of your manuscript pages equals a book page, you can easily monitor your progress to control length. You probably will get between one and one-third and two and one-third manuscript pages per book page. Once you reach your maximum bp for a chapter, simply delete a sentence or paragraph for every sentence or paragraph you add. This same rule applies for revisions in which overall book length must stay the same.

Disaster Control Guidelines for Length

Following Hippocrates, the following solutions for correcting length problems are ordered in terms of the principle of least intervention. In addition, following the principle of the conservation of energy and matter, solutions aim to preserve content in some form while cutting length.

Scenario A: Your chapter is too long and there is simply no way you can cut it without destroying its brilliance and integrity.

Solution 1: Scour for wordiness and tighten your prose (see Chapter 6). Especially look for strings of unnecessary prepositional phrases, unnecessary qualifying remarks and disclaimers, and any gratuitous-seeming or jargony elaborations. Change every sentence to active voice.

Solution 2: Search for paragraphs you can drop. Especially drop a paragraph whose source citation is more than ten years out of date, unless this source is an essential classic. Also, ruthlessly drop paragraphs that are in any way tangential or digressionary, however amusing or clever. Then consider dropping extra examples and applications, shortening them, or substituting more economical ones.

Solution 3: Check that you have the prescribed number of pedagogical features and chapter elements. Choose the best ones and then combine, condense, move, or drop any extras, however good they are. Consider repurposing the best of them for use in your ancillaries or supplements.

Solution 4: Where possible, condense and convert portions of narrative to a figure or table. For example, the formula for estimating length took only 12 lines of type but essentially replaces 54 lines of manuscript preceding it.

Solution 5: Where possible, depending on your evaluation of their importance for your purposes, drop long figures or tables and preserve the content in condensed or summarized narrative form. For example, "Research clearly shows that sleep deprivation has a negative effect on productivity in the workplace (Smith, 2002)" might easily replace a graph occupying one-third of a book page.

Solution 6: Ask your editor for suggestions or assistance in reducing the length of the chapter. It is important to identify and discuss any dropping of whole topics or headings and sections. Your editor might have reason to believe that some of your proposed cuts will compromise meeting customer needs. Avoid cutting any elements that are part of the publisher's book plan, because this is the plan for marketing, advertising, promoting, and selling your book, which is already underway.

A development editor or a professional copyeditor who is knowledgeable in your subject area also can help you cut. Especially if you are working with a development editor (who ideally has seen you through thick and thin over the course of a year or more), never deliver a surprise for final manuscript. If in taking matters into your own hands you have exercised poor judgment, the development editor may not have time at that point to "save" your book. Editors are required to hand off your manuscript to the compositor or packager by a certain date regardless of its readiness. If your book is significantly not ready, it is likely to be cancelled or postponed at great loss to all.

Scenario B: You did not pay attention to length. Your book is now in production and you have been informed that the compositor's castoff puts it at 100 book pages over length.

Solution: Consult with your publisher. You may have to drop chapters, cut appendices, lose figures and tables, and make other painful radical changes. Dropping topics now will require resetting your chapter and table of contents into type and making up new pages, which would add greatly to the cost of production and also essentially makes the prepublication promotion a lie. Any forced changes to the book design (if changes to design specs are permitted at all) also could put your book as much over budget as adding signatures. The best solution to this scenario is to avoid it like the plague.

Avoid Length Creep in Revisions

Development editors can help prevent length problems by performing length estimates on a chapter-by-chapter basis and warning you of any "length creep" between drafts. Without such help, you need to be able to monitor length yourself.

It is easy to get lazy about maintaining length, and length creep is the result. If you compare the 1st, 3rd, and 6th editions of a popular introductory textbook, you may see physical evidence of this phenomenon. An introduction to psychology textbook, for instance, may become ever longer and more dense and bulkier on the bookshelf. Students have to pay a lot more for this book but have no hope of getting through it in a semester, and instructors must pick and choose which chapters to assign and which to discard from the course.

Length creep is caused by continually adding new material without deleting the old. Revisions, in their attempt to update sources and address reviewers' requests for more coverage of this and that, are especially prone. There is only one way to prevent length creep, and that is to drop before adding: word for word, sentence for sentence, paragraph for paragraph, figure for figure, box for box.

Production managers have a bag of tricks for handling length problems, but you should not count on combinations of the following as solutions to length problems.

- **Running a line long:** an extra line of type is added to each page, which gives your book a crowded appearance with very small margins at the top or bottom.
- **Reducing leading around heads:** space is removed above and below A- and B-heads, which also gives your book a packed look.
- **Running photos in the margins:** vertical photos are printed exceptionally small in the margins so they don't take up text space, which can detract from the visual presentation of your book.
- **Reducing type size:** elements of your book are produced in smaller type, which makes for a dense, less readable text.
- **Double- and triple-columning:** elements of your book are produced in two, three, or four columns to fit more on a page, which also can make for a dense, less readable book.

Some things cannot be done, however, and in the last analysis, there is only so much anyone can do with the absolute limit of a physical page. The only sensible thing to do is to plan for and control length from the beginning. For example, an average of 12 manuscript pages per chapter (with a range from 9 to 20) was the planned length for this book. As you can see, then, it is entirely within an author's power to deliver a manuscript of appropriate length.

Why Schedule Is Important

Just as the physical page has absolute limits, so has the time frame for publishing a textbook. Why is the time frame so important? For one thing, as you read in Chapter 2, if your book is not available in time for customers to see and order it well before the first term of its copyright year, it is dead at the gate. To be in the running, textbooks need to be in the warehouse by the preceding summer or fall, the earlier the better.

Also, your publisher is in competition to capture market share, and the early bird gets the worm. Sales representatives having to field a late book find that professors have already made their choices and have ordered current editions for their courses from competitors. Needless to say, the loss of investment is not just your publisher's; it is yours as well. Late books, even very good ones, do not have an opportunity to succeed.

Late first editions are not as vulnerable, because they lack market recognition and a track record. However, late revisions of established textbooks are at great risk. Because of this vulnerability, sales representatives in the field attempt to "roll" their customers, that is, to get them to order, sight unseen, the new edition of a book customers are using presently in their courses. The loyalty factor often drives these rollover sales, but if the new edition and its supplements are not ready in time, the trust factor kicks in, and you and the company lose business. Thus, schedules, along with budgets and book lengths, are bottom lines.

Types of Schedules in Publishing and Key Dates

In commercial textbook publishing, your project probably will have the following basic schedules.

Publishing Schedules

Drafting Schedule: dates by which chapters, revised drafts, and final complete manuscript are due

Reviewing Schedule: dates by which portions of manuscript are sent out for peer review and reviews are received and honoraria paid

Production Schedule: schedule for setting your book into type, including dates by which copyedited final manuscript and stages of proof are sent to you for corrections and dates by which proof must be returned

Marketing Schedule: schedule for presenting, advertising, promoting, and selling your book

Manufacturing Schedule: schedule for printing and binding your book

Supplements Schedule: dates by which samples and final manuscript for each supplement are due

Fulfillment Schedule: dates by which books and supplements are sold, ordered, in stock, inventoried, and shipped

As you might suspect, slippages in schedule can have a disastrous ripple effect on outcomes. The following dates, spanning a period of as much as two years or more, are the chief benchmarks in producing major market textbooks, although the precise order varies according to publishers' unique systems and procedures.

Scheduling Benchmarks

- Final book plan approval
- Manuscript complete
- Reviewing complete
- Sample manuscript to design
- Budget and production schedule approval
- Marketing plan approval
- Final manuscript and permissions complete
- Release to production
- Manufacturing initial pricing review
- Design approval
- Copyediting complete
- Release to composition
- Proofreading complete
- Art and photo approval
- Final page proof
- Pages out complete
- Indexing complete
- Cover design approval
- Finals to printer
- Art and photo package to printer
- Press okay
- Bound book to warehouse

You need to meet schedules during the development, drafting, reviewing, and production stages. Your most important date is "final manuscript complete," because other than reviewing nothing will be done for your book until you deliver your manuscript. During the production stages, you need to meet schedules for checking or correcting and turning around copyedited manuscript and one or more stages of proof.

As noted previously, your last real chance to make minor changes to manuscript is in the copyediting phase. Any changes you make to proofs ("author's alterations" or "AAs") are charged against your book. Now that authors see computer-generated page proof rather than unpaged typeset galleys, if your changes are too great, page make-up artists have to redo the pages on the computer at significantly greater cost.

Scheduling problems often strain author–publisher relations and cause other difficulties. Consider Author Z, who no longer answers his phone to avoid talking to his editor. He is experiencing excruciating time pressure and feels guilty about putting a strain on relationships with loved ones and losing touch with the rhythms of family life. He also feels angry and frustrated about having to neglect or under-perform various professional obligations. Yet he is working days, nights, and weekends and can't seem to let go of manuscript that seems less than perfect, regardless of due dates. He resents acidly the editor's constant reminders about deadlines. The editor, meanwhile, does not know what is going on and therefore cannot help. Author Z has not expressed his feelings and automatically interprets every contact with the editor as just another crack of the whip.

Author Z has a problem. Getting a college textbook published in time should not and need not cause personal and professional hardships and author–publisher misunderstandings. Author Z needs a better attitude, a stronger support network, and a more structured approach to managing time.

Develop Your Own Drafting Calendar

How can you avoid becoming like Author Z? To start, by far your best option is to develop and monitor your own drafting calendar, based on your own personal, professional, and family needs in relation to the due date for "manuscript complete." Sample pages from a drafting calendar are presented in the chapter appendix. You can develop a calendar by taking the following steps.

1. Ask your editor for the schedule of core due dates. Count the number of weeks from now until the "manuscript complete" due date and divide by the number of chapters. This tells you how many weeks or days you have to draft or revise each chapter. Everyone works at different rhythms and paces, but as a rule of thumb, regard a rate of a chapter a week as a bare minimum, based on full-time drafting.
2. Consult your appointment schedule and subtract the weeks or days you will not be drafting, including professional obligations, conferences, office and classroom hours, exam grading, vacation travel, personal commitments, family obligations, and holidays. Adjust your estimate accordingly for how much time you will have realistically to draft or revise each chapter.
3. Enter your personal due dates chapter-by-chapter on a planning calendar, allowing one or two days for each mailing of batched chapters. Batching manuscript often helps the publisher with workflow, as reviewing and any developmental editing can be done in installments. Adjust your calendar to allow more time for longer, less developed, or more difficult chapters.

4. Stop and reflect on your calendar. Can you really do it? Should you plan now to get someone to help you on specific chapter components, non-drafting tasks, or other authoring responsibilities? What can you do for backup or a Plan B?

Send your drafting calendar to your editor, and note any concerns you have. If you do not provide a drafting schedule, the editor should construct one, send it to you for your approval, and revise it according to your response. Make sure both you and your editor are clear and in agreement on scheduling. Some editors will want you to revise as you go along by creating interim draft chapters, while others will want you to wait until your draft is complete before you revise.

The editor needs a solid drafting schedule to create a reviewing schedule. Reviewers typically are lined up and contracted for in advance according to their availability. The editor tells them when they can expect to receive manuscript and when the reviews are due back. If your chapters are late, reviewers might have only a few days to respond. Worse, reviewers often drop out because they are no longer available, and the editor has to reduplicate time and effort to find replacements. Late reviews, in turn, can create further delays. In a worst-case scenario, your book gets fielded without reflecting any of the expert and market feedback for which the publisher has paid.

Disaster Control Guidelines for Schedule

Suppose you realize at some point that you are not going to be able to make critical deadlines. First-time authors are especially prone, as they are not wise to the magnitude of their undertaking. Common reasons for delays, in addition to the usual distractions and life events, normally include the following.

- Underestimation of the time required
- Over-optimism about abilities (biting off more than you can chew)
- Cold feet (loss of confidence in your knowledge or ability)
- Preoccupation with face-saving (fear of exposure or criticism)
- Writer's block (difficulty expressing yourself in writing)
- Perfectionist retention (difficulty letting go of less-than-perfect manuscript)

If unforeseen life events or reasons such as the above will prevent you from completing the manuscript in time, it is important to notify your editor immediately. The editor can help you address concerns and even arrange to get you help. You and your editor and publisher may negotiate to extend the time, hire help, postpone the book, or terminate the contract.

The time usually can be extended briefly, say, up to six weeks. If extra time won't solve the problem, it's possible that a hired hand can be brought in to take over some chapters or authoring tasks, an option that usually is written into publishing contracts to guarantee that the publisher will get a product. Alternatively, the publisher might be persuaded to pay an additional advance or grant for you to buy extra help—a research assistant, for example, or a keyboarder, transcriber, or photo or permissions researcher.

If extra time and help won't solve the problem, your book may need to be postponed. Postponing the book is difficult and costly, however, and can have a ripple effect on the company's publishing plan. Your book might have to be delayed two years, for example, if the company has another similar product for the year following your original publication date. Cancellation is a last resort.

Here are some strategies for managing your time and resources to prevent scheduling disasters.

- With your calendar schedule in hand, consult the copy of your drafting outline on which you have recorded your length planning. Then further subdivide drafting tasks in relation to the time you have set out for them. For peace of mind, standardize your personal commitment as much as possible. For instance, you might establish the goal of completing a working draft of one A-head section of your outline per working day. Then stick to this, working until you've completed a section of text. Keep your length planner and drafting calendar handy, along with your mechanics and style checklist and your apparatus and pedagogy checklist (see Chapter 13).
- Set up economies and efficiencies for accomplishing authoring tasks. For example, you might schedule blocks of time for library research on a chapter-by-chapter basis, and you might set aside every other Tuesday for consulting with coauthors or updating your permissions log (see Chapter 15). Also preserve time for rest and recreation in your schedule, including self-rewarding activities for personal benchmarks achieved.
- Formally prepare family members, friends, colleagues, students, and department chairpersons or deans for the personal and professional challenge you are undertaking in writing a textbook. As much as possible, find ways to enlist the support of these people and include them in your project. Be creative. The fruits of having a strong support network can lead to getting a semester sabbatical, having a chapter class-tested, or spending

quality time with a spouse, child, or student who is assisting you in some meaningful, practical way. Even children might enjoy photocopying, cutting and pasting figures, alphabetizing the glossary, or feeding you intelligence from the Internet.

- Find or create and provision an environment conducive to writing, and develop a writing habit. Many writers report that they are able to produce manuscript through the self-discipline of writing at particular times or writing for particular durations of time. Find out what works for you and stick to it.
- When your schedule for drafting manuscript is complete, develop a new calendar for completing permissions, responding to reviewing suggestions; revising for final draft; following through with any remaining frontmatter, endmatter, and nondrafting authoring tasks; and meeting the production editor's schedule for turning around copyedits and proofs.

Thus, as with length, managing schedule is entirely within your control, barring the unforeseen. If the unforeseen happens, and if it promises to compromise your schedule by more than two weeks or to compromise it in some way that cannot be made up later, tell your editor right away. It may not be too late to postpone without incurring losses, and there may be some remedy or relief. Editors usually have access to a range of talent and services to help authors complete their projects in time.

APPENDIX
Sample Pages from a Drafting Calendar

May 2008						
Sun	Mon	Tues	Weds	Thurs	Fri	Sat
27	28	29	30 Ch. 6 to ed.	1 SO 101 Office	2 Draft 7A	3
4	5 Draft 7B SO 304	6 SO 101 Office	7 Draft 7C	8 Office Dr J–1PM	9 Draft 7D	10
11 Celia's Birthday	12 SO 304	13 SO 101 Office	14 Grades Due	15	16 Draft 7E	17 Library
18 Library	19 Faculty Meetings	20 Office Ch. 7 to ed.	21 Draft 8A	22 Office	23 Draft 8B	24 Track Meet
25	26 Draft 8C	27 Draft 8D	28 Draft 8E	29 Draft 8F	30	31 Ch. 8 to ed.

June 2008						
Sun	Mon	Tues	Weds	Thurs	Fri	Sat
1	2 Library	3 Draft 9A	4 Library	5 Draft 9B	6 Concert	7
8 Gradua-tion	9	10 Draft 9C	11 Draft 9D	12 Draft 9E	13	14 Ch. 9 to ed.
15	16 Draft 10A	17 Library	18 Draft 10B & C	19 Draft 10D	20 Draft 10E & F	21 Library
22	23 Draft 10G	24 Ch. 10 to ed.	25 Draft 11A	26 Draft 11B	27 Draft 11C	28 Vacation week
29 _____	30 _____	1 _____	2 _____	3 _____	4 _____	5 _____

15

Do Permissions Right

IN COLLEGE TEXTBOOK PUBLISHING, requesting and tracking grants of permission for use of others' work is usually the author's task. The publisher might provide the service of paying the grant fees as part of the cost of production. Some large houses maintain permissions departments and may agree to evaluate authors' permissions or conduct permissions research.

Copyright Law

Copyright law is reasonably clear on the subject of what permissions you need, although there are gray areas from which new issues often arise. The latest issues relate to electronic publishing and intellectual property rights on the Internet. Ask your publisher for permissions guidelines. It is such a critical matter that even small houses have policies and guidelines. To learn more about copyright law and the permission process, you might consult one or more of the following sources.

Selected Sources on Copyright Law

10 Big Myths about Copyright Explained: **templetons.com/brad/copymyths**

Besenjak, C. *Copyright Plain and Simple*, 2nd ed. Career Press, 2001.

Copyright Clearance Center: **authors.copyright.com**

Copy Law: **copylaw.com**

Digital Millennium Copyright Act,1998: **copyright.gov/legislation/dmca.pdf**

Fishman, Stephen. *The Copyright Handbook: What Every Editor Needs to Know*. NOLO, 2006.

Guide to Citing Government Information Resources: **library.unr.edu/depts/bgic/guides/government/cite.html**

Kozak, Ellen M. *Every Writer's Guide to Copyright and Publishing Law*, 3rd ed. Holt Paperbacks, 2004.

Stim, Richard. *Getting Permission: How to License and Clear Copyrighted Materials Online and Off*, 2nd ed. NOLO, 2004.
U.S. Copyright Office: **loc.gov/copyright/search**

As a rule of thumb, you can use and cite 300 words inclusively from any one book-length source without permission, and publishers increasingly risk up to 500 words. With citation you also can use up to five percent of journal articles or other works that are less than book-length. You must have permission, however, for any part of a poem, song, speech, letter, e-mail, unpublished thesis or dissertation, child's artwork, or student's writing. By law, the authors of these works or their legal guardians own the copyright. Likewise, individuals' responses to questionnaires constitute protected speech and may not be published without a release or written permission.

You must have permission to use (reproduce), adapt, or abridge all figures and tables regardless of the number of words they contain, as well as for most photos, cartoons, and illustrations. To "adapt" any text is to change some of its words or parts, or to add new information to it. To "abridge" is to leave out words or parts, or to shorten (condense) it.

Whether textual material is permissionable or not, always use quotes or the indented excerpt format, and cite the source. Cite sources directly below figures and tables. If you have already received a grant of permission to use a figure or table by the time you submit chapter manuscript, also include the credit line after the source. For instance, some grantors will request that you write "Used with permission of. . . ." Otherwise, provide a credit line manuscript as soon as all permissions for a chapter are in. In some houses a production editor or packager performs this service for you.

Public Domain and Paraphrases

Public domain includes most (but not all) material published by the United States government; various classes of historical and documentary materials; expired copyrights; and matters of public record, such as vital statistics and news articles without bylines. There are murky areas. Government reports might contain copyrighted material, for example, requiring permission.

Some authors seek to avoid the necessity for permissioning sources by paraphrasing text—restating using other words or forms. Contrary to popular belief, however, paraphrases are not safe from litigation for copyright infringement. For example, changing the order of words in a quotation, changing or dropping articles or pronouns, and adding or dropping items in a list do not constitute legal paraphrase. Quotations must be substantively rewritten in your own words to satisfy the rule for paraphrase. At the same time, creating derivative works (e.g., the same model using different labels or the same story using different names for characters and a different ending) without permission also is illegal unless you are writing a parody.

Fair Use and Other Restrictions

It is a common misconception among academics that speech for educational purposes is protected in some way against claims of copyright violation. And this may be true inside classroom walls and in scholarship generally. However, a whole new scrutiny of such use arises as soon as money comes into the picture. Unlike the "free speech" that takes place in your classroom, your textbook will be sold commercially for profit, which means that educational use will no longer be regarded as fair use.

Also keep the following facts in mind.

- As of April 1989, everything created in the United States is protected whether or not it carries a copyright notice.
- Nothing is in the public domain unless the copyright owner explicitly puts it in the public domain in writing. This includes postings to computer networks and discussion groups.
- All e-mail is automatically copyrighted and owned by the original creator or sender.
- Fair use applies only if you are directly writing a commentary on, reporting on, or educating about a work itself, not if you are only writing about the subject of the work.
- Fair use involves short excerpts that are attributed and do not ruin the commercial value of the work they come from.
- You must get permission from your publisher to quote from your own previously published work.
- Raw data from any source are not copyrightable.
- Never assume that a colleague would appreciate free publicity by being quoted at length and cited in your textbook. Request permission.
- Written permission to use works of minors or photographs of minors must be obtained from a parent or guardian.
- In most circumstances, photos cannot be used without written model releases from anyone in the picture who can be identified, as well as the photographer, photo agency, or news syndicate. (An exception is photographs of scenes at public sites or events in which identifiable individuals may appear.)
- Most copyright infringements involve suits in civil court. However, commercial copyright violations involving more than 10 copies and/or value over $2,500 is a felony.

Permissioning Internet Sources

If you want to use something in your book that you find online, you must request permission, unless a grant of release is appended to the online material. If you do not see a copyright statement at the end of the material or elsewhere on the website, contact the webmaster and request information about the copyright holder. Then send a letter or e-mail explaining how and where you wish to use the work, and request information for a proper credit line. You may receive a form and fee request in response. In any case, keep a hardcopy file of any grants of permission.

The editorial style guidelines you are using for your textbook (see Chapter 6) will have information on how to cite online sources. As an alternative, consistently use the Columbia Online Style, which lists the author, the title of the selected work (in quotes), the title of the larger work where the selected work resides (the name of the website, if different from the name of the author), the publication date (or date last revised), the URL (universal resource locator, or online address), and the date you accessed the work.

Example: Citing an Online Source
Editorial Freelance Association, "Fair Practice Code," 2007, the-efa.org/res/code_TOC.html, accessed September 10, 2007.

Permissioning Photos and Art

Permission is necessary for any artwork (illustration) from another source, unless (1) the subject is common knowledge in your field or must be rendered in a certain way (such as a representation of the human brain) and (2) your publisher is planning to have it redrawn or rendered in a different style. For example, if your chapter on speech and language disorders requires a labeled diagram of vocal apparatus, an artist may legally create an original drawing of the human vocal apparatus based on a number of photos and illustrations in anatomical reference books, to which your labels are then added. Chance resemblances between your diagram and a diagram of the human vocal apparatus in some other text could arise solely because of the uniformity of human anatomy. If your diagram is a copy of another one or a facsimile, however, you would need permission.

Use artworks from their primary sources if at all possible. If art from a secondary source credits the primary source of the art, you need permission only from the primary source. However, if the secondary source adapted or redrew the art and you are using that, you will need permission from both the primary and the secondary sources. As with text permissions involving works in the public domain, there are gray areas. If you wanted to publish a translation from the Greek of the *The Periplus of the Erythrean Sea* along with the map, for instance, you would be wise to choose a translation from the 19th century that is in the public domain rather than one found on a contemporary historian's website, even if the historian cites an earlier source.

The same principle applies to figures and tables. That is, suppose you want to use a table in the pubic domain, such as a statistical chart on arrests from the U.S. Department of Justice. You see this chart in a competing textbook with the U.S. Department of Justice cited as the source in the credit line. But if you thought it would be safe to use that table, you would be wrong. That textbook author may have modified or abridged the table, in which case you would be infringing copyright. Thus, you should always try to get your materials, even public domain materials, from their original sources.

Photographs also must be permissioned and credited, although a corpus of copyright-free images does exist online. The source of a copyright-free image nevertheless should be credited. Snapshots you take yourself are not free; they involve carefully obtaining signed releases from recognizable subjects, even (especially) family members and neighbors.

Specific images you choose for your textbook can be traced (by you or by the publisher's photo researcher) only if you provide complete information about the sources, including the names and addresses of copyright holders. If the copyright holder of an unreleased photo you want to use cannot be found, then you cannot use the photo. Even then, specific images may not be traceable or may not be available (or affordable) when found. Photo researchers rely mainly on your photo specs and captions as guides, a subject of Chapter 16.

Cost of Permissions

Individual permissions can range from gratis to shockingly expensive, and overall costs can mount significantly. Scientific textbooks, textbooks with extensive illustration programs, and literature anthologies are especially dear. A one-time use of a single cartoon cel from a syndicate or movie can cost $300 or more. Permissions fees for an undergraduate textbook on human evolution might exceed $8,000, not counting the permissions researcher's fee. If the publisher is disbursing payment for fees, these costs typically are charged against your book.

Textbook authors who have relied heavily on others' works often become more creative when they have had a few surprises or see how permissions fees can add up. You might be asked to pay $1,500 for a page from a children's book whose copyright owner is its author.

Materials regarded as essential to a course of study are not safe from high (some would say excessive) fees imposed by an individual author, a famous person's estate, or certain publishing conglomerates. More than one history, mass communication, and literature textbook has chosen to reduce usage of the texts of speeches of Martin Luther King Jr., for instance, to keep overall permissions costs in line.

If the copyright owner is a publisher or a professional organization, you generally will find reasonable standard fee scales. Many publishers, journals, and stock photo agencies have standard rates. An article from a professional journal might be permissioned for $35 per page, for example, and a photo for use as a four-color, full-page chapter opener might be permissioned for $500.

Professional associations often request that you also obtain permission from the authors as well, as a courtesy. Some publishers have grant forms that require payment prior to publication or set a time limit for payment beyond which the permission will be void. Pay these requests promptly, or forward the forms to your publisher for prepayment.

Whatever wording you use in your initial request to the copyright holder, permissions typically are good for only one edition of a specified print run of a particular title. Because of the possible costs involved, if you are responsible for doing all your own permissions research, you would be wise to find out the fee policies of sources in advance and to choose only the best and most essential material to use in your textbook. Commercial textbook companies typically take responsibility for photo research and may assist you in text permissions by helping to locate the names and addresses of copyright holders.

Sources of free and low-cost images include the Library of Congress, state and local historical societies and museums, labor and trade associations, NASA and other federal organizations, and some archived image banks on the Internet. Internet photos and clip art require careful research and selectivity, however. Recently, for instance, Google produced 158 million sites in response to a keyword search on "free stock photos," and those photos included a great many that one would not want to see in a textbook on any subject.

Developing a Permissions Log and Tracking Requests

However permissions are being handled for your textbook, you will need a permissions log for each chapter. This is the best way to make permissioning easier on yourself and others. For each chapter, identify permissionable material as you go along and record intended requests on a six-column table or log. The contents of such a log are shown below, but there are alternatives. Your publisher may have its own detailed record-keeping and tracking letters and forms for you to use. A sample permissions log is presented in the chapter appendix.

Minimum Contents of a Permissions Log

Title: Chapter number, working chapter title, and date

Column 1: Manuscript page number (msp) on which the material appears

Column 2: The complete source of that material (including page numbers)

Column 3: The name and address of the copyright holder (to be filled in when you find out; the actual copyright holder may not be the same as the source)

Column 4: The date of request (to be filled in when you send your letter of request)
Column 5: The date of grant (to be filled in when you receive the grant of permission)
Column 6: The amount of the fee you or your publisher must pay in order to use the material. Sometimes the "fee" may be a complimentary copy ("comp") of your textbook when it is available.

If the publisher's Author Guidelines does not provide a form for logging and reporting permissions, ask your editor for one. Publishers' forms may have additional columns for identifying the specific rights granted.

As you develop your permissions log, take the time to make two photocopies of the permissionable material and the page on which it appears. One set goes out with your request (so the grantor can see what you are doing with it), and one set stays in your file to help you keep track. If you later decide to cut the material, or if you have to drop it because you cannot locate the copyright holder, the fee is too high, or permission is denied, then you can conveniently forward this extra copy to your editor or production coordinator in time to keep it out of print in your book. All you need to do then is notify copyright holders that the material they gave you permission for is not being used after all. It is far better to cancel a permission than to be without.

So, when you complete your draft, you will have a permissions log for each chapter and two copies of each piece for which you are requesting permission. By that time you should have researched the sources, located copyright holders, and sent out your letters of request. In fact, it is better not to wait to apply for permissions, as they can take months to obtain. For addresses and phone numbers, research copyright holders online or consult the most recent LMP (*Literary Market Place*), online or in the reference section of your campus or public library. Sort your pieces by publisher or copyright holder for efficiency. You can make multiple requests to the same grantor in one mailing.

Requesting and Handling Grants of Permission

If your publisher has not sent you a sample form letter for requesting permission, ask for one. Getting the wording right is important for legality, and every company has its own requirements. You need to know if you should request world rights, foreign language rights, reprint rights, rights to digitized versions, and so on. Also determine the planned publication date for your book, the estimated page count, whether it will be case bound or paperback or both, the number of copies your publisher plans to print, and the price for which the publisher plans to sell it. Grantor companies often request this information and sometimes base their fees on the size of print runs and price. Your letter will go something like the following.

Introduction: I (we) and (the publisher) would like permission to (use, reprint, abridge, adapt) the following material in (your name(s)), (title of your book), (publication date), (page count), (paperback or case bound), (size of print run), (initial pricing).

<Insert here the complete source of the material, including the page numbers and the number of words or lines you want to use>

Body: Your publisher's legal statement about rights requested and various disclaimers, such as assuming that the signer is the legal copyright holder.

Conclusion: Your signature, the date, and various write-on lines for grantors to sign and date.

Enclosure: A copy of what you are requesting permission for and the context in which you are using it.

Make two copies of each letter, one for you and one for your publisher. Large grantors will respond to your letter by sending you their own special form to fill out. Your request for permission is not officially made until you receive, fill out, and return this form.

As grants come in, write the date received on your permissions log. Then, when you submit the final draft of your manuscript for production, include your completed permissions logs, copies of your requests, and the originals of the grants. Many grantors will state the precise wording they want you to use in the credit line. As much as possible, insert credit lines on your final manuscript.

Keep a copy of the grants for your files. Publishing houses without functioning permissions departments, large and small, have been known to lose such files in production, misplace them during housecleaning or staff turnovers, or lack the will to find them in dead storage. If your book goes into another edition two or three years later, your copy of the first-edition permissions grants could prove invaluable. As mentioned earlier, textbook permissions are almost always granted for one time use only. If you want to reuse material in a new edition, therefore, you likely will need to reapply.

Disaster Control Solutions for Permissions

Scenario A: You procrastinated on permissions and now you don't have time to do it:

Solution 1. Quickly go through a copy of each chapter with a marker and identify everything you think you need permission for. Give this manuscript to a fulltime helper or hired hand along with your publisher's form letter for requests. Have the helper make the permissions logs, research the addresses and phone numbers, generate the request letters, do the mailings, and track the grants.

Solution 2. Immediately notify your publisher. Ask the publisher to hire a professional permissions researcher. This cost will be charged directly or indirectly against your royalties.

Scenario B: It's late and you are worried that you will not receive outstanding permissions in time.

Solution 1. Phone copyright holders and beg. Get a verbal agreement, a fee estimate, and the name and title of the person you speak to. Record and date this information in a phone log. Include the phone log with the permissions logs when you submit the final manuscript.

Solution 2. Immediately notify your editor and ask for reassurance.

Scenario C: You did not get or could not afford all the permissions you wanted.

Solution 1. Convert selected tables to figures and vice versa. You do not need permission for an original table you create from someone's labels in a figure or for an original figure you create using someone's labels from a table. Just credit the source of the information.

Solution 2. Cut any unpermissioned quotes to 299 (or 499, depending on the standard being used) words or less per source (this includes words of one character).

Solution 3. Interweave paraphrases of material from two or more different sources, and list all the sources together in one parenthetical citation (separated by semicolons).

Solution 4. Substitute for or drop any remaining unpermissioned material, however painful it may be.

In all the above scenarios, it is crucially important to notify your editor or production coordinator immediately of any changes you are making to final manuscript. While you are dropping a figure, the publisher might be paying an artist to draw it. The best solution by far is to avoid permissioning problems by not procrastinating and by working within a budget.

The more you can do for your book on your own the better. You can even enhance your textbook's value visually. The next and last chapter guides you in developing your figures and tables, art and map specs, and photo program.

APPENDIX
Sample Permissions Log

Chapter 7 Mutual Funds, 9/10/07					
Msp	Source	Copyright Holder	Letter Out	Grant In	Fee
2	"Mutual Fund" (definition), InvestorWords (financial glossary), investorwords.com/3173/mutual_fund.html, 2007.	InvestorWords, investorwords.com/licensing.html	6/2	7/24	75
4	Kling, Arnold, "Regulate Mutual Funds?" Library of Economics & Liberty, econlog.econlib.org/archives/000513.html, July 8, 2004	Arnold Kling, webmaster@econlib.org	6/4	8/1	0
11	Frankel, T., and A. T. Schwing, Regulation of Money Managers: Mutual Funds and Advisers, 2nd ed., Aspen, 2006: ix–x	Aspen Publishers. Aspenpublishers.com/licensing/	6/4	7/14	35
22	Investment Company Institute, "Shareholder Sentiment about the Mutual Funds Industry 2006" (pdf table), Mutual Fund Fact Book, icifactbook.org, May 2007	Investment Company Institute, 1401 H Street NW, Washington, DC, 20005, 202-326-5800 webmaster@ici.org	6/6	9/3	125
24	"Mutual Funds Scorecard, July 31, 2007," Business Week Online, bwnt.Business week.com	Morningstar Inc., 225 West Wacker Dr., Chicago, IL 60606 312-696-6000	6/6	—	—

continued on next page

Chapter 7 Mutual Funds, 9/10/07					
31	U.S. Securities and Exchange Commission, "The SEC Mutual Fund Cost Calculator," sec.gov/investor/tools/mfcc-intsec.htm, 02/28/2006.	SEC, 100F Street NE, Washington, DC 20549, 202-942-8088 Press Inquiries: 202-551-4120	6/8	—	—

16

Enhance Your Textbook's Value Visually

PRESENTATION REFERS to the tangible, physical characteristics of your book—how it feels in the hand and how it looks as it pages. Your publisher's choice of a trim size, paper weight, paper opacity, binding type, cover, book design, art style, and palette (if color is involved) all affect presentation.

Consider how you evaluate a textbook. Very likely you begin by holding the book open by the spine in your left hand and rifling the pages with the fingers of your right hand. You are looking for content, but you are strongly influenced by your impressions of what you see as the pages flip past your eyes. Professional sales reps call this the "flip test," and it usually is the first step in a buying decision.

The Importance of Presentation

The visual presentation of your book is important in marketing and selling it to customers. Depending on the budget, based on the sales projection, you may have opportunities to enhance your text visually. For example, you might include a specified number of tables, figures or illustrations, and photographs that have pedagogical value and enhance the text's visual interest. At signing, negotiate with your publisher the numbers of these elements that your book can have. The cost of acquiring and producing them will create restrictions.

Textbook publishers have diverse standards for treating visual elements, to which you must conform. For instance, you might need to include tables within your narrative if they will be typeset, or on separate sheets if they will be treated as art or will appear in a four-color design. You might be required to provide camera-ready or plate-ready figures on disk yourself, or your publisher might gather all your figures into an art manuscript and commission an artist to create them. Find out, therefore, what your contract requires exactly and what your publisher will need.

If your editor does not provide you with guidelines for preparing figures, tables, and photos, ask for them. If you are doing your own development, you continually will want to remain mindful of opportunities to present information visually. The following sections describe ways to visualize information that you can use in your textbook, beginning with the basic graphic organizer.

Using Graphic Organizers

A graphic organizer is a visual representation of a chapter, topic, sequence, or concept. In a chapter opener, a graphic organizer prepares students for the content you intend they should learn. For example, a diagram or flowchart might convey the progression of ideas you develop in the chapter, while a concept map or web might trace relationships among the topics subsumed under the chapter's unifying concept. Thus, at the beginning of chapters or sections, graphics function as "advance organizers" (see Chapters 10 and 11). Readers have a chance to recognize a basic relationship in advance of reading about it. Graphic organizers also can contribute to exposition within the body of chapters or at the end of a chapter to summarize or connect up data. This example shows an advance organizer for a chapter on the securities industry.

Example: An Advance Organizer

Securities and Exchange Market Flow

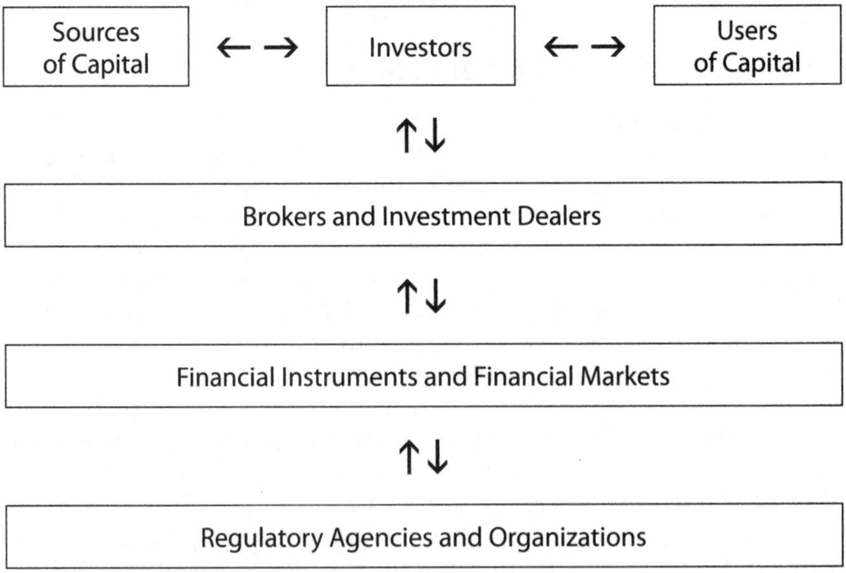

Visualizing verbal information is an art, and some authors and editors are more talented in this art than others. Yet, whatever your subject area and talents, the possibilities are worth the effort. Begin by determining the basic purpose of the information you want to illustrate, and then make some experimental sketches. There always is more than one way to convey ideas visually. Evaluate the likely effectiveness of the visualizations as a piece of art, and choose one that seems to work. For example, what visual representation might show the difference between a longitudinal research design and a cross-sectional research design? How might you show a dynamic systems model for language acquisition or other benchmarks in human development? What visualization might convey the physics of dispersion in wavelength or show how a transponder works? This chapter's appendix offers graphical templates for showing how information can be organized for a number of instructional purposes.

Presenting Figures and Tables

In college textbooks, figures and tables are more commonly seen than graphic organizers. Technically, a table presents numerical information in tabular form, while a figure presents information graphically or through illustrations. There are four basic types of figures.

- Charts and matrices with cells containing text
- Line, bar, and pie graphs
- Conceptual graphics (such as diagrams, flowcharts, concept maps, or graphic organizers)
- Rendered art (representational drawings or paintings, sometimes called "line art")

Some publishers refer to any figures that have to be drawn, rather than simply typeset or reproduced from film or digital media, as "art."

Common practice in commercial publishing requires you to provide each figure as a full-size printout, photocopy, sketch, or tearsheet on its own separate manuscript page. Recall that each figure and table is identified with a double number (e.g., Figure 2.4 would be the fourth figure in Chapter 2), and appears with a title, complete source, credit line if needed, and preferably a caption. If captions are planned, every figure should have one. Figure captions go beyond the figure title to elaborate on the content, call attention to something in the figure, or partly interpret it for the reader.

Figures (plus any tables not embedded in the manuscript) are keyed to text by using the assigned double numbers. For example, Figure 2.4, above, would be keyed on the manuscript on a separate line to mark the best location for it, as a kind of placeholder, like this:

<Insert Figure 2.4>

The notation alerts the copyeditor and later the compositor or page make-up artist of the existence of numbered "art" and its desired location. The sidewise carets (or alternatively an enclosing circle) alert production people that the insertion note itself is not to be set into type as part of the book (unless otherwise indicated, as in the above example of an insertion note). Sometimes the production editor marks a circled DNS on the manuscript for "Do Not Set."

The best location for each figure and table is at the end of the paragraph in which you call the reader's attention to it. It is good practice to refer to each figure by number within the chapter narrative as you discuss the content the figure serves. Your text reference can be parenthetical (e.g., see Figure 2.4), or you may refer to the figure in a sentence. In some subject areas, such as mathematics, a figure often immediately follows the referring sentence.

Use Figures and Tables Appropriately

Many authors treat figures and tables as ancillary to the text or purely decorative, and neither refer to them nor relate the information they contain to the sections of text in which they appear. This is not good practice. For figures and tables to have pedagogical value, their presence, relevance, and significance must be explained, however briefly, in the narrative or in a caption (or both).

Another common misconception is that figures and tables replace text. However, in good exposition the function of tables and figures is to elucidate text, not substitute for it. Therefore, figures and tables should not introduce new information without text support. Figures and tables also should not contain any terms or concepts that are not defined in the text narrative.

Provide Narrative Context for Figures and Tables

Following are some examples of alternative ways to refer to your figures and tables within the narrative and to key them for location. Note the differences in style.

Example of Narrative Context A:

> Principles of Gestalt psychology rest on the observations of Max Wertheimer, Kurt Koffka, and Wolfgang Köhler that people perceive whole units rather than bits of sensation, that the whole of sensation is more than its parts. In Figure 6.3, for example, you readily see a circle even though bits of the circle are left out. This illustrates the principle of closure, which states that people organize their perceptions so that they are as simple and logical as possible, filling in gaps in perceptions as needed.
>
> <Insert Figure 6.3>

Example of Narrative Context B:

Principles of Gestalt psychology rest on the observations of Max Wertheimer, Kurt Koffka, and Wolfgang Köhler that people perceive whole units rather than bits of sensation, that the whole of sensation is more than its parts. Look at Figure 6.3, for example. What do you see?

<Insert Figure 6.3>

Your ability to see a circle even with parts of it missing illustrates the principle of closure. In closure, people organize their perceptions so that they are as simple and logical as possible, filling in perceptual gaps as needed.

Example of Narrative Context C:

Principles of Gestalt psychology rest on the observations of Max Wertheimer, Kurt Koffka, and Wolfgang Köhler that people perceive whole units rather than bits of sensation, that the whole of sensation is more than its parts. The principle of closure, for example, states that people organize their perceptions in the simplest and most logical way, filling in perceptual gaps as needed. For instance, people can readily recognize and identify incomplete forms (see Figure 6.3).

<Insert Figure 6.3>

In the manuscript, the illustration for Figure 6.3 would appear on its own separate sheet with the figure number, title, source, credit line, and possibly a caption, although some publishers prefer to have captions in a separate manuscript. According to the publisher's wishes, the sheet with the figure might be placed in context, following the page that refers to it, or in a separate art manuscript consisting of all the figures for the chapter, gathered at the back of the chapter manuscript.

If a figure comes from a published source, provide a good-quality photocopy or original tearsheet. To modify a previously published figure, adapt or edit it on the page, as needed, writing clearly in soft pencil or pen if only a few words are involved. Otherwise, type the changes. Compositors do not like to set type or re-key from handwriting and may refuse to do so or may charge the publisher a penalty fee. That fee gets charged against your book.

Preparing Art and Map Specs

If your figure is a computer graphic you created, provide both hardcopy and disk copy. This is a good time to explore to the limit the graphical and art capabilities of your software, including the generation and placement of labels and symbols in a diagram. If an artist or cartographer is assigned to your book, however, you need only provide a sketch and a specification sheet (or "specs") to enable the artist-specialist to render what you want (regardless of your sketching talent). Your specs might include the following information.

- Figure or map double number and title
- Manuscript page number on which the figure or map is keyed to appear
- Source (and credit line, if possible)
- Permission status
- Relative importance in the chapter (e.g., 1 = most important)
- Suggested approximate size (e.g., 1/4, 1/3, 1/2, 2/3, 3/4 page)
- Labels (e.g., showing A-, B-, and C-level headings)
- Brief note to artist or cartographer explaining in words what you want

Note, however, that artists as a rule prefer to receive information visually. Many go by what they see rather than taking time to read descriptions or explanations. Make your note to the artist brief, and do not attempt to dictate the specific size, design, or colors to be used in the art. The artist must follow the publisher-approved book designer's plan, and actual sizing is done by people in production according to page make-up and design options for art treatments.

Following are some suggested criteria for determining the relative importance of a figure or map, based on a three-point scale with 1 as "most important."

Importance of Art Piece	Rating
Necessary to make sense of text	1
The chapter's visual showpiece	1
Has other pedagogical value	2
Augments or enriches exposition	2
Is fun but pedagogically optional	3
Is uninteresting but obligatory	3

Your rating will help determine how much time and, therefore, money to lavish on each piece. Such a rating also helps in deciding what to drop if overlengthage or permissions problems require cuts. Nevertheless, you may find that your publisher has different standards or is not at all interested in your ratings of relative importance. Author input on production tasks is a traditional nicety that many twenty-first-century editors don't have time for, have forgotten, or ignore.

The size of a piece on the page can be an indication of importance or merely of the amount of information a figure is attempting to convey.

Readability and length are factors in determining the size of art objects, which normally is determined by the publisher's agents. As a rule of thumb, keep figures and tables to one book page or less, preferably less. Exceptions include chronologies (which might need a whole spread), comparative grids, and appendices (which might have several pages of tabular information). Sizing is an exact measurement in picas and, as noted above, relates to the book's design and budget.

The labels for each figure or map may be set from your art spec. In most cases you should type labels one to a line in the order they appear in the figure (left to right, top to bottom, or clockwise). Distinguish between umbrella labels and subordinate ones to show their relationship or relative importance. Otherwise all the labels might be set in the same size type, which might make interpretation difficult. Labels for maps and figures with insets should be organized by the differentiations within their keys.

Here is an example of a labeled sketch and the typed labels sheet that would accompany it. Labels for a map spec would be done in a similar fashion.

EXAMPLE: Art Sketch

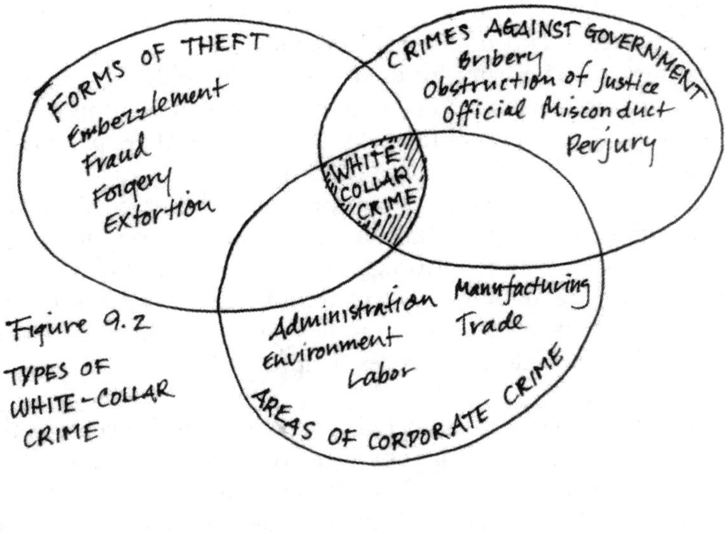

EXAMPLE: Typed Labels Sheet for Art Sketch

Figure 9.2 Types of White Collar Crime

FORMS OF THEFT
- Embezzlement
- Fraud
- Forgery
- Extortion

CRIMES AGAINST GOVERNMENT
- Bribery
- Obstruction of justice
- Official misconduct
- Perjury

AREAS OF CORPORATE CRIME
- Administration
- Environment
- Labor
- Manufacturing
- Trade

Visualizing Information and Creating Original Figures

Authors often find it difficult to create pedagogical figures beyond simple bar graphs and matrices. With a little imagination, however, charts and graphs can be embellished for greater visual interest. A common method of embellishing graphs is to choose an appropriate metaphor for the information being conveyed and then to represent the metaphor visually through objects or colors. News media do this all the time to attract attention. For example, stairs, elevators, or escalators might represent rising and falling commodities market, or a single commodity might be shown as a mountain climber summiting or tumbling down the chart.

Effective metaphors are simple, such as a pencil for scholastic achievement in a bar graph, where pencil length stands for student performance in different countries. Another familiar example is the dollar bill divided into percentages of expenditures or revenues.

What metaphors are apt for data sets in your field? For example, for the rate of global warming? For voting behavior in relation to gender? For runaway depreciation of the baht? For imports of pepper and cloves to Spain in the 16th century? For the hardness of minerals? For the distance of stars? Sometimes the thing itself is all that is needed. Imagine how much more exciting the formula for fractal geometry might be, for instance, if framed within a form generated by that formula.

As noted before, delivering verbal information visually is an art, but you don't have to be an artist to do it, just able to think a bit divergently. You might find the following process helpful.

1. Identify the main components of an important concept, analysis, process, or synthesis that you want your chapter to communicate. Discover them by asking: What is most important about this chapter (or section)? Why do readers need to know it? What is most critical for them to remember about it? What do I want them to come away with after reading it?
2. State the main idea that results from this line of questioning. For example, suppose you come up with the following statement for Chapter 2 of your macroeconomics textbook: Analysis of economic decisions is based on five fundamental principles—opportunity cost, marginal cost, diminishing returns, spillover, and reality.

3. Now, determine and draw the relationships among the principles. For instance, the principles might be of equal importance, as in the example of principles of economic decision making, or else might be contingent on each other in some way, as in a causal or chronological relationship.
4. Then determine and draw the relationships between each principle and the economic decision to which it leads. For instance, opportunity cost applies to decisions to sacrifice something for something else. The marginal cost principle applies to decisions to make small changes. The principle of diminishing returns applies to decisions to expand. Spillover applies to benefits external to one's own decisions; and the reality principle applies to decisions to the use of one's actual purchasing power.
5. Whatever relationships you state, experiment with different ways to represent them visually. Keep it simple, using as few short labels as possible to fully convey the point. Choose or create your own design elements to express the idea or metaphor, such as icons, arrows, geometric shapes, other symbols, or line drawings. Following is an attempt at a figure for the five economic principles. Does it work?

EXAMPLE: Creating Art

Principles of Economic Analysis

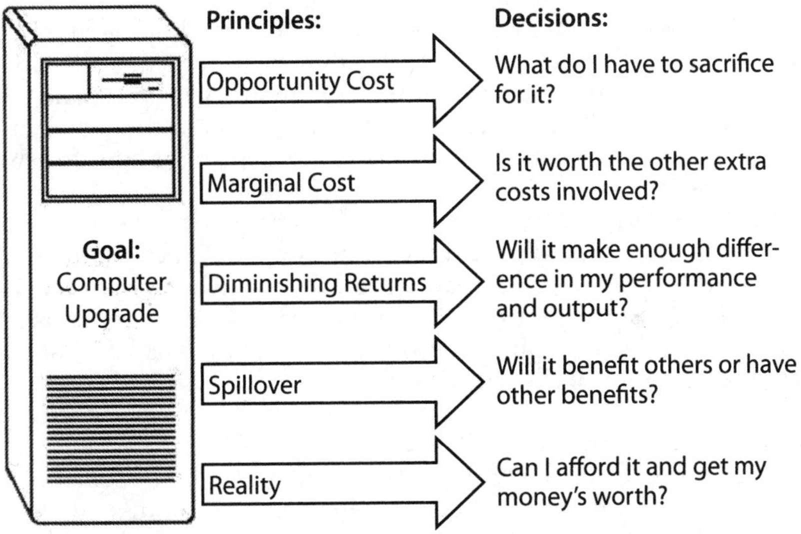

This macroeconomics example addresses the theoretical principles governing a phenomenon. Other types of statements might address other qualities (see also the chapter appendix). How could you represent each of the following qualities visually if x stood for a concept, condition, situation, or object in your field?

- Different approaches to x
- Degrees of x
- Stages of x
- Types of x
- Steps in the process of x
- Positive and negative aspects of x
- Causes and effects of x
- Factors to consider in solving x
- Changes in x over time
- Similarities and differences between x and y

Planning a Photo Program

Technically, photographs are any image on film or digitized media, regardless of content. The content might be a document, a drawing, a cartoon, a famous painting, a page of a book, or a facsimile, in addition to the images one normally thinks of as photographs. In publishing, any digital image or image on film is treated as a photograph, and all photographs must be researched, permissioned, and credited.

Photos often are obtained from individual freelance photographers responding to a publisher's "needs list," and also from stock agencies; film and video archives; museums; news agencies, television networks, and other media sources; chambers of commerce; other government sources, such as the Department of Labor, the Library of Congress, and state historical societies; business and industry sources; and professional and public service organizations. Larger commercial publishing houses might maintain in-house stock photography for their specific needs.

Many authors mistakenly regard photos as window dressing or decorations for their book. In textbooks, however, as much as any other pedagogical element, images teach. You can remain mindful of this fact by framing questions that readers can answer by looking at the picture or by relating chapter content to the image. Images should be chosen for their pedagogical value to the learner.

Evaluating and Choosing Images

If the publisher is obtaining the images or film for photo requests, you will need to provide photo specs—a description of the desired images and their location in relation to chapter content. If possible, include a photocopy or tearsheet of an image like the one you want, as well as a likely source. However, if you supply guide photos to aid the photo researcher, be sure to identify them as such or you may find them reproduced in your textbook. Typically, the photo researcher and editor solicit and select one to three images for each photo spec that you or your development editor provides. You then view the images and choose or approve them. For major market books, the publisher's agents pick most of the photos, do the permissions research, and pay the use fees, which normally are charged against your book.

Photographs, both black and white and color, can be very expensive to obtain and reproduce. Different rates apply based on the size at which the image will be reproduced on the page. Because of the costs, high visibility, and market sensitivity of photographs, and because of technical matters concerning image reproducibility and print quality, most college houses retain control over final photo selection. The market, sales projection, and budget for your book will determine the number of photos you will be allowed, whether they will be four-color or black and white, and whether you or the publisher will be responsible for getting them. These decisions will be part of your contract negotiation.

In undergraduate textbooks, chapters typically have a chapter-opening photo and one or more internal photos. If you are supplying images for your book personally, unless you are trained in photographic techniques, do everyone a favor and hire a professional photographer. Your snapshots very likely will not be good enough for reproduction and your low-resolution digital images will not print large enough with sufficient quality. If you have existing images that you must use, consider hiring an expert to scan them and enhance their reproducibility using Adobe PhotoShop or other image manipulation software. Your publisher usually can arrange to have this done for you as needed.

The visual and verbal content of photographs can be a critical issue in educational publishing. Customer complaints often involve images regarded as misleading, offensive in some way, or outdated. This is especially true in elementary and secondary school publishing, where more than one textbook has failed in adoptions because of the photo program alone. Also, untrue or injudicious photo captions can be seen as unethical and have been known to lead to libel or defamation suits. For example, you would not print a scene with recognizable children and adults at a day care center with a caption about child sexual abuse. Following are some general rules of thumb for selecting and captioning photographs.

- Reject images that reflect stereotypes of any kind (racist, classist, sexist, ageist), unless stereotyping is the subject.
- Choose images that accurately represent people, places, and subjects, that fairly portray population diversity overall, and that show balance in your treatment of the subject.

- Reject images with salacious or suggestive content, especially involving children.
- Check that any foreign language print evident in images is not profane or otherwise unacceptable to your audience.
- Reject images containing commercial brands or trademark labels or slogans, unless advertising or popular culture is the subject. (Permission must be obtained from the trademark owner.)
- In captioning, do not ascribe characteristics to people or imply conditions, unless you can verify empirically and ethically that those characteristics or conditions are present. For example, you would not identify a recognizable child in a stock agency photo as hearing impaired, poor, pregnant, or infected with HIV. Also take care in making attributions about public figures.
- Reject images with dated hair and clothing styles, outdated technology (including car and computer models) and passé social contexts, unless your subject or purpose is historical.

Writing Photo Specs

Writing photo specs is an authoring task, although editors may write specs for managed textbooks. Photo specs are double-numbered by sequence in each chapter. Like figure specs, photo specs are keyed to text to show the optimal location in the chapter. In locating images, consider the best way to achieve the right kind of visual impact and pedagogical payload for your book. You might space images evenly throughout a chapter to suggest both richness and continuity, or you might pair or cluster images to achieve a particular aim. Note, however, that photo placement on a page is a technical matter, ultimately decided by the publisher's agents.

Submit photo specs (or photos) and a photo caption manuscript along with your text manuscript. Your publisher should supply guidelines for writing photo specs, which need to be worded briefly in a way that non-experts in your field can understand. The best photo specs include a brief description of what has to be in the picture and the concept the picture serves. The best captions provide comprehensive factual information or ask application questions.

Examples of Photo Specs and Captions

Photo 11.1 Chapter opener: Japanese and American businesspersons shaking hands in a corporate setting. Illustrates the chapter theme of international business.

Photo 11.2 Msp. 17 Iraq "free zone" black market.
CAPTION: Unofficial, or "black," markets are free markets that operate outside the control of the government. Black markets arise wherever a currency is not fully convertible, but the term

also is used to describe the buying and selling of goods that are officially or legally unavailable.

Photo 11.3 Msp. 31 Okavongo power plant in Botswana, Africa, with workers.
CAPTION: The World Bank funded this power plant project in Botswana through the International Monetary Fund. International development banks such as the World Bank give loans and assistance for government guaranteed projects. Funding is designed to improve national economies and stimulate international trade and investment, but critics have questions.

Be realistic in your photo specs. With all the pictures there are in the world, even professional photo researchers have difficulty filling specs that are over-specific or over-detailed, as well as those that describe rare or improbable sights. "A smiling eight-year-old Eskimo playing wheelchair basketball in a traditional parka with white fur trim" just isn't going to happen. And if it did happen, you would need to provide the specific name, date, and place so that the photo researcher could find out if a professional photographer was present who might have taken such a picture.

At the opposite extreme are photo specs that are not specific enough for the photo researcher to find, such as "a mug shot of that serial rapist they executed recently," or that are too abstract, such as "an illustration of capitalism."

Publishers sometimes commission photo shoots for textbooks with particular needs. For example, a college house might create in-house stock for its series of textbooks for teachers on special education.

The Art of Writing Captions

Many authors (and some editors) miss teaching opportunities by treating visual elements strictly as illustration. Images are left captionless or are given a few uninspired lines of general self-evident information. Yet good descriptive captions can reinforce learning. Visuals also offer opportunities for readers to interact with text through reflection, critical thinking, and application. Give some thought to captioning your figures, tables, and photos in meaningful, pedagogically useful ways. Captions might briefly interpret graphs, draw conclusions from statistics, provide background information, or ask questions of the reader.

For example, compare the following treatments of photographs for textbooks on English composition, marine biology, and foundations of education. In each case, which caption, A or B, probably would have greater value to the learner?

Examples: Caption Quality

<Photo of Ichabod Crane illustration>	
Caption A: In characterization, a writer describes the qualities and peculiarities of a person.	**Caption B:** In characterization, a writer describes the qualities and peculiarities of a person. Using the guidelines on p. 87, write a characterization of this imaginary person.
<Photo of clownfish with anemone>	
Caption A: By "inoculating" themselves against the anemone's venom, these clownfish gain protection from predators.	**Caption B:** By "inoculating" themselves against the anemone's venom, these clownfish gain protection from predators. In this example, how does the autoimmunity of one species contribute to the adaptation of another?
<Photo of parent helping child with homework>	
Caption A: Parental involvement is an important factor in academic achievement.	**Caption B:** Parental involvement is an important factor in academic achievement. Which of Eisner's six functions of parental involvement are represented in this picture?

In every case, you probably chose Caption B. These captions all share the following three characteristics.

1. The reader must "read" the image; that is, the reader must take time to look at "this imaginary person," "this example," and "this picture."
2. The reader must interpret the image in terms of main concepts presented in the textbook (i.e., the concepts of characterization, autoimmunity and adaptation, and parental involvement).
3. The reader must do something or answer a question that demonstrates comprehension or application (i.e., use specific guidelines to write a characterization, explain an adaptive relationship in nature, apply a specific functional model to a case).

Education research supports the intelligent use of visual information in textbooks at all levels of academic attainment. Try to develop your art program so that every chapter has tables, figures (possibly including maps), and photos that will contribute to the pedagogical value, visual continuity, originality, and appeal of your textbook. If possible, avoid the "usual suspects." For example, how many chapters on evolutionary forces use a microscopy image of sickled blood cells to illustrate balanced polymorphism? Could you show an African American child being treated for sickle-cell anemia instead? Or an African child eating fava beans and thereby risking the expression of Glucose-6-Phosphate Dehydrogenase Deficiency? Or Peruvian cholera victims in 1991, pointing out that carriers of the genes for cystic fibrosis were immune?

Putting It All Together

"Putting It All Together" is hardly original for the last heading in a nonfiction work that aims to teach, but it is apt. It's hard to end a book on writing and developing a college textbook. Textbook authors tend to have the same difficulty, with last chapters taking longer to arrive at the editor's desk. In actuality, for both the author and the editor, so long as a book is in print, work is never done.

This book has attempted to convey some of the complexities of providing sound print support for a course of study in higher education while also providing a product that can compete successfully in the marketplace and make money for both its author and publisher. In keeping with the theme of this chapter, this book closes with a graphic organizer summarizing those complexities. In writing and developing your college textbook, I wish you the best of luck. Yes, you can do it, and yes, it's worth it.

Writing and Developing Your College Textbook: The Essentials

Understand Your Market
Decide Your Mission
Find Your Audience
Know Your Competition

Get Signed
Choose a Publisher
Establish a Relationship
Negotiate a Contract

Develop Your Textbook
Write a Table of Contents
Plan Your Apparatus
Plan Your Pedagogical Features
Plan Your Presentation

Prepare Your Manuscript
Choose Your Style
Find Your Voice
Draft to Length
Draft to Schedule
Do Permissions

APPENDIX
Ways of Visualizing Information

Purpose: To illustrate a process

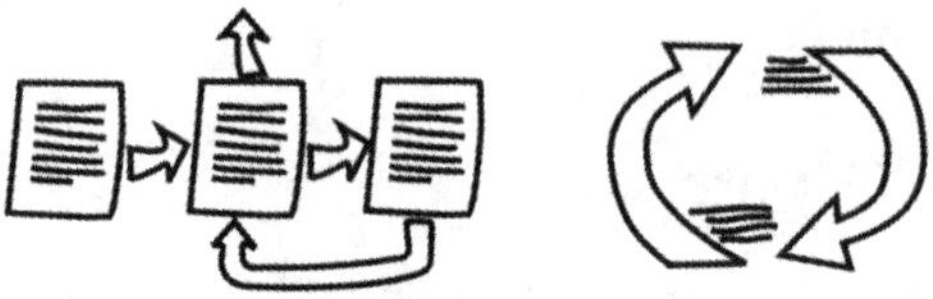

Purpose: To summarize steps in a procedure

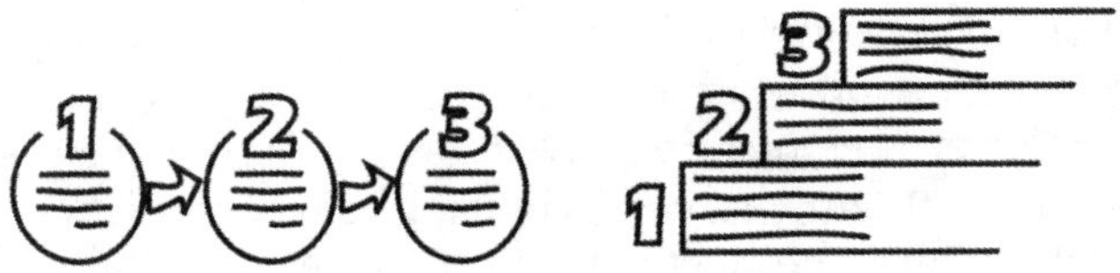

Purpose: To trace a sequence of events

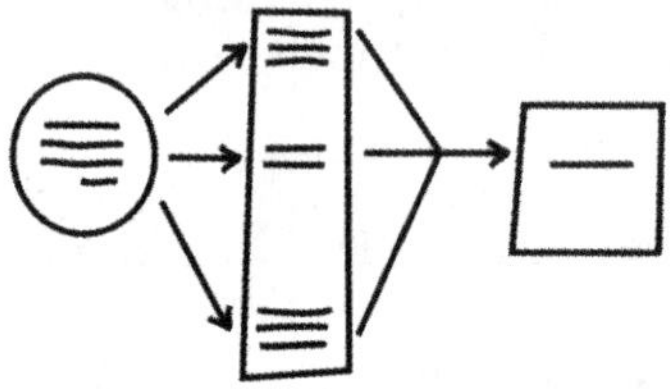

Purpose: To indicate cause and effect

Purpose: To show effects of or influences on a subject

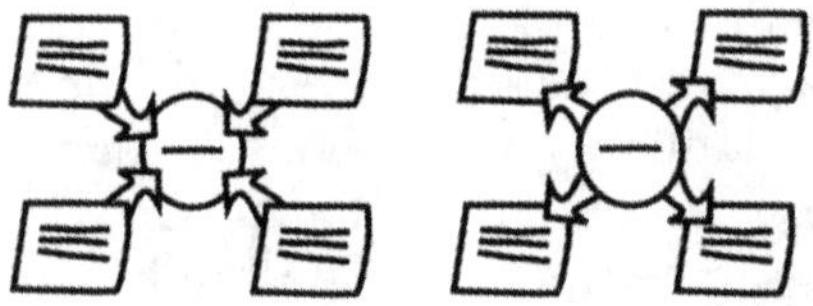

Purpose: To explain the relationship among topics

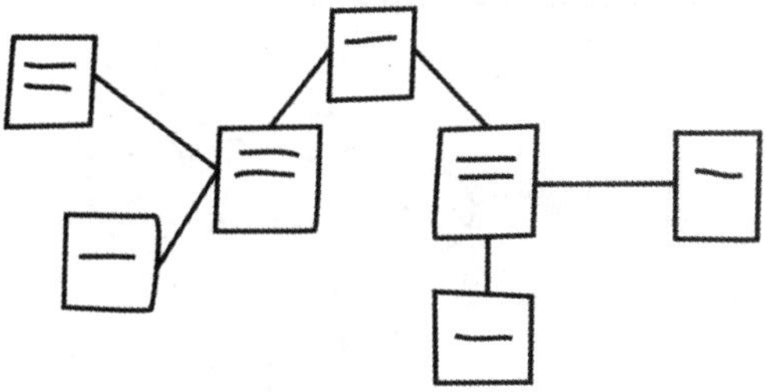

Purpose: To classify information

Purpose: To show the parts of a whole

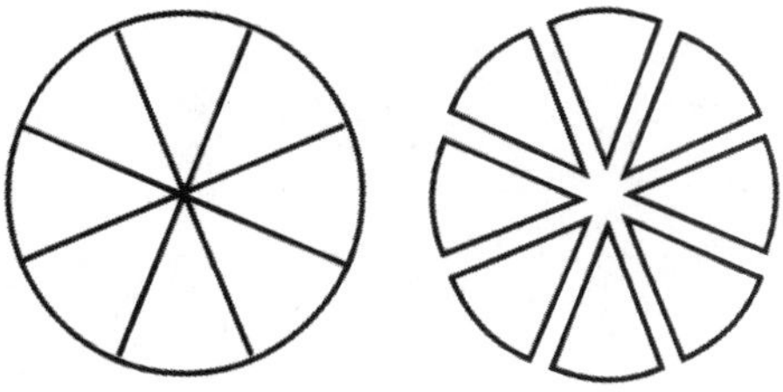

Purpose: To illustrate the relationship of parts to a whole

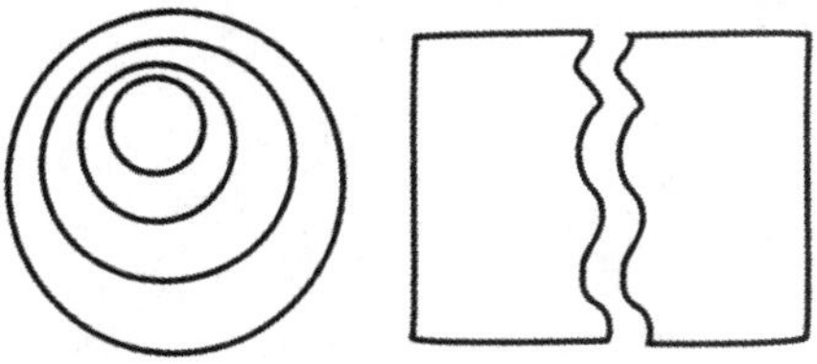

Purpose: To show the relationship of ideas to a concept

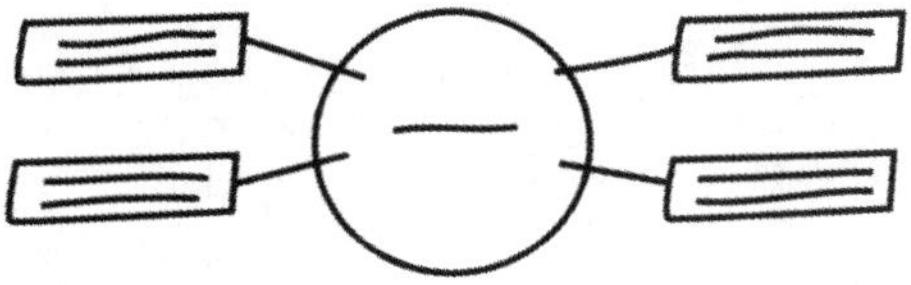

Purpose: To trace a logical extension of ideas

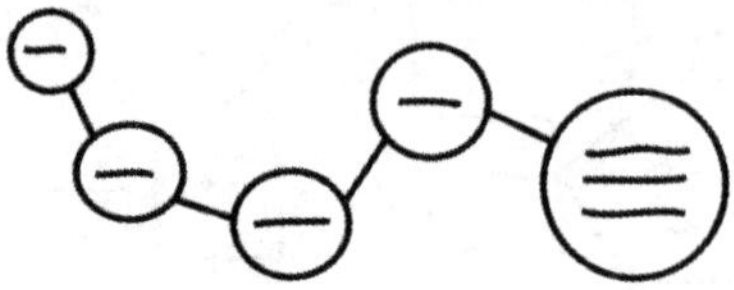

Glossary

A-book (or AA, AAA) A high-investment, typically four-color, title.

Abridge Change text by omitting words or paragraphs to shorten it.

Academic presses Smaller commercial presses that publish upper-tier course supplements and scholarly works with minimum investment.

Acceptable manuscript (also publishable manuscript, satisfactory manuscript) A completed draft that the publisher deems publishable by some standard.

Active learning Self-directed learning through experience or through interaction with text or other information sources.

Acquisitions 1. Publishers' purchases of other companies. 2. publishing phase that ends when you submit an acceptable manuscript for which you are under contract.

Acquisitions editor (AE) Publishing professional (also called series editor or sponsoring editor) responsible for getting you under contract to provide a work for publication and for presenting your project to the company and its agents.

Adapt Change text by altering words or adding material to make it fit your purpose.

Adopt (or adoption) Order a text for a course.

Advance organizer A pedagogical device (graphical or textual) that prepares readers for learning chapter content by identifying the categories or framework in which the topics are related.

Advances Payments in advance of earnings, which are deducted from future royalties.

Affective objectives Learning objectives that specify desired changes in feelings or values.

Agent (see Literary agent)

Agreement Legal contract for publishing your book ("the Work").

Ancillaries Student supplements without which your textbook would be incomplete, such as a website in a text–web hybrid or a text-dedicated workbook.

Annotation (or anno) A brief identifying description, often used in marginalia in textbooks, especially in instructor's editions.

Apparatus Regular elements of your textbook structure, such as the way chapters or sections open and close.

Art manuscript A separate compilation of the figures for your textbook to be rendered by an artist or computer graphics specialist.

Art specs A descriptive list of requested content for the creation of original figures for your textbook.

Audience The people who will buy and read your textbook.

Audit clause Clause in a publishing contract expressly granting the author the right to audit (or have audited) the publisher's accounts for the author's book.

Author-centered Characteristic of textbooks that give primacy to the author–expert in exposition.

Author Guidelines (or AG) The publisher's preferences and instructions for manuscript preparation and submittal.

Authorial voice Who you are as a person and teacher, as revealed through your writing.

Authoring Writing and publishing a college textbook and in a timely manner attending to all the nonwriting tasks associated with that process.

Author profile Characteristics that publishers look for in an author.

Author's Alterations (AAs; also author's corrections, ACs) Changes an author makes to content after the manuscript has been set into type or page proof has been generated.

Authorship Observance of the values, responsibilities, and behaviors involved in authoring.

Author team Two or more coauthors who directly collaborate on a textbook manuscript.

B-book A medium-investment, typically two-color, title.

Backlist Formerly published titles in a subject area the publisher serves.

Bibliography An alphabetized list of all the sources you consulted as you wrote your textbook, whether or not you had occasion to mention them or cite them in the body.

Binding Mechanical means by which pages of a book are permanently put together.

Blog A shared, personal, chronological web log on any subject.

Bloom's Taxonomy A well-known rubric that classifies cognitive objectives in terms of six levels of complexity (from low to high: knowledge, comprehension, application, analysis, synthesis, and evaluation).

Book design Decisions about the appearance of the interior of a book and its cover.

Book organization The division and sequencing of course content into the parts and chapters of a textbook.

Book outline 1. The preliminary drafting outline you send to the acquisitions editor with your prospectus. 2. The revised drafting outline that serves as a basis for your table of contents.

Book pages The number of pages in a manuscript based on printed pages.

Book plan The publisher's plan for publishing, marketing, and selling your book.

Bound book date Benchmark in the publishing process when your book has been manufactured but is not yet for sale.

Buyback Retailer's offer to repurchase a textbook to resell as a used book.

C-book A low-investment, typically one-color, title.

Captions 1. The numbers and titles of figures, tables, and photos. 2. Brief descriptions, interpretations, or questions to readers about the content of figures, tables, and photos.

Case studies Pedagogical features for case-based instruction and analysis.

Cast-off The compositor's length estimate of a manuscript in terms of the calculated number of book pages.

Chapter closer (or closers) Pedagogical elements at the end of a chapter, as part of the chapter apparatus.

Chapter outline The heading structure and titled features in terms of which a chapter is presented.

Chronological development Chapter development organized in terms of story, process, or change.

Chunking In learning theory, optimizing learning by delivering meaningfully related useful information together at one time rather than discretely.

Clarity Clearness of expression and meaning.

Coauthor One of more authors with whom you publish a work and share royalties along with contractual obligations.

Cognitive objectives Learning objectives that match levels of cognitive functioning: knowledge acquisition, comprehension, application, analysis, synthesis, and evaluation.

Cognitive psychology Interdisciplinary study of thinking, learning, perception, intelligence, and memory.

Coherence The quality of writing that shows sequentiality, integrity, or togetherness.

College textbook publishers Larger commercial publishers of textbooks and supplements for undergraduate and graduate courses.

Commercial textbook publishing Publishing textbooks as a business with the goal of making a profit.

Comparative review Review of a revision compared to its last edition.

Comp copies Free samples to prospective customers.

Competition analysis Analysis of directly competing textbooks for a course.

Competitive review Review of a book or manuscript compared to leading competing books by other publishers.

Complete manuscript Manuscript that contains all the planned elements, including frontmatter, apparatus, pedagogy, figures and tables, source notes, endmatter, and so on.

Composition (comp) A stage of production during which your book is set into type and other pre-manufacturing tasks are accomplished.

Compositor Publishing professional responsible for putting your book into type and providing page proofs.

Conceptual organizers Verbal or visual devices for showing the relationships among the qualities or characteristics of a concept or among concepts.

Conclusion As part of the chapter closer, a unifying thought, an interpretation, or a statement of significance of the chapter content.

Concrete examples Specific empirical or non-abstract examples, such as facts, observations, evidence, or cases.

Condense Change text by shortening it through abridgments.

Confidentiality clause Clause in publishing contracts that forbids the author from disclosing the terms of the contract.

Consistency The quality of regularity or conformity in the application of style and in the treatment of apparatus and pedagogy.

Contributed work An anthology or any one work in which chapters authored by different individuals are compiled.

Contributing Writing original materials for a textbook or its package on the work-for-hire basis, such as a series of boxes, a chapter, or a study guide.

Co-publisher A publishing company that partly subsidizes your self-publishing initiative and assists with marketing.

Copyeditor (CE) Specialist in publishing who corrects or queries errors, ambiguities, or inconsistencies in spelling, grammar, punctuation, usage, or meaning.

Copyright holder The person or entity that holds the rights to publication and use of a work and can tell you who and where the copyright owner is.

Copyright infringement Illegal use of another's work in your book.

Copyright law A body of laws that defines and regulates the ownership and transfer of intellectual property.

Copyright owner The person or entity that owns the rights to publication and use of a work, whose permission you need.

Copyright year The year for which your publisher legally registers copyright for your book, which is not the same as the year your book is published and may be sold, which typically is in the year prior to your copyright year.

Correlations (in textbook publishing): 1. pedagogical connections and page cross-references between chapter content and the content in a supplement or ancillary; 2. specific designations of test items in relation to chapter content.

Cover letter Letter to the publisher to accompany a prospectus, including a list of enclosures and information about manuscript status and your availability.

Credit line A line of type crediting the source of a photo, figure, table, or excerpt.

Critical thinking questions Questions to students in the chapter pedagogy or apparatus that require the use of critical thinking skills.

Critical thinking skills Skills that enable learners to define and clarify problems, judge information, draw conclusions, and problem solve.

Crossover trade Trade books that are marketed to education markets or books by academic authors that are marketed to the trade.

Crowdsourcing Soliciting data or content from the public online.

Customization Process of altering or augmenting textbook content for a course.

Custom publishing An emerging publishing industry in which instructors author or customize books and materials, sold through the college bookstore for their own courses or departments.

Debates Pedagogical features that present opposing views on chapter content.

Debundling Practice of selling textbooks separately from their supplements.

Desktop publishing Creating high-quality documents with text and graphics on a personal computer.

Development 1. Publishing phase during which you draft and revise your manuscript in response to editorial input, marketing plan, and peer reviews. 2. A complex recursive process through which your manuscript is brought to market level and prepared for production through a collaboration between editors and authors.

Developmental review Hands-on review of a book or manuscript compared to the publisher's development and market plans for it.

Development editor (DE) Publishing professional responsible minimally for seeing that the writing, organization, and content of your textbook are at market level and competitive.

Development plan A detailed description of the measures that will be taken to develop a manuscript into a market-ready textbook.

Difficulty level As distinct from reading level, the degree of conceptual and logical abstraction in text and the extent to which it is supported by exposition, concrete example, or reasoned argument.

Digitization Practice of converting print to electronic content.

Direct instruction Direct transmission of information that all students are expected to master.

Distribution Industries involved in distributing (selling) products; a step in the fulfillment phase of the publishing process.

Discussion questions Questions to students that are appropriate for verbal interaction in the actual or virtual classroom.

Double number Convention in numbering figures and tables in which the first number indicates the chapter, followed by a decimal point, and the second number indicates the particular figure or table in the series.

Drafting calendar An author's personal calendar for realistically apportioning time for authoring tasks based on the "manuscript complete" due date.

Drafting checklists Authoring tools in which you remind yourself of all your final decisions about writing mechanics and style, and the form and content of your textbook.

Drafting schedule Dates by which your chapters, revised drafts, and final complete manuscript are due.

Dumbing down Perceived debasement of a text by abridging or amending the content to make it easier to acquire.

Economies of scale Savings from buying in bulk and applying business solutions across all units of a company.

Editorial Chief function of personnel involved in the acquisition and development of textbook manuscripts.

Editorial style A system of stylistic conventions for preparing manuscript, such as Chicago Style, APA, MLA, CBE, and so on.

Educational psychology The application of theory and research from the disciplines of psychology to all aspects of learning and teaching.

Educational publishing Industry devoted to producing books for preK–12 students; also called el-hi publishing.

Elements of style Word choices and usages; sentence and paragraph constructions; writing rules, conventions, and formats; and your personal distinguishing communication values and expression of self.

Emphasis The quality in writing that shows focus, interest, and control.

Endmatter 1. All the elements that follow the last paragraph of narrative in a chapter (chapter closers). 2. All the elements the follow the last chapter of a book (backmatter), such as appendix, glossary, and index.

Endnotes Notes citing complete sources of material (referenced through either parenthetical source citations or superscript note numbers) that are gathered at the end of a chapter or by chapter at the end of a textbook.

Epigrams Brief quotations relating to chapter content, often used as an element in the chapter opener.

Errata A list of errors and corrections to text given after a work is published.

Events of instruction In educational psychology, the functional steps in a direct instruction lesson.

Expert review Specialized review of a portion of a book or manuscript by a subject expert.

Expository writing Narrative prose in the service of explanation, description, or analysis.

External competition Textbooks from other publishers for the course your book targets.

Fact checking Editorial function of checking that your facts are correct, accurate, and current.

Fair use Legally defined conditions in which another's work can be used without permission, especially uses that do not destroy the commercial value of the original work.

Feature strand A type of feature, distinguished through title and design, that appears regularly with different relevant content in the body of chapters throughout the textbook.

Figures Labeled illustrations and representations in a textbook, such as drawings, diagrams, charts, and graphs.

Flat Four discontinuous printed pages of a book, which (when folded, assembled with other flats, and cut) show the correct numerical sequence (imposition) of pages.

Focus groups Potential adopters or users of a textbook whom marketing managers gather together and involve in a roundtable discussion of the book's strengths and needs.

Focus questions As an element in chapter openers, a set of questions that follow or are embedded in the chapter outline to guide student study.

Folios Typeset page numbers.

Fonts Styles of type, such as Arial or Times New Roman.

Footnotes Notes citing complete sources that appear at the bottom of the pages on which the referenced material appears, as designated by superscript note numbers.

Frontlist The current or coming year's titles in the company's publishing plan.

Frontmatter All the parts of your book that precede the opening page of the first chapter, especially the table of contents (TOC) and the preface.

Fulfillment Publishing phase during which your textbook is sampled, sold, and delivered to customers.

Fulfillment schedule Dates by which books and supplements are sold, ordered, in stock, inventoried, and shipped.

Galleys Unpaged typescript produced mechanically, seldom done in today's electronic publishing, but sometimes used erroneously to refer to page proof.

Gender bias Negative portrayals of people on the basis of their sex or socially constructed maleness or femaleness (opposite: gender-fair).

Glossary An alphabetical listing of vocabulary items (key terms and concepts) with their definitions.

Grants Cash awards in advance of earnings that are not deducted from royalties and do not have to be returned.

Graphic organizers Visual representations of a chapter, topic, sequence, or concept, such as a flowchart, concept web, or diagram.

Heading structure The system of headings and subheadings in terms of which a chapter is organized.

Hierarchical development Chapter development organized on the basis of classification and analysis.

Higher education publishing Industries that serve post-secondary educational, professional, and occupational markets.

Honoraria Small amounts of money that may be paid as a courtesy to peer reviewers or contributors.

Horizontal development Chapter development organized on the basis of topical parallelism.

House style Writing conventions that a publishing house adopts, to which your manuscript ultimately must conform.

Hypothetical examples Imaginary or abstract examples, not as good as concrete examples.

Ideology Your personal political philosophy or other "isms" that are not the subject of discourse and therefore do not belong in your textbook.

Imposition The layout of pages in flats, resulting in the correct sequence of page numbers when the book is assembled.

Indemnity clause Clause in a publishing contract that holds the publisher harmless (not financially responsible) in the event that they are sued because of something you did in your book that is illegal. You must warrant and represent, for example, that your work is original.

Index An alphabetical listing of significant topics in your book and the pages on which information on those topics may be found.

Indexer Publishing professional responsible for writing indexes for books.

Information processing Area of learning theory that focuses on how people process, store, and remember information and experience.

Institutional affiliation Your title and rank at the school, college, university, company, or corporation where you work, suggesting your qualifications for writing a textbook.

Instructional design Term for the structure (or architecture) of information delivery in computer-mediated teaching.

Instructional goals Teaching objectives, but not the same as learning objectives.

Intellectual property Original expressions of ideas in the form of writing, music, art, performances, brand names, and so on.

Intellectual property rights Area of law and specialty of lawyers dealing with copyright law.

Internal apparatus (also interior apparatus) Pedagogical elements of a chapter that appear systematically between the chapter opener and the chapter closer, such as vocabulary glosses, marginalia, and interim reviews.

Internal competition Your publisher's products by other authors for the course your textbook targets.

Introduction As an element in chapter openers, a brief description of the contents of a chapter, preparing readers for acquiring the information.

Launch Official release of a book's production budget once final manuscript is complete.

Leading Space on a page between lines of type and above and below other typographical elements, such as headings and captions.

Learning design Term for the structure (or architecture) of information delivery in computer-mediated learning.

Learning objectives As an element in chapter openers, statements specifying what students are expected to know or be able to do after studying the information.

Learning objects Term for modular digital media from which online lessons or courses can be assembled.

Learning outcomes 1. As an element in chapter openers, statements specifying the changes students can anticipate in their beliefs, attitudes, behavior, or skills as a consequence of reading the chapter. 2. What students will accomplish as a result of meeting the learning objectives.

Learning theory Ideas and research on how learning takes place and how learning is optimized.

Length creep The tendency for textbooks to increase in length from edition to edition.

Length estimate A calculation of the number of printed book pages that a typescript manuscript will fill.

Level of investment The publisher's designation of your book as an A-, B-, or C-book, indicating how much money will be spent on it.

Levels of development Minor, moderate, or full development or involvement of a development editor.

Levels of edit Minor (light), medium, or full (heavy) line editing of manuscript by a copyeditor.

Levels of heading A-, B-, C-, and D-heads, distinguished through type design and size, which range from the most inclusive to the most specific categories of information in terms of which a chapter is organized.

Line art Figures that need to be drawn (versus rendered art, which is an artist's illustration).

List A publisher's books in print in a department or subject, including frontlist and backlist.

Literary agent Fee-for-service author's representative who presents book proposals to publishers.

Literary Market Place (LMP) A significant, comprehensive source of information about all aspects of the publishing industry.

Mainstream text 1. A textbook that contains what is expected or usually taught in the course for which it was written. 2. A textbook with appropriate and non-idiosyncratic content.

Major market book Term for a textbook with a large market and a high projection of sales.

Managing editor Editor responsible for channeling many titles through the drafting stage into production.

Manufacturing Publishing phase that ends with shipments of your printed and bound book to the warehouse.

Manufacturing schedule Dates on which your textbook is printed, covered, bound, and shipped to the warehouse.

Manuscript (ms, plural mss) A work or portion of a work in double-spaced typescript form.

Manuscript complete Benchmark in the publishing process when the publisher accepts your final complete manuscript.

Manuscript pages The number of pages in a manuscript.

Manuscript preparation General term for the rules and conventions for submitting a complete, acceptable manuscript.

Map specs Instructions, labels, and models for the creation of original maps for your textbook.

Marginalia Internal pedagogical elements that are printed in the margins of pages in your textbook.

Market 1. In this context, the field, course, departments, instructors, and students who will use your textbook. 2. Competing producers, buyers, and sellers of textbooks.

Market fit The appropriateness of a product for its market in relation to other products.

Marketing Bringing a product to the attention of prospective customers; a phase in the publishing process.

Marketing schedule Dates on which your textbook is announced, promoted and advertised, presented to the sales force, and sampled to customers.

Market level The course level (introductory, second-tier, graduate) and the intellectual level of the audience.

Market penetration Extent to which the sales base for a product is secured or can be predicted accurately.

Market research Investigations into what customers need, want, or will buy.

Market savvy Publisher talk describing authors and editors who realize the importance of meeting marketing needs for a book to succeed.

Market segmentation The division of the market for a product into constituent types, e.g., community colleges and four-year colleges are segments of the same market.

Market specialization Extent to which marketing efforts for a product target a particular market segment.

Mark-ups Additions to the price of a textbook that college stores make to provide a profit margin.

Mass market books Books for sale in supermarket chains, department stores, military base stores, and similar venues.

Merger Combination of two or more publishing houses.

Metavoice An overarching authorial voice that reconciles the voices of coauthors.

Mission Your compelling reason, purpose, or goal in writing your textbook.

Models (or how-tos) Pedagogical features that apply or demonstrate practices, procedures, principles, theories, or laws.

Motivation Internal state that activates and directs goal-oriented behavior.

Multiple submissions The practice of sending out a prospectus to more than one publisher at one time (also called simultaneous submission).

Narrative context The textual environment in which readers make sense of the elements of apparatus, pedagogy, and art (figures, tables, photos).

Networking Communicating with colleagues and potential customers about your project and gathering information that will help you craft a successful product.

Niche market A small, technical, or non-mainstream market with a comparatively low sales projection.

Nondirect instruction Planned learning experiences by which it is intended that students will acquire information on their own or through interaction with peers or others.

Notes Information about your identified sources that enables readers to locate or access them, expressed in footnotes or endnotes.

Open access A collective name for movements and initiatives to make information and course content available for free online.

Openers (or chapter openers) The pedagogical elements at the beginning of a chapter, as part of the chapter apparatus.

Open source Any software program in which users or developers may freely access the source code and modify the program as they wish.

Out of print (OOP) No longer being published.

Out-of-print clause Clause in a publishing contract that defines when a book is regarded as no longer published.

Outsourcing Having key publishing tasks performed by offsite or offshore vendors.

Overdevelopment Providing more content or topical differentiation than is needed for comprehension or for meeting the learning objective.

Overlengthage Term indicating that your book will have too many pages.

Overview As an element in the chapter opener, a brief explanation of the connections between the chapter at hand and previous chapters, units, or the course.

Packager A private company that your publisher subcontracts to produce your textbook.

Page count The actual number of pages in a book or manuscript.

Page make-up artist (also page layout artist) Publishing professional who fixes the appearance of each page of your textbook.

Page proof Preliminary, designed layouts of typeset pages, showing how your book will actually look and read when corrected and printed.

Pagination The numbering of pages in the frontmatter and body of a text.

Palette In four-color books, the array of colors chosen for the design.

Paraphrases Rewritings of another's written text using different words and phrases.

Parenthetical source citations Citations that identify sources by author's last name and the year of publication in parentheses at the end of the relevant sentence or paragraph.

Parts Sections of text that correspond to units of knowledge or units of instruction.

Passive voice Use of forms of the verb "to be," creating dull, wordy writing.

Pedagogical devices Regular internal elements in a chapter that serve a pedagogical purpose, such as glossary annotations, statements of main points, or interim reviews.

Pedagogy Regular written elements of your textbook other than narrative, such as features, which you intend will have educative value.

Pedagogy pitfalls Dangers of bad practices in using pedagogy and misuse of textbook features.

Pedagogy plan An editorial plan for the chapter apparatus and pedagogical features that will appear throughout your textbook.

Peer reviews Reviews of your manuscript by others who are experts in your field or have taught the course for which you are writing a textbook.

Permissioning The process of sending letters requesting permission to use others' material in your book, receiving the grants of permission, paying the use fees, and adding the credit lines.

Permission fees Money charged for the use (rental) of an image in your textbook.

Permissions General term in textbook publishing for complying with copyright law.

Permissions log A form for recording and tracking permissioning needs, including information about copyright owners, rights requested, restrictions, and fees.

Permissions researcher Publishing professional responsible for evaluating permissioning needs, contacting copyright owners, and keeping records of permissions grants and fees.

Photo specs List of requests for photos to be researched.

Picas In publishing, with points, the units of measure used in typesetting and page layout.

Plant costs Costs of manufacturing (printing, binding, and shipping) your textbook.

POD Print on demand. 1. A manufacturing service offered by some printers in which publishers can have a small number of copies printed at one time. 2. A publishing service in which authors pay to have a vanity press publish a few copies of their work.

Political correctness In textbook publishing, a characteristic of writing that is not offensive or insulting to customers and readers.

Postprint Online publication of a previously published journal article.

Preliminary book outline The drafting outline or working table of contents (TOC) that accompanies a prospectus.

Preprint A version of an article (usually an abstract) published online in advance of the publication of the article in a journal.

Presentation A general term for the physical appearance of your book in all aspects (trim size, fonts, color, design, illustration, bulk, cover, etc.).

Print run Printing of a specified number of copies of your book.

Prior knowledge Information and skills that learners need or can use to access and acquire new knowledge.

Primary market The specific customers who will adopt your book for their courses.

Primary sources Pedagogical features based on passages from literature or excerpts from documents, first-person accounts, artifacts, or exhibits.

Production Publishing phase during which your final complete manuscript is set into type and sent out to be manufactured.

Production editor (PE) Publishing professional responsible for preparing your manuscript to be sent for manufacturing.

Production schedule Dates on which your manuscript is copyedited, set into type, proofread, corrected, indexed, and sent to the printer.

Professional associations Organizations for the advancement of fields of study or practice that may act as publishers.

Professional book A book for practitioners in your field, which is by definition not a textbook (see STM and PTR).

Profiles Pedagogical features that offer descriptive accounts of particular examples or exemplars of chapter content.

Proofreader Publishing professional who compares typeset pages with manuscript to ensure that the typescript is error free.

Prospectus A proposal; a comprehensive description of your textbook and analysis of its market to interest a company in publishing it.

PTR A genre of publishing encompassing professional, technical, and reference books.

Public domain Legally defined intellectual property that you can use without permission because it is published by the government, is a matter of public record, is sufficiently old or has an expired copyright, or consists of raw data.

Publishing cycle The movement of a manuscript through the five phases of book publishing (acquisition, development, production, manufacturing, fulfillment) over the course of two or more years.

Publishing ethics Business ethics of publishers.

Publishing process The five phases of publishing: manuscript acquisition, editorial development, book production, book manufacturing, and book fulfillment.

Publishing schedules The dates by which benchmarks in each of the five phases of book publishing are achieved.

Publish or perish Expression in academe referring to the traditional requirement that scholars publish in their fields to be regarded as successful.

Readability tests Formulae for determining the grade level or intellectual or cognitive level at which text is written.

Reading level (also called comprehension level), largely subjective judgments about the appropriateness of writing for an audience based on vocabulary, sentence length, sentence construction, and paragraph length.

Rebranding Process of integrating the book lists or produce lines of acquired or merged companies.

Reference books Professional and technical resources, including online databases, which by definition are not textbooks.

References An alphabetized listing of all the works you actually refer to or cite in the body of your textbook.

Reflection questions Questions to students that require self-referential thinking and expression.

Release to production Benchmark in the publishing process when your complete and final manuscript is turned over to a production editor.

Reproduce Use text as-is, without adaptation, abridgment, or condensation. **Resource management** Developing a system for gathering and organizing information and sources for drafting a manuscript and carrying out other authoring tasks.

Returns Unsold new books that bookstores return to the publisher, representing unrealized income.

Review analysis Chapter-by-chapter comparison of reviewers' comments as a guide to development or revision.

Reviewing 1. Your expert evaluation of another's manuscript, establishing a relationship with a publisher. 2. A stage of development in which your manuscript is sent out for professional peer review.

Reviewing schedule Dates on which reviewers are contacted and chapters of manuscript are sent out for review, reviews received, and honoraria paid.

Review questions Questions to students that guide their study and test preparation after they have read a chapter.

Revision 1. A published new edition of your textbook representing an altered version of it. 2. The act of changing the form and content of your textbook.

Revision cycle The period of time that elapses between one edition of your textbook and the next.

Rollovers Customers who have been automatically switched (rolled over) to a new edition of their textbook in use.

Royalty income Your taxable income from royalties, which you disclose on Schedule C.

Royalties Regular payments to you based on a percentage of net sales of your textbook.

Royalty rate The percentage of net sales you will receive after the publisher recovers advances paid to you against royalties.

Royalty schedule Incremental changes in the royalty rate and when royalties will be paid over the life of an edition, based on the number of sales.

Royalty statement An accounting of sources of royalty payments and any offsets, usually issued at least twice a year.

Rule of two Convention in formal outlining of having two or more subheadings for each heading, also applied to the construction of text headings.

Sample chapters 1. Chapters that you submit with your prospectus for consideration prior to signing. 2. Chapters that your editor submits for design prior to turning over your manuscript for production.

Sampling Sending of free advance copies (also called comp copies) of your book to potential customers for their inspection.

Satisfactory manuscript clause Clause in a publishing contract that makes the payment of advances and royalties contingent on acceptance of a manuscript that the publisher deems publishable.

Scenarios Brief descriptions of simulated or real-life situations, usually involving named characters, usually set off from basal text.

Scholarly publishing An industry focusing on the publication of scholarship and research, especially in journals.

Scope and sequence Phrase from preK–12 (or el-hi) publishing referring to the range of content a textbook will cover and the order in which it will be presented.

Secondary market Individuals, groups, or institutions that may be interested in buying your textbook (other than those who will adopt it for their courses).

Seeding adoptions Publisher practices that increase the likelihood of customers adopting your book, such as soliciting reviews or contributions from those with comparatively higher enrollments.

Self-assessment In textbook publishing, opportunities for students to assess whether they are meeting the learning objectives.

Self-publishing Becoming an independent publisher and writing, producing, marketing, selling, and shipping your own book by yourself.

Series editor Acquisitions or sponsoring editor responsible for managing a series of related titles.

Shadow text A textbook alternative; a comprehensive study guide for a course.

Signature Thirty-two book pages (half signature is sixteen; quarter signature is eight; an eighth is four).

Signing 1. Stage in the acquisitions process in which you and the publisher sign a legal contract to publish your book. 2. Entering into a contractual agreement with a publisher to produce a work.

Sizing In book production, determining the sizes and locations of figures, tables, photos, and art.

Skill sets Term for the skills that students need and/or acquire to meet learning objectives.

Source citations Identifications of your sources of information.

Sponsoring editor Editor responsible for recruiting authors, signing titles, and presenting them to the publisher.

STM A genre of publishing encompassing scientific, technical, and medical books.

Story Your book idea, stated succinctly in terms that can be used to market and sell your book.

Student-centered Characteristic of textbooks that give primacy to the student-learner in exposition.

Style 1. The way you use words to express yourself in writing. 2. The system of conventions you adopt to format your writing for your subject area, such as APA, MLA, etc.

Style sheet A list of important or expected writing conventions to be observed.

Subject-centered Characteristic of textbooks that give primacy to the subject or academic discipline in exposition.

Subsidiary rights Other salable rights to your book, such as serial rights, electronic rights, foreign language rights, recording rights, and others.

Subsidy publishing Industry based on author-paid publishing services for self-publishers.

Subvention The practice of having authors contribute to the costs of publishing their low-volume, high-cost works.

Summary As part of the chapter apparatus, brief descriptions reviewing in full the content of a chapter or answering the focus questions.

Supplements Print and non-print materials for students and instructors, offered as accompaniments to your textbook, such as a test item file, instructor's manual, videotape, or website.

Supplements schedule Dates on which supplements authors are commissioned and samples and final manuscript for each supplement are due.

Supplement tie-ins Pedagogical devices that link content in the student text with that of supplements included in the textbook package.

Table of contents (TOC) Also chapter outlines. A sequence of functional, pedagogical headings and subheadings that direct student learning of chapter content.

Tables Numerical information in tabular form, typeset but typically set off from basal text.

Tearsheet Pages cut or torn from a printed book and affixed to standard-size paper, on which corrections are written for a revised edition.

Termination clause Clause in a publishing contract that defines the terms for canceling the contract.

Text sections Parts of a chapter that begin with an A-head.

Textbook package A textbook and its supplements and ancillaries.

Thematic boxes Pedagogical feature strands that express a theme in different contexts throughout a textbook.

Tone The quality of voice in your writing that reveals your affective response toward your subject, reader, and self.

Topical balance The relative weight or importance given to topics, expressed in the number of words or amount of space devoted to them.

Topical development The relationship among topics in a chapter, expressed in the amount and specificity of information given about them.

Topical outline (also called writing outline) Guides the author, and is different from the system of headings that makes the table of contents (TOC).

Track changes Microsoft Word editing tool that enables authors and editors to share working manuscript.

Trade book publishers Publishers of adult nonfiction, fiction, and books in other genres for sale in bookstores.

Trim size The actual physical dimensions of your textbook (e.g., 6×9, 8×10).

Turnover The first stage of production following the turning over of your manuscript to the production editor, typically involving production review, packager bidding, cover design request, budget analysis, and scheduling.

Undeclared bias Influential writing that is secretly slanted in a way that naive readers do not detect.

Underdevelopment The provision of insufficient content or topical differentiation for comprehension to take place or for meeting the learning objective.

Unity The quality of writing that shows centrality, relevance, or belongingness.

University presses Scholarly publishers affiliated with, and often subsidized by, one or more colleges or universities.

Unsolicited manuscript Manuscript sent to a publisher without prior notice, query, or consent.

Unwarranted assumptions Untrue ideas you have about your readers, or assumptions that stem from ignorance of their identities, backgrounds, etc.

URL Universal Resource Locator, the Internet address of an information source.

User review Review of a textbook by an instructor who uses or has used it (versus a nonuser review).

Vanity presses Companies that produce books for self-publishers with limited distribution and sales.

Vignettes Brief descriptions of simulated or real-life situations, usually embedded in basal text.

Visual metaphors Pictorial or graphical representations that suggest or evoke the information being conveyed.

Visualization The skill of imagining verbal or conceptual information in graphical form or as representational art.

Voice The way you speak to your audience, revealing who you are and your attitudes toward your subject and your reader.

Wholesalers Jobbers or brokers who buy and sell textbooks in bulk.

Wiki 1. Name for software that creates a collaborative website in which anyone with access may contribute, remove, or alter content. 2. A website created through wiki software.

Wordiness The habitual use of more words than are needed to adequately convey facts and ideas.

Work-for-hire 1. Non-royalty-bearing contract based on fee for service. 2. A person, such as a freelance editor, who performs such service.

Working draft A non-final version of a chapter or manuscript; a work in progress. (Also used in working manuscript and working TOC.)

Writing outline (also book outline or drafting outline) A formal, hierarchical, logically exhaustive sequence of topics to be covered in a chapter—not the same as a table of contents (TOC).

References

10 Big Myths about Copyright Explained. http://www.templetons.com/brad/copymyths.

2007 AP Stylebook: http://www.apstylebook.com. (General reference.)

Academic Small Publishers Listserv: http://finance.groups.yahoo.com/group/Academic-Education. (General reference.)

Acq Web: http://acqweb.library.vanderbilt.edu/law. (General reference.)

Advisory Committee on Student Financial Assistance. *Turn the Page: Making College Textbooks More Affordable*. ACSFA, 2007.

American Association of University Presses: http://www.aaup.org. (General reference.)

American Library Association: http://www.ala.org. (General reference.)

American Society of Journals and Authors: http://www.asja.org. (General reference.)

Applebaum, Judith. *How to Get Happily Published*. Harper and Row, 1992.

Association of American Publishers, *Author's Guide to College Textbook Publishing*: http://www.publishers.org/highered. (General reference.)

———. *College Learning Materials: More than a Textbook*, 2007: http://www.publishers.org/highered. (General reference.)

Association of American University Presses: http://www.aaup.pupress.princeton.edu. (General reference.)

Association of Authors' Reps: http://www.aaronline.org. (General reference.)

Association of Canadian Publishers: http://www.publisher.ca. (General reference.)

Author's Guild: http://www.authorsguild.org. (General reference.)

Baker, John F. University Presses: Hanging On in Tough Times. *Publishers Weekly*, June 2, 1997, 42–44.

Balkin, Richard, and Nick Bakalar. *A Writer's Guide to Book Publishing*, 2nd ed., Plume, 1994.

Barket, Malcolm E. *Book Design and Production for Small Publishers.* Londonborn Publications, 1990.

Bauman, M. Garrett. Textbook Writing 101. *Chronicle of Higher Education*, July 4, 2003, http://www.chronicle.com/weekly/v49/i43/43b00501.htm.

Beach, Mark, and Eric Kenly. *Getting It Printed: How to Work with Printers and Graphic Imaging*, 3rd ed. North Light Books, 1999.

Bell, Patricia J. *The Prepublishing Handbook: What You Should Know Before You Publish Your First Book*. Cat's Paw Press, 1992.
Bennett, Christine I. *Comprehensive Multicultural Education*. Allyn and Bacon, 1990.
Berkowitz, Eric N., Roger A. Kerin, and William Rudelius. *Marketing*. Moseby, 1986.
Bernstein, Leonard. *Getting Published: The Writer in the Combat Zone*. Morrow, 1986.
Besenjak, C. *Copyright Plain and Simple*, 2nd ed. Career Press, 2001.
Bibliofind (rare and out-of-print books): http://www.bibliofind.com. (General reference.)
Bloom, B. S., M. D. Engelhard, E. J. Frost, W. H. Hill, and D. R. Krathwohl. *Taxonomy of Educational Objectives*. David McKay, 1956.
Bodian, Nat G. *Direct Marketing Rules of Thumb*. McGraw-Hill, 1995.
Boice, Robert. *Professors as Writers*. New Forums Press, 1990.
Book Industry Study Group: http://www.bisg.org. (General reference.)
Boswell, John. *The Awful Truth about Publishing*. Warner Books, 1986.
Branscomb, Anne W. *Who Owns Information? From Privacy to Public Access*. Basic Books, 1994.
Bronner, Ethan. Textbooks Shifting from Printed Page to Screen. *The New York Times on the Web*, December 1, 1998. http://www.nytimes.com/library/tech/98/12/biztech/articles/01school/etex.
Brower, David. David Brower's Why Textbook Writing Matters in Academia. *Dateline UC Davis*, October 28, 2005. http://www.dateline.ucdavis.edu/dl_detail.lasso?id=8495.
Brown, Laura, R. Griffiths, and M. Rascoff. University Publishing in a Digital Age. *Ithaka*, July 23, 2007. http://www.ithaka.org/stragic-services/university-publishing.
Bunnin, Brad, and Peter Beren. *Writer's Legal Companion*, 3rd ed. Addison Wesley Longman, 1998.
Burgett, Gordon. *The Writer's Guide to Query Letters and Cover Letters*. St. Martin's Press, 1991.
———. *Publishing to Niche Markets*. Communications Unlimited, 1995.
Byron, D. L. and Steve Broback. *Publish & Prosper: Blogging for Your Business*. New Riders Press, 2006.
Canadian Press Stylebook, 14th ed. (and *Guide de rédaction*). Canadian Press, 2007. http://www.cp.org.
Canadian Publishers' Council: http://www.pubcouncil.ca. (General reference.)
Cantor, Jeffrey A. *A Guide to Academic Writing*. Praeger, 1993.
Capriccioso, Rob. Throwing Down the Book. *Inside Higher Education*, August 29, 2006. http://www.insidehighered.com/news/2006/08/29/textbooks.
Cardoza, Avery, *Complete Guide to Successful Publishing*. Cardoza Publishing, 2002.
Cheney, Theodore A. Rees. *Getting the Words Right: How to Revise, Edit and Rewrite*. F&W Publications, 2005.
Chronicle of Higher Education: http://www.che.com. (General reference.)
Cleaver, Barry, et al. *Handbook Exploring the Legal Context for Information Policy in Canada*. Faxon, 1992.

Coghill, Anne M. and Lorrin R. Garson. *The ACS Style Guide: Effective Communication of Scientific Information*, 3rd ed. American Chemical Society and Oxford University Press, 2005.

Cole, David. *Complete Guide to Book Marketing*. Allworth Press, 2004.

Columbia Guide to Online Style, 2nd ed.: http://www.columbia.edu/cu/cup/cgos2006/basic.html. (General reference.)

Cook, Claire Kehrwald. *Line by Line: How to Edit Your Own Writing*. Houghton Mifflin, 1985.

Copy Law: http://www.copylaw.com. (General reference.)

Copyright Clearance Center: http://authors.copyright.com. (General reference.)

Crawford, Tad. *Business and Legal Forms for Authors and Self-Publishers*, 3rd ed. Allworth Press, 2005.

——— and Kay Murray. *The Writer's Legal Guide*, 3rd ed. Allworth Press, 2002.

Daniels, John D. and Lee H. Radebaugh. *International Business*, 4th ed. Addison Wesley, 1986.

Digital Millennium Copyright Act,1998: http://www.copyright.gov/legislation/dmca.pdf. (General reference.)

Driscoll, Marcy P., Mahnaz Moallem, Walter Dick, and Elizabeth Kirby. *How Do Textbooks Contribute to Learning?* Paper presented at the 1992 Annual Meeting of the American Educational Research Association, San Francisco, CA.

DuBoff, Leonard. *The Law in Plain English for Writers*, 4th ed. Sphinx, 2005.

Dunne, Patrick. The Selling of 'Complimentary' Textbooks: Boom or Bust for Marketing Education? *Marketing Education Review* 3 (Summer 1993): 9–15.

Earth Science Library: http:// library.usgs.gov. (General reference.)

Educational Writers Association: http://www.ewa.org. (General reference.)

Education Week: http://www.edweek.com. (General reference.)

Egan, Kieran. *The Educated Mind*. University of Chicago Press, 1997.

Einsohn, Amy. *The Copyeditor's Handbook: A Guide for Book Publishing and Corporate Communication*. University of California Press, 2000.

Engelhardt, T. Gutenberg Unbound. *The Nation*, March 17, 1997, 18–29.

Epstein, Jason. *Book Business: Publishing Past, Present, and Future*. W. W. Norton, 2002.

ERIC Clearinghouse for Higher Education: http://www.eriche.org. (General reference.)

Evans, Tonya M. and Susan Gordon Evans. *Literary Law Guide for Authors: Copyrights, Trademarks and Contracts in Plain Language*. FYOS Entertainment/Legal Write Publications, 2005.

Faculty Online: http://www.facultyonline.com. (General reference.)

Feeney, Mark. Beyond the Voodoo Stick. *Boston Globe Magazine*, January 16, 1993, 10–18.

Fishman, Stephen. *The Copyright Handbook: What Every Editor Needs to Know*. Nolo Press, 2006.

Frankel, T. and A. T. Schwing. *Regulation of Money Managers: Mutual Funds and Advisers*, 2nd ed. Aspen Publishers, 2006.

Frohbieter-Meuller, Jo. *Writing: Getting into Print: A Business Guide for Writers*. Glenbridge Publishing Ltd., 1994.

Fry, Edward. Fry's Readability Graph: Clarification, Validity, and Extension to Level 17. *Journal of Reading* 21 (1977): 242–252.
Gagne, R. M. and M. P. Driscoll. *Essentials of Learning for Instruction*, 4th ed. Prentice-Hall, 1988.
Germano, William. *Getting It Published: A Guide for Scholars and Anyone Else Serious About Serious Books*. University of Chicago Press, 2001.
Gillen, Stephen E. Ten Tips for Your Next Book Deal. *Academic Author* (1997):1. Also available online, http://www.taaonline.com.
Gitlin, T. The Dumb-Down. *The Nation*, March 17, 1997, 28.
Goldfarb, Ronald L. *The Writer's Lawyer: Essential Legal Advice for Writers and Editors in All Media*. Times Books, 1989.
Gorman, Michael. The Sleep of Reason, Part I. *Web 2.0 Forum*, *Britannica Blog*, June 11, 2007, http://www.blogs.britannica.com/blog/main/2007/06/web-20-the-sleep-of-reason-part-i.
———. Jabberwiki: The Educational Response, Part II. *Web 2.0 Forum*, *Britannica Blog*, June 26, 2007, http://blogs.britannica.com/blog/main/2007/06/jabberwiki-the-educational-response-part-i.
Guide to Citing Government Information Resources: http://library.unr.edu/depts/bgic/guides/government/cite.html. (General reference.)
Hafner, Katie. Seeing Corporate Fingerprints in Wikipedia Edits. *The New York Times*, August 19, 2007.
Harris, Lesley Ellen. *Canadian Copyright Law.* McGraw-Hill Ryerson, 1992.
Haynes, Anthony. *Writing Successful Textbooks*. A&C Black, 2001.
HED Up-Date: A Quarterly Publication of the Higher Education Division of the Association of American Publishers (Winter 1993).
Hegde, M. N. *A Singular Manual of Textbook Preparation*, 2nd ed. Singular Publishing Group, 1996.
Henderson, Bill. *The Publish It Yourself Handbook*. Pushcart Press, 1987.
Henry, Celia M. Birth of a Textbook. *Chemical & Engineering News* 80, no. 26 (July 1, 2002): 22–25.
Hupalo, Peter. I. *How to Start and Run a Small Book Publishing Company*. HCM Publishing, 2002.
Investment Company Institute. *A Guide to Understanding Mutual Funds*, 2006. http://www.ici.org.
Jaschik, Scott. New Model for Scholarly Publishing. *Inside Higher Education*, July 14, 2006. http://www.insidehighered.com/news/2006/07/14/rice.
Jones, Hugh. *Publishing Law*, 3rd ed. Taylor & Francis Group, 2006.
Judd, Karen. *Copyediting: A Practical Guide*, 3rd ed. Crisp Publications, 2001.
Kakutani, Michiko. Books of the Times: Young Minds Force-Fed with Indigestible Texts. *The New York Times*, April 29, 2003.
Kenley, Eric and Mark Beach. *Getting It Printed: How to Work with Printers and Graphic Imaging*, 4th ed. F&W Publications Inc., 2004.
Kirkpatrick, David D. Dictionary Publisher Going Digital. *The New York Times*, August 21, 2000.
Kirsch, Jonathan. *Kirsch's Handbook of Publishing Law.* Acrobat Books, 1994.
Kling, Arnold. Regulate Mutual Funds? *Library of Economics and Liberty*, July 8, 2004. http://www.econlog.econlib.org/archives/000513.html.

Kneedler, P. California Assesses Critical Thinking. In *Educational Leadership*. Association for Supervision and Curriculum Development, 1985.
Kozak, Ellen M. *Every Writer's Guide to Copyright and Publishing Law*, 3rd ed. Holt Paperbacks, 2004
Kremer, John. *1001 Ways to Market Your Books*, 5th ed. Open Horizons, 2000.
———. *1001 Ways to Market Your Books*, 6th ed. Open Horizons, 2006.
Lanham, Richard. *Revising Prose*, 3rd ed. Allyn and Bacon, 1992.
Learning Annex. *The Learning Annex Guide to Getting Successfully Published*. Carol Publishing Group, 1992.
Lee, Marshall. *Bookmaking: The Illustrated Guide to Design and Production*, 3rd ed. W. W. Norton & Company, 1997.
Lepionka, Mary Ellen. *Writing and Developing College Textbook Supplements*. Atlantic Path Publishing, 2005.
———. How to Reach the Education Market: Determining K–12 Market Fit, Market Placement, and Market Appeal. *The Independent*, November 2005: 9; 11–14.
————_____. Insights on Educational Publishing–Part I and Part II. *SPAN Connection* (April and May 2006): 9; 22.
———. *Textbook Authorship* blog, http://atlanticpathpublishing.com/blog/blog.html.
Levine, Mark. *Negotiating a Book Contract: A Guide for Authors, Agents, and Lawyers*. Moyer Bell, 1994.
Library of Congress: http://www.oc.gov. (General reference.)
Library Spot (library of libraries): http://www.libraryspot.com. (General reference.)
Lichtenberg, James. The New Paradox of the College Textbook. *Change* 12 (September/October 1992): 11–17.
Literary Market Place: http://www.literarymarketplace.com. (General reference.)
Luey, B. *Handbook for Academic Authors*, 4th ed. Cambridge University Press, 2002.
Madison, Charles Allan. *Irving to Irving: Author–Publisher Relations, 1800–1974*. R. R. Bowker, 1974.
Mankiw, N. Gregory. My Rules of Thumb. *American Economist* 40 (Spring 1996): 14–19. Also available online, http://post.economics.harvard.edu/faculty/mankiw/papers/My_Rules_of_Thumb.pdf.
———. On Textbook Writing. *Greg Mankiw's Blog*, March 4, 2007. http://gregmankiw.blogspot.com/2007/03/on-textbook-writing.html.
Masterson, Pete. *Book Design and Production: A Guide for Authors and Publishers*. Aeonix Publishing Group, 2005.
McHugh, John. *Managing Book Acquisitions: An Introduction*. McHugh Consulting, 1995.
———. *Book Publishing Contracts: An Introduction*. McHugh Consulting, 1996.
Michener, James. *James A. Michener's Writer's Handbook*. Random House, 1992.
Miller, Casey and Kate Swift. *The Handbook of Nonsexist Writing: For Writers, Editors and Speakers*, 2nd ed. Lippincott, 1988.

Miller, George A. The Magical Number Seven, Plus or Minus Two: Some Limits on Our Capacity for Processing Information. *Psychological Review* 63 (1956): 81–97.
Miller, M. C. The Crushing Power of Big Publishing. *The Nation,* March 17, 1997, 11–18.
Moxley, Joseph Michael. *Publish Don't Perish: The Scholar's Guide to Academic Writing and Publishing*. Praeger, 1992.
Munger, David and Shireen Campbell. *Researching Online,* 5th ed. Pearson Longman, 2001.
Munn, N. The Ethics of Textbook Writing. *American Psychologist* 3 (1948): 88–90. Also available online, http://www.comnet.ca/~pballan/Munnethics.htm.
Munroe, Mary H. The Academic Publishing Industry: A Story of Merger and Acquisition. 2007. http://www.niulib.niu.edu/publishers.
National Association of College Stores. Where the New Textbook Dollar Goes. NACS, 2007. http://www.nacs.org/common/research/textbook$.pdf.
National Writers Union. *Freelance Writer's Guide* (including *Guide to Freelance Rates and Standard Practice)*, 2nd ed. National Writer's Union, 2000.
National Writers Union (BizTech Contracts Glossary): http://www.nwu.org/nwu. (General reference.)
Para Publishing: http://www.parapublishing.com. (General reference.)
Paradigm Online Writing Assistant: http://www.powa.org. (General reference.)
Parsons, Paul. *Getting Published: The Acquisitions Process in Scholarly Publishing*. University of Tennessee Press, 1989.
Pickert, Sarah H. Preparing for a Global Community: Achieving an International Perspective in Higher Education. *Ashe-ERIC Higher Education Reports*. George Washington University, ERIC Clearinghouse on Higher Education, 992 (EDO-92-2).
Pinkerton, Linda F. *The Writer's Law Primer.* Lyons and Burford, 1990.
Powell, Walter W. *Getting into Print: The Decision Making Process in Scholarly Publishing*. University of Chicago Press, 1985.
Powers, Ella. Textbook Report–A New Edition. *Inside Higher Education*, October 31, 2007. http://www.insidehighered.com/news/2006/10/31/textbooks.
———. Who Controls Textbook Choices. *Inside Higher Education*, March 16, 2007. http://www.insidehighered.com/news/2007/03/16/unc.
Poynder, Richard. Bertelsmann Springer Is Sold to Private Equity Firms. *Information Today Inc.*, May 27, 2003. http://newsbreaks.infotoday.com/nbReader.asp?ArticleId=16696.
Poynter, Dan. *The Self-Publishing Manual, How to Write, Print and Sell Your Own Book*, 8th ed. Para Publishing, 1995.
———. *The Self-Publishing Manual: How to Write, Print and Sell Your Own Book,* 16th ed. Para Publishing, 2007.
PMA—The Independent Book Publishers Association: http://www.pma-online.org. (General reference.)
Publishers Weekly: http://www.publishersweekly.com. (General reference.)
Publishing Law: http://www.answers.com/topic/publishing-law. (General reference.)

Publishing Law Center: http://www.publaw.com. (General reference.)

Purdue Online Writing Lab: http:// owl.english.purdue.edu. (General reference.)

Quint, Barbara. Thomson Learning and Gale Under New Management Following Sale. *Information Today Inc.*, May 21, 2007. http://newsbreaks.infotoday.com/nbReader.sp?ArticleId=36230#top.

Rankin, Elizabeth. *The Work of Writing: Insights and Strategies for Academics and Professionals.* Jossey-Bass, 2001.

Ravitch, Diane. *The Language Police.* Knopf, 2003.

Ripoff 101: How the Current Practices of the Textbook Industry Drive Up the Cost of College Textbooks. CALPIRG, January 2004; Second edition, The State PIRGS, February 2005: maketextbooksaffordable.org.

Rose, M. H. and Angela Adair-Hoy. *How to Publish and Promote Online.* Griffin Trade, 2001.

Rosenthal, Morris. *Print-on-Demand Book Publishing.* Foner Books, 2004.

Ross, Tom and Marilyn H. Ross. *The Complete Guide to Self-Publishing,* 4th ed. Writer's Digest Books, 2002.

Seidman, Michael. *From Printout to Published: A Guide to the Publishing Process.* CompuPress, 1988.

Self-Publishing Listserv: http://finance.groups.yahoo.com/group/Self-Publishing. (General reference.)

Shatzkin, Leonard. *In Cold Type: Overcoming the Book Crisis.* Houghton Mifflin, 1982.

Shea, Nina. This is a Saudi Textbook. (After the intolerance was removed). *The Washington Post*, May 21, 2006. http://www.washingtonpost.com/wp-dyn/content/article/2006/05/19/AR2006051901769.html.

Shepard, Aaron. *Perfect Pages: Self-Publishing with Microsoft Word.* Shepard Publications, 2006.

———. *Aiming at Amazon: The NEW Business of Self-Publishing.* Shepard Publications, 2007.

Silverman, Franklin H. *Authoring a Textbook or Professional Book: A Guide to What Publishers Do and Don't Want Authors to Know.* CODI Publications, 1993.

———. *Self-Publishing Books and Materials for Students, Academics, and Professionals*, 2nd ed. CODI Publications, 2000.

———. *Self-Publishing Textbooks and Instructional Materials.* Atlantic Path Publishing, 2004.

Simba Information Inc. *Educational Marketer* 26, no. 3 (August 21, 1995).

Skelly, Stacy. Publishers Respond to ACSFA Report. *American Association of Publishers*, June 5, 2007, http://www.publishers.org/main/PressCenter/HigheerEdACSFA.htm.

Skillin, Marjorie E., and Robert Malcolm Gay. *Words into Type*, 3rd ed., Pearson, 1974.

Slavin, Robert. *Educational Psychology: Theory and Practice*, 8th ed. Allyn and Bacon, 2005.

Small Publishers Association of North America: http://www.spannet.org. (General reference.)

Society of Academic Authors: http://www.sa2.info. (General reference.)

Society for Scholarly Publishing: http://www.sspnet.org. (General reference.)

Spiegler, Michael F. *A Complete First Course in Textbook Writing: NSF Chautauqua Short Course*, August 4–6, 2007, http://www.providence.edu/CTE/Textbook+Writing.htm.

———. *Handbook for College Textbook Writing*. Forthcoming.

Stainton, Elsie Myers. *Author and Editor at Work: Making a Better Book*. University of Toronto Press, 1982.

Stim, Richard. *Getting Permission: How to License and Clear Copyrighted Materials Online and Off*, 2nd ed. Nolo Press, 2004.

Strunk, William, Jr. and E. B. White. *The Elements of Style*, 4th ed., Allyn and Bacon, 2000.

Tarutz, Judith A. *Technical Editing: The Practical Guide for Editors and Writers*. Perseus, 1992.

Text and Academic Authors Association: http://www.TAAonline.net. (General reference.)

The Authors Registry: http://www.authorsregistry.org. (General reference.)

Thompson Sews Up Reuters. *TheStreet.com*, May 15, 2007. http://www.thestreet.com/_tscrss/newsanalysis/mediaentertainment/10356810.html.

The Writer's Friendly Legal Guide. Writer's Digest Books, 1989.

Tufte, Edward R. *Envisioning Information*. Graphics Press, 1990.

Tyson-Bernstein. *A Conspiracy of Good Intentions: America's Textbook Fiasco*. Council for Basic Education, 1988.

University of Chicago Press. *The Chicago Manual of Style*, 15th ed. University of Chicago Press, 2003.

Unwin, Stanley. *TheTruth about Publishing*. Academy Chicago, 1982.

UPI Stylebook and Guide to Newswriting, 4th ed. Capital Books, 2004.

U.S. College Publishers. Simba Information Inc., July 2007.

U.S. Copyright Office: http://www.loc.gov/copyright/search. (General reference.)

Van Til, W. *Writing for Professional Publication*, 2nd ed. Allyn and Bacon, 1986.

Verkaik, Robert. Wikipedia and the Art of Censorship. *The Independent*, August 18, 2007.

White, Jan V. *Editing by Design: Word and Picture Communication for Editors and Designers*. R. R. Bowker, n.d.

Woll, Thomas. *Publishing for Profit*, 2nd ed. Chicago Review Press, 2002.

———. *Publishing for Profit*, 3rd rev. ed. Chicago Review Press, 2006.

———. *Selling Subsidiary Rights: An Insider's Guide*. Fisher Books, 1999.

Writer's Guild: http://www.wga.org. (General reference.)

Yudkin, Marcia. *Internet Marketing for Less than $500 a Year*, 2nd ed. Independent Publishing Group, 2001.

Zinsser, W. *Writing to Learn*. Harper & Row, 1988.

———. *On Writing Well*, 5th ed. Harper & Row, 1994.

Index